D1263537

THE
SALES
GURUS

OTHER BOOKS IN THIS SERIES

The Marketing Gurus
The Management Gurus

THE

SALES

GURUS

LESSONS FROM THE BEST

SALES BOOKS OF ALL TIME

ANDREW B. CLANCY

**AND THE EDITORS AT SOUNDVIEW
EXECUTIVE BOOK SUMMARIES**

PORTFOLIO

PORTFOLIO
Published by the Penguin Group
Penguin Group (USA) Inc., 375 Hudson Street, New York, New York 10014, U.S.A.
Penguin Group (Canada), 90 Eglinton Avenue East, Suite 700, Toronto, Ontario, Canada M4P 2Y3
(a division of Pearson Penguin Canada Inc.)
Penguin Books Ltd, 80 Strand, London WC2R 0RL, England
Penguin Ireland, 25 St. Stephen's Green, Dublin 2, Ireland (a division of Penguin Books Ltd)
Penguin Books Australia Ltd, 250 Camberwell Road, Camberwell, Victoria 3124, Australia
(a division of Pearson Australia Group Pty Ltd)
Penguin Books India Pvt Ltd, 11 Community Centre, Panchsheel Park, New Delhi – 110 017, India
Penguin Group (NZ), 67 Apollo Drive, Rosedale, North Shore 0632, New Zealand
(a division of Pearson New Zealand Ltd)
Penguin Books (South Africa) (Pty) Ltd, 24 Sturdee Avenue, Rosebank, Johannesburg 2196, South Africa

Penguin Books Ltd, Registered Offices:
80 Strand, London WC2R 0RL, England

First published in 2010 by Portfolio Penguin,
a member of Penguin Group (USA) Inc.

10 9 8 7 6 5 4 3 2 1

The summaries of the following books are published for the first time in this volume: Be a Sales Superstar
by Brian Tracy; How to Master the Art of Selling by Tom Hopkins; Ziglar on Selling by Zig Ziglar; The Winning
Attitude by John Maxwell; Selling to Zebras by Jeff Koser and Chad Koser; Sales Essentials by Stephan Schiffman;
and A Seat at the Table by Marc Miller. The other summaries have been previously published by Soundview
Executive Books Summaries.

Permission acknowledgments appear on the last page of the respective selection.

LIBRARY OF CONGRESS CATALOGING IN PUBLICATION DATA
Clancy, Andrew B.
  The sales gurus : lessons from the best sales books of all time / Andrew B. Clancy and the editors at
Soundview Executive Book Summaries.
     p. cm.
  Includes bibliographical references and index.
  ISBN 978-1-59184-338-2
  1. Selling. 2. Selling—Abstracts. I. Soundview executive book summaries. II. Title.
  HF5438.25.C526 2010
  658.85—dc22
                                                                    2010004024

Printed in the United States of America
Set in Joanna MT with ITC Franklin Gothic

To SGC and WJC for the foundation.

To MVC for what we're building on it.

ACKNOWLEDGMENTS

I am extremely grateful to a number of individuals who helped in the creation of this book. While selling is often seen as a solitary profession, there are numerous individuals whose collaborative efforts help a single salesperson to greater success. I feel fortunate to be part of a group whose goal in publishing this book is to push each sales representative who reads it to the highest level of achievement.

Soundview's president, Josh Clement, deserves a great deal of credit for his commitment to grow and reshape the business during a time of great change in the publishing industry and uncertainty in the economy. Publisher Rebecca Clement is the person who gave this project shape and substance and helped give it the cohesion it requires for maximum impact.

Soundview is very fortunate to have Sabrina Hickman as its representative to the publishers whose works appear in this collection. She is given the gargantuan task of corralling works from all corners of the globe, and her mastery of a very difficult task cannot be overstated.

As an editor, I know the challenges of attempting to pull the best out of a writer. This is why I must give great thanks to Sarah Dayton at Soundview and Jillian Gray at Portfolio. Sarah's suggestions helped push me forward in the early stages, and Jillian provided simple, pinpoint guidance to make this book an essential resource for sales professionals. Thanks as well to all at Portfolio, including Adrian Zackheim, Adrienne Schultz, and Brooke Carey, for continued belief in Soundview's product and our collaboration.

A final debt of gratitude must be given to Soundview chairman George Y. Clement. Many of the people whose names appear on this page have benefited from his trust, knowledge, and determination. His commitment to quality and unflagging devotion to the customer are the principles that continue to drive Soundview forward into bold, new directions.

CONTENTS

THE
SALES
GURUS

INTRODUCTION

The sales department of any organization is the engine that drives the business forward. It moves at a frenetic pace and relies on the interaction of each of its parts to deliver the necessary solutions to prospects and customers alike. And as with an engine, when something is wrong, it's obvious to everyone and there's a true sense of urgency to return it to peak performance.

The Sales Gurus is intended to save salespeople and their managers a good amount of effort and frustration in the process of building a more successful sales force. This collection contains eighteen summaries of sales books from some of the most prolific salespeople in a variety of fields. Fortunately for readers, they are able to receive one-on-one instruction from an all-star coaching panel without incurring the cost of travel or lecture attendance fees. Our intention is to provide the most complete resource to help sales professionals improve their prospecting, presentation, negotiation, and closing skills.

Sales is a profession that can never rest on its achievements. Each quarter demands new and improved rates of success. This process begins with prospecting, a skill that involves more than simply picking up a phone and scrolling through numbers on a call list. To help refine a salesperson's abilities, Jeff and Chad Koser present *Selling to Zebras*. This summary provides salespeople with tips to take the guesswork out of prospecting. Steve Kaplan's *Bag the Elephant!* takes prospecting to the next level and offers solutions for targeting top-level, high-dollar businesses. The prospecting section finishes with Marc Miller's *A Seat at the Table*. Miller aims to help sales professionals partner with their prospective customers and eliminate the adversarial stigma that prevents buyer and seller from finding solutions.

Once an introduction to a prospect has been secured, the salesperson's attention turns to making the sale. The myriad ways to combine customer and product (or service) can occasionally boggle a salesperson's mind. Salespeople often rush to close without first fully understanding the nature of the customer's need. Without the necessary preparation, the sale can be lost within moments of walking through the prospect's door. We attempt to remove some of the confusion by presenting a selection of sales-boosting strategies all intended to raise a representative's performance.

Our in-depth look into sales presentations begins with *Exceptional Selling* by Jeff Thull. Thull takes readers through the best ways to increase sales while reducing wasted effort. Michael T. Bosworth and John R. Holland put a salesperson's focus squarely on the prospect with *CustomerCentric Selling*. This summary provides sales professionals with excellent insight into integrating a customer's goals with the need for the salesperson's product.

Dialogue between seller and buyer is a key area overlooked by sales trainers. The importance of verbal communication is not lost on Thomas A. Freese, whose *Secrets of Question-Based Selling* teaches salespeople verbal cues to spark interest. For those sales representatives who struggle with delivering their message to the customer, we have included Jerry Weissman's *The Power Presenter* to help boost a seller's confidence and presence. Weissman is a top-ranked speaking coach and has helped many CEOs use presentations to push their companies to new heights.

After presentations are given, a sale often goes to the bargaining table. At this point, salespeople will benefit from reading Roger Dawson's *Secrets of Power Negotiating for Salespeople*. Dawson instructs sellers to master the initial interaction because the entire negotiation rests on what is laid out at that critical point. Negotiation, like all aspects of a sale, is highly dependent on good use of time. Todd Duncan's *Time Traps* helps salespeople master the art of time management. The salesperson who refuses to waste his or her own time will never waste a moment of his or her customer's day.

Sales managers are a critical part of the sales process, which is why we've made their responsibilities the subject of the next section. We start by including *The Ultimate Sales Machine*, by Chet Holmes. His twelve key strategies for sales mastery are "blackboard material" to be hung in every sales office. A critical skill for sales managers to pass on to their representatives is the ability to distinguish a worthy prospect from a time waster. *The Dollarization Discipline*, by Jeffrey J. Fox and Richard C. Gregory, takes this concept a step further and provides an analytic strategy to attach real dollars to potential customers. Once sales are made, there is nothing more important than tracking them. In *Making the Number*, Greg Alexander, Aaron Bartels, and Mike Drapeau teach readers to use sales benchmarking as a means to power up the bottom line and expand a company's market share.

The final section of *The Sales Gurus* is dedicated to an all-star panel of coaching talent. Readers will receive advice and sales strategies from some of the most famous names in the field. This section starts with Tom Sant's *The Giants of Sales*, a collection of the wisdom of Dale Carnegie, John Henry Patterson, Elmer Wheeler, and Joe Girard. This is followed by the insight of one of the most notable names in the history of sales: Zig Ziglar. Including his *Zig Ziglar on Selling* in this collection bridges the past and present of sales strategy. We also feature Tom Hopkins and his book *How to Master the Art of Selling*. This book is one of the great compilations of selling strategies of the last several years.

From here, the collection moves to Brian Tracy, whose *Be a Sales Superstar* gives new and experienced salespeople additional ways to improve their numbers. Stephan Schiffman, one of the top sales trainers in terms of both volume and results, provides *Stephan Schiffman's Sales Essentials* to increase a salesperson's focus on tactics that really work.

The Sales Gurus concludes with a motivational title from legendary management coach John C. Maxwell. Sales is not an easy road. It's a difficult profession filled with rejection and the pressure to make one's numbers. Maxwell's *The Winning Attitude* provides sellers with a needed injection of self-assurance and positive reinforcement.

When examined as a whole, this collection features decades of wisdom that resulted from thousands of sales presentations, some successful and some not. The authors of the books contained in *The Sales Gurus* have treaded the well-worn path to many a CEO's door. What they've learned along the way is presented here for each salesperson to read and remember on their own journey to becoming a sales guru.

For more information on any of the authors or summaries featured in this book, visit www.summary.com.

SELLING TO ZEBRAS

by Jeff Koser and Chad Koser

It's easy to see that in today's fiercely competitive market, selling is a jungle. Salespeople are expected to capture the ever-fleeting attention of prospects and close more high-dollar sales in less time than in the past. One failed close can make the difference between a successful quarter and missing one's numbers. A jaded public with limited resources does nothing to help the salesperson differentiate the big game from the time wasters. With their book *Selling to Zebras*, Jeff and Chad Koser end the debate and clearly define your strongest customers.

It certainly doesn't benefit sales professionals to use a scattershot method in hope of hitting as many potential customers as possible. The authors contend that the average salesperson wastes 85 percent of his or her time chasing prospects that have little to offer. Finding the right prospect, they argue, should be as easy as spotting a zebra on the plains. A salesperson's job is to pounce like a waiting lion and bring the prey back to the pride of his or her company. Just as there is no mistaking that pattern of black and white stripes for another animal, the ideal prospect should be something a salesperson recognizes on sight. The Kosers help to refine the salesperson's vision and bring the stripes out of the solid mass of prospects that he or she faces on a daily basis.

According to the authors of *Selling to Zebras*, the targeting of one's prime category of prospects is a company-wide initiative. The Kosers recommend seeking input from all functional levels of an organization. This helps the entire company zero in on finding and selling to the right customers. The hidden benefits of this approach include more focused efforts and a sense that everyone in the organization is "speaking the same language" when it comes to the customer. A top-to-bottom approach prevents excess effort from being expended in the attempt to get everyone in an organization on the same page. It also makes every individual in an organization a reliable contact point for the potential customer. Regardless of who picks up the phone at the seller's office, the customer will not have to experience the frustration of being passed from person to person until his or her question is answered.

Readers of *Selling to Zebras* will be impressed with the Kosers' focus on helping salespeople create the perfect prospect's profile. The authors point out that there are identifiable, objective characteristics that can be used to ensure that the right person receives the sales pitch every time. Jeff Koser helped create and evolve the Zebra method of selling during his thirty-year career in management and sales consulting. During his time as chief operating officer of Baan Supply Chain Solutions, Koser was able to help grow the company's revenues tenfold in less than five years. It was the similarities among his best clients that helped Koser realize that certain companies with specific needs were more likely to be receptive to his company's products. *Selling to Zebras* is a salesperson's survival guide to tracking the right prospects and coming out of the jungle alive and well.

SELLING TO ZEBRAS
How to Close 90 Percent of the Business You Pursue Faster, More Easily, and More Profitably
by Jeff Koser and Chad Koser

CONTENTS

THE SUMMARY IN BRIEF

In many ways, salespeople are like lions. Lions need sharp focus to catch enough food to survive, but not all lions hunt the same way. Young lions often fail to focus on prey that they can catch and that will effectively feed the pride, whereas the experienced lion knows that the better strategy is to focus on prey that is worth the energy to pursue, like a zebra.

In a typical year, most salespeople in our complex business environment work a limited number of opportunities. So spending time and money on an unqualified prospect can be a tremendous drain on a company. When salespeople pursue every opportunity that catches their attention, they exhaust their limited resources until they have nothing left to continue to hunt. Ultimately, even the business that could have been won is often lost, making survival in the wild world of sales increasingly difficult.

Selling to Zebras can help you identify the perfect prospects for your company—your Zebras—and develop a sales process that will help you close deals 90 percent of the time. Coauthors Jeff and Chad Koser provide specific tools, models, and spreadsheets you can customize to make the Zebra way the best way for your company to do business.

In addition, you will learn:

- How to increase close rates
- Why it is important to shorten sales cycles
- How to increase average deal size
- How to reduce discounting and increase margins
- How to make better use of scarce resources
- What makes customers happy; creating a stable of great references

THE COMPLETE SUMMARY

Hunting Zebras

There was a time when more activity produced greater results, but too much has changed to make that approach workable in today's sales environment. There are more competitors in every industry, and they have better access to information. They figure out your strengths and work hard and fast to emulate them. Prospects are now saying that it's hard to distinguish among different options. To most prospects, everyone in the market looks the same and many of the competitive differences that companies can claim don't seem to matter.

As products begin to appear equal, price becomes more important to customers. Margins have been bled from many industries because India, China, and other developing countries are creating downward price pressure. Their low-cost development and manufacturing resources contribute to the lowest-cost game. Sales are lower, and there is more competition than the market can support.

It doesn't matter if you sell tangible or intangible products and services, large- or small-ticket items—the activity-based sales approach no longer works. Sales can no longer be a numbers game. Old-school methods targeting sheer volume of leads and knocking on every door with equal vigor have been proven vastly ineffective, not to mention expensive. Effort alone is no longer enough to be competitive. If effort is the key to your strategy, you will go hungry.

Instead of chasing anything that moves, why not hunt Zebras? It's time to heed the old cliché about working smarter, not harder.

The Zebra

Your Zebra is the prospect that is a perfect fit for your company—and not just from a product or solution perspective. It is a prospect that you know you can win based on identifiable, objective characteristics—and Zebras are the only prospects a salesperson should pursue.

We call this perfect prospect a Zebra because once you've identified the characteristics of your Zebra, you can quickly and easily spot it amid all the other prospects. A Zebra's stripes tell you exactly what kind of animal you're looking at—you can't mistake a Zebra for any other animal, so you know for sure when you have one.

Most good salespeople have an instinct for Zebras. You know in your gut when you've found a prospect that offers you a good chance. It's the perfect prey, and the time and money you spend pursuing this prospect are going to pay off. But you still pursue lots of prospects that aren't Zebras because you believe that if you work hard enough, you can close those deals, too. This is a fallacy that most salespeople believe. Putting your energy toward the wrong focus is just as detrimental to sales success as being unfocused.

Part of the reason you pursue less-than-ideal prospects is because you can't articulate what makes a Zebra a Zebra.

Why You Need the Zebra

Some of the wasted effort in sales is a consequence of the fact that most sales are initiated by a prospect, often with a request for proposal (RFP) or a request for information (RFI). As salespeople, we expend much of our energy keeping ourselves involved in the competition of customer-initiated and customer-driven sales cycles where we never had a chance to win in the first place. We feel we must respond, and we do so without fully qualifying the opportunity, considering the resources we're expending to pursue it, or evaluating how likely it is that we'll win the business.

Another element that has pulled our attention toward activity levels and away from results is the advent of customer relationship management (CRM) systems. The proliferation of CRM systems has automated the collection and analysis of data, which makes it easy to generate reports on sales activity. The activity that we enter into CRM systems falsely encourages us, implying that we're productive simply because our activity levels are high. Problematically, companies and individuals end up using CRM systems to measure the quantity of sales activity rather than the quality, requiring salespeople to spend countless hours logging the quantitative data.

But CRM systems also offer the benefit of collaboration and the ability to measure actual progress and productivity. Unfortunately, most companies do not take advantage of this asset. Using the Zebra model in conjunction with a solid CRM can actually help you identify and overcome your sales hurdles.

The Zebra Buying Cycle

If you follow the way of the Zebra and apply analysis, process, focus, and discipline, this results-driven approach will offer greater reward with less work. To help you do this, use the Zebra Buying Cycle.

We use the phrase "buying cycle" rather than the traditional "sales cycle" for good reason. A sales cycle is named as such because traditionally the salesperson seeks someone to sell to. The Zebra Buying Cycle process targets the person who is going to buy from you—the person with decision-making power, who defines the company's business issues, who is responsible for the promises that will get the project approved and for achieving and reporting the end results. This person is referred to here by the generic name Power.

When Power is presented with a solution that addresses key pain points, he or she has the authority to make the decision to buy. So another critical element of the Zebra Buying Cycle is identifying the pain points needed to reach Power and make the most of your time and resources. Why waste your time selling to someone who doesn't want your solution or doesn't have the authority to buy?

This process is different from anything you have ever tried. First, you are selling to Power, and Power, unlike lower-level managers, is paid to evaluate risk, make decisions based on that risk, and carry out a plan of action in support of those decisions. Second, the process enables you to give Power everything he or she needs to make a decision in the shortest possible time. During the cycle, you'll give Power information that

- predicts very specifically the value he or she can expect to achieve;
- makes the decision-making process easy;
- describes the best process for evaluating your solution and what it will take in terms of time and resources;
- clearly explains what his or her company will lose by not moving forward with your solution.

THE SALES PIPELINE

*Y*ou say that if you pursue only Zebras, you'll risk selling less than you are now. It's true that when you first start focusing on Zebras, your potential sales pipeline will decrease in overall value. But if you're closing 90 percent instead of 15 percent, this short-term discomfort will be worth it. And because you won't be wasting time on prospects that will never buy from you, you'll have more time to pursue quality accounts where you add unique value.

You'll have time to strategize the accounts that are worth your valuable time and sales resources. You'll be able to review your Zebras, determine and leverage your strengths, and identify and devise strategies to address your weaknesses. This is the real strength of the Zebra way. The more you identify and chase Zebras, the faster the deals in your pipeline will turn into revenue, the less discounting will be required to close business, and the faster your business will grow.

Develop Your Zebra Profile

The Zebra profile outlines the characteristics of those companies that represent your best opportunities. It is the best tool for quickly, easily, and accurately identifying the Zebras among your prospects—without relying on gut instincts.

By focusing on your prospects' size, culture, industry vertical, source of decision-making power, and overall look and feel, you'll be able to sell far beyond features, functions, and even solutions to determine a mutually beneficial fit.

When you learn how to identify and sell to Zebras, you'll dig all the way into your prospects' core values. Then you can look at—and sell—solution fit, but not from a typical feature or function perspective. A better approach is to analyze solution fit from the perspective of the customer's business issues—Power's pain points. Determining and selling to these pain points is absolutely critical to your success because they are what drive decision-making behavior.

The Zebra Team

The first step you must take toward creating a Zebra profile is to pull together your Zebra team. The information gathering and analysis required in the Zebra process should involve input from a variety of departments. It's important to include all of the major functional areas of your business in the creation of your Zebra team because they may have insights that you would not consider.

For instance, the legal department may have important points to make about negotiations with your best customers. Human resources may have input on staffing changes necessary to better support the actual needs of your Zebras.

The Source of Your Zebra Profile: Your Best Customers

Finding companies that are your Zebras is all about identifying the types of companies that have a need for the specific things that make your solution more compelling than your competition's. To do this, begin by thinking about your existing customer base in terms of which customers you would use as references. It sounds intuitive and maybe even simplistic, but once you dissect the traits that make them good customers, you will unlock the key to identifying good prospects to pursue—to finding your Zebras.

Although you want to focus on your best customers to define what your Zebra is, it's also important to know what your Zebra is not. This will allow you to quickly assess prospects that are anti-Zebra and eliminate them from your pipeline. Take a look at your most recent sales losses and ask yourself these questions:

- How do the losses differ from your recent wins?
- Which competitor won the business?
- Why did that competitor win?

Once you've compiled a list of your best customers and some basic information about their characteristics, you are ready to begin creating your Zebra Profile using the seven categories (company characteristics, operation characteristics, technology characteristics, service characteristics, access to Power, funding, and return on investment, or ROI).

WHAT IS A ZEBRA?

A Zebra is a perfect sales prospect:

   A Zebra's business needs match the promised benefits of your company's solution.

   A Zebra fits with your company philosophically, demographically, politically, and culturally.

   A Zebra likely buys the way you sell.

   A Zebra allows you access to Power.

   A Zebra is ready to buy if the return on investment is right.

   A Zebra is the sum of the company operational technology and service characteristics that define your best customers.

Spot Your Zebra

The next step on the Zebra Buying Cycle is to spot your Zebra. Determine who your best prospects are and are not by comparing them to your Zebra profile. You've compiled a lot of information about your Zebra, but you have limited information about each of your prospects. So how do you compare and contrast those two sets of information easily without wasting a lot of time and resources just to discover that a prospect isn't a good fit?

The Push-Button Zebra

The Push-Button Zebra, or PBZ, is the most effective and efficient way to analyze the prospects in your pipeline. It allows you to quickly and easily identify those prospects that offer you the best opportunity to see a return on your investment of time and resources. And it makes it easy to implement the Zebra process in your organization because it's a tool everybody will be willing to use.

Creating your own PBZ is pretty simple because you've already done the heavy lifting of creating your Zebra profile. To turn your Zebra profile into a PBZ, follow these steps:

- Step 1: For each attribute category of your Zebra profile, identify the most important characteristics of a true Zebra and a true non-Zebra (your worst prospect). These are the characteristics that will immediately let you know if you do or do not have a Zebra in each of the categories.
- Step 2: For each category, create a short description (fifty to seventy-five words) of your Zebra's characteristics. Then develop a brief description of what your anti-Zebra—a very poor prospect—would look like. In the PBZ spreadsheet, you can insert these descriptions as comments relating to the brief descriptions you created for each attribute. This creates a solid foundation for analyzing a prospect.
- Step 3: Insert all of this information into the spreadsheet and begin scoring prospects. Simply enter a score from 0 to 4 for each attribute (0 being the worst, 4 being the best). Once you've scored a prospect on each attribute, add up the scores for a total. This total is your Z-score.

While the PBZ is often used to quickly evaluate prospects and can get you to a Z-score in just a few minutes, it is also a living document. You may have enough information about a prospect to score it low in most attributes and rule it out as a good opportunity right away. More likely, though, you'll have a fair amount of information and you'll do an initial score that is not entirely conclusive. As you progress through the Zebra Buying Cycle and learn more about the prospect, you'll continue to update the PBZ. Before you invest more resources to progress through each stage of the cycle, you'll revisit the PBZ to verify that the prospect is still worthy of pursuit.

What to Do with a Z-Score

You may be tempted to remove a low-scoring prospect from your list. If this is your first pass through the PBZ and the resulting score is low only because you don't have sufficient information, continue to pursue the opportunity until you have enough information to reach a valid score.

If this prospect has a midrange score, indicating that there might be some risk in pursuing the opportunity, but is a key account and is in one of your preferred verticals, meet with Power before you remove the opportunity from your pipeline. Meet with Power early, before wasting valuable resources. Once you feel like you've reached a final score, if the prospect is still on the lower end of the "some risk" category, you should seriously consider removing it from your pipeline.

If a prospect has a midrange score, you should assess where you are strong and where you are weak and develop a strategy to improve upon your weaknesses. If you are not at the right executive level in the deal, you might decide to invest enough time to get to Power. If you are still in the lower end of the "some risk" category after meeting with Power, you should consider exiting the deal.

And of course, if a prospect scores high as a Zebra, pursue, pursue, pursue! Don't stop unless or until you discover information that would make you lower the score.

The main thrust of the Zebra philosophy isn't about walking away, although that is a possibility. All opportunities are reviewed against the profile before you pursue a prospect and before each major step in the Zebra Buying Cycle. From there you make a decision to engage or stay engaged. This way your eyes are open to all the possible strengths and weaknesses that determine your chances for mutual success with a prospect. The idea is to evaluate each opportunity before you use, or continue to use, any sales resources to pursue it.

Define Power's Pain Points

For most of your sales career, you've probably believed that the success of your product or solution is tied to how well it addresses the operational needs of your customer, right? If you sell software, you are successful at selling it because the people who use it like the three-way financial matching capability, finite scheduling, solid-model three-dimensional views, or other features and functions that drive the value associated with using it. If you sell earth-moving equipment, you probably think you've been successful because of the pay-load capacity of your equipment, the 960-horsepower diesel power plant, or the plush, air-conditioned cabin. You can always make a sale by emphasizing features and functions, right? Guess what? You're wrong! That's not why they bought.

Features and functions are important to middle managers, and most companies sell to these managers. But this usually results in a continuous selling-and-reselling process where you sell to the middle managers, and they sponsor you to the executive or, worse, they become the ones who try to sell your solution to their boss, boss's boss, or boss's boss's boss. This is one of the primary reasons why sales cycles are so long and unpredictable. The better way we have been describing requires that you start and stay with Power. To do that, you have to determine the executive-level pain points your solution can address.

Power's Pain Points Are Different

Take a moment to consider the selling points you've relied on in the past. They probably relate to the functionality of your product, the special features and/or the key differentiators compared to competitors' products. In short, they are probably operational selling points. And you may believe that to move beyond those basic selling techniques you simply have to show that your product or service offers a positive or even substantial ROI.

With that, you'll have what you need to sell at the executive level—because executives are concerned only with what the numbers tell them. Wrong! Today, a positive ROI is not enough. Power likely has a number of projects with positive ROIs but doesn't have the budget to approve all of them. You have to prove that your project or product can address problems that Power is responsible for solving. You will probably have to use numbers to support those claims, but the numbers have to be tied to specific business issues.

Once you've identified Power's pain points in your prospect, what do you do with that information? Well, one of two things will happen: The pain points will align with the pain points your solution addresses or they won't. If they do, then you have more proof that you're working with a Zebra. This type of proof is particularly important if the original Zebra score was borderline. This information might not directly improve that score, but it might give you more insight into some of the characteristics of your prospect that will improve the score. Regardless, even if the score is borderline, if you think Power's needs align with your strengths, then you need to keep pursuing the prospect.

Predict the Value of Your Solution

To sell to Power, we have to be able to convince Power that we have a solution that will address his or her pain points. The pain points, as we've said, are the only things that will drive Power to spend money. So identifying those pain points is critical, but proving that you can create a valuable solution to address them, one that has been successfully implemented in other companies, is also necessary. Otherwise, why would Power buy from you?

The process for developing the data and tools you'll need to make this statement to Power and support it is straightforward:

- Conduct audits of the customer base to uncover the quantifiable value your solution has produced by solving the executive-level pain points.
- Gather specific data about your prospect (if you haven't already).
- Use your research and knowledge of the value your solution has created in the past to predict the value you can create for the prospect.

Uncovering the Value You Create

Now you need to answer the question What value has been generated for my existing customers by addressing their executive-level pain points? You'll be able to take the answer to this question and extrapolate from it to answer the same question for your prospect.

Every company's survey will be different because it will be based on its product and industry. But there are some general types of information you should be trying to gather to help you understand the very specific value you've been able to create:

- Basic data about the company, including industry, annual revenue, and total annual expenditure in the area of your solution or product
- Savings data—including savings the company expected to and actually achieved by using your product
- Feedback about why the company bought your solution

What you want to create from the survey process is a clear definition of how your product drives value for your customers—both direct value (bottom line) and indirect (productivity enhancements). These elements are your value drivers. You will likely start the survey process with a hypothesis of what you believe to be the value you create, and you will use that hypothesis to help you create the survey. The survey will then help you refine your claims and back them up with customers' quantifiable results and quotations. In the end, the greater part of your sales message will be pulled directly from your customers. You will turn your sales force into messengers of your customers' ideas and achieved value.

Predicting Your Value

Using the data you've gathered, you will be able to create a financial model that supports your Zebra efforts. The characteristics of a Zebra are important, but if you can't quantify the value you can generate for your Zebras, all of your research won't convince prospects that you are a perfect fit for them. Power needs financial proof of the value you say you've created for other customers.

Keep in mind that your ultimate goal is not to justify a solution but to justify and sell *your* solution. Many companies have an ROI model that justifies a decision to buy a solution, any solution—even solutions that their competitors are offering.

Power-Level Sales Tools

Using the model you've created from customer data and prospect information, you can now predict the value you will create for your prospect. How you present that prediction of value is just as important as the validity of the prediction. You could give Power a host of spreadsheets with detailed information about your company and theirs, or you could distill that information to make better use of their time and yours.

In the Zebra model, you generate three sales tools once you input your data:

- **Financials.** Power-level financials to use in communicating the predicted value generated by your solution. These are the numbers Power wants to see.
- **The Value Waterfall.** While the financials show the overall results a company can expect from a project, they won't necessarily hit Power's hot buttons, or pain points. The Value Waterfall will show, in a quantifiable way, the specific and unique value of your solution and why Power should care. It is a graphical representation of value created by the various functional components of your solution.
- **Payback Period Graph.** Because payback period is so closely aligned with risk, the model automatically produces a payback period graph so you can demonstrate that your solution is low risk.

Meet with Power

Have you ever gotten to the end of a sales cycle only to find that the enthusiastic non–decision makers couldn't help you get a deal done, in spite of their best efforts? Many salespeople have experienced this: The person you've been relying on to sell your solution to upper management didn't know what they didn't know—what it would take to get a buy order approved inside their own company.

It can be difficult for salespeople to get appointments, much less appointments with real decision makers. So it's hard to say no when the first appointment is with somebody other than the final decision maker. But this is exactly what you have to do. One factor that contributes to the tendency to say yes when you should say no is the activity-for-activity's-sake approach, or using hustle as a substitute for formulating and executing a truly effective strategy.

Deals that die or take months to close are a result of selling at too low a level. This is why it is critical for you to begin working at the executive level and maintain that through the entire cycle. It helps you identify those accounts you should be pursuing, ensures that you're spending time and resources fruitfully, and gives you the tools to sell at the executive level.

When you request a meeting with Power at a prospect you believe is a Zebra, you must provide him or her with everything he or she needs to decide to grant you that meeting.

Acing the Meeting

The objective of your meeting with Power is to get Power to sponsor your value-verification process. Partnering with the prospect to verify your value will help confirm that you can create the value you've told Power you can create.

How do you get Power to approve the process? The same way you got Power to meet with you: identify and confirm the business issues; confirm that Power would like to address the issues; describe how the value you predict can be created; and prove you have created value in the past. Typically, you will use a presentation to give Power everything needed to make a decision to partner with you to verify the value in one twenty-minute meeting. You'll need to communicate the mutual cost of the value verification and when Power can expect results.

JUST SO YOU KNOW

1. It usually takes about seven phone calls to talk with an executive at a Global 2000 company.
2. You will be relegated and delegated to the management level that matches the image you project in those calls.

Partner to Verify Your Value

Value verification is one of the most exciting parts of the Zebra Buying Cycle. It gets you inside a company to discover exactly what your products can do for the prospect. This is your best selling time.

Value verification avoids the dreaded "show-up and throw-up" sales demonstration by providing confirmation of two things for the prospect: Power's pain points exist and align with your solution, and you can create the value you claim to generate by addressing these pain points.

To achieve everything you need to achieve, you must have the right team in place. From your company, bring your sales team, the people who are responsible for determining the necessary components of the product or solution, and the people who will be responsible for the implementation. The prospect's team should include the people who will be involved in implementing, managing, and using your product or solution. These are the members of management whom Power has identified will help you uncover the process improvements and solutions components that, if implemented, will drive the value possible with your solution.

The same survey used to determine the value you've created for your existing customer base will be used to establish your partnership with new prospects. That survey is given to Power to help him or her identify who is best equipped to answer your survey questions. Your survey will include only those questions that will help you uncover the big savings areas.

Depending on the complexity of your solution, the value verification occurs over one or two days and requires between five and thirty man-hours of the prospect's time. The goal of all this work is to come to an agreement on the level of savings possible for each value driver.

Once you've adjusted your prediction of value, you'll build your value road map, which is the final presentation you will make to Power. The road map presentation describes the before-and-after picture of each process associated with each value driver.

The Presentation to Power

You should schedule a two-hour meeting with Power and the value-verification team. You'll need plenty of time to present findings on each of the business issues or value drivers and address any question Power has. During the meeting you'll discuss

- before-and-after processes;
- the value you were able to verify;
- your solution, through the road map that demonstrates how your solution eliminates steps, reduces errors, and saves time and money;
- the financial justification for the project;
- a commitment from Power to do business.

The presentation you coauthor with the prospect's value-verification team defines the present state, the future desired state, and your solution components, which, when implemented, will create the verified value.

Contract and Force Success

Many salespeople dread contract negotiations. They know that even though it seems like the deal is done, it could still fall apart at any minute because of some surprise detail or a fight over cost. Enter the power of the Zebra.

In the Zebra Buying Cycle, contract negotiations come after you have already presented and verified your solution's value, provided financials that show how a decision to buy your product compares with all other uses of available capital, explained the key Power pain points your solution can address, and presented the solution cost, including every element necessary to make the value possible. Having accomplished all of these steps ahead of time, you are fully prepared to leverage them during the contract negotiations; you are in a powerful position to get the business, hold your price firm, and complete a win-win contract in a timely manner.

A sales representative's job doesn't end when a deal is closed. The job ends when the customer achieves the original project goals set during the sales process, the goals established during the value verification. If you approach every sales call and every strategic discussion with this focus in mind, the positive, committed energy will be evident to your prospects, and you'll be able to leverage that commitment to their success for greater and greater results.

The Force Success Implementation Plan

So the contract has been signed, but your job isn't done yet, is it? It's not done until your client has achieved the value you've told them is possible. You made a deal (with the customer): Pay us this amount of money and this is what you'll achieve. If you don't hold up your end of the bargain, your credibility in the market will suffer—and so will your sales.

Forcing success means ensuring that the implementation plan you designed will enable your client to repeat the level of success that others have achieved with your solution. The Force Success Implementation Plan is configured to address Power's pain points. And Power's sponsorship and the process owners' buy-in from the value verification will fuel the implementation and help to eliminate some of the typical problems that crop up. And when problems do surface, you will be in a powerful position to address them.

You now have everything you need to sell to your Zebra, close the sale, and ensure that your new customer is a happy one. You know what you need to make your product successful and how to sell it that way.

BAG THE ELEPHANT!

by Steve Kaplan

When it comes to mammals that walk on terra firma, there is none greater than the elephant. In the world of sales, the elephant is the one titanic customer that can radically impact a salesperson's revenue. However, much like the namesake pachyderm, sales elephants are elusive, intimidating, and not to be tangled with unless one is adequately prepared. Steve Kaplan is the author whose mission is to help salespeople tame the savage beasts of giant corporate customers. His book *Bag the Elephant!* provides the necessary instructions to accomplish what many salespeople view as a near-impossible task.

Kaplan knows the territory of elephant hunting quite well. The marketing company he started in his basement had modest showings during its early years. Kaplan knew that if he didn't begin to target more profitable prospects, his business would go the way of the wooly mammoth. That's when he hit upon the notion of going after big game. His pursuit of elephants took a giant leap forward when he threw his lasso around the neck of one of the biggest bulls walking the global business veld, Procter & Gamble. His company then propelled itself to sales of more than $250 million and a global network of employees in twenty-one countries. Kaplan currently operates several businesses, including The Difference Maker Inc., an executive coaching and training company.

His success led him to share what he had learned by writing *Bag the Elephant!* Kaplan carefully created his metaphor and connected the size, pace, and temperament of big businesses with the traits of the elephant. As he notes on his Web site, "Elephants are also smart, sometimes dangerous, uniquely individual and equipped with long memories—all reasons for you to be super-cautious and respectful when dealing with them."

Bag the Elephant! is a great title because its foremost priority is to help salespeople overcome the most common question in dealing with big clients: Does a large business need my goods or services? Kaplan demonstrates in specific examples how to pierce the tough exterior of a corporate elephant. He is not afraid to explore the inner workings of a large company and exploit its own mechanisms to help a salesperson. Red tape, to Kaplan, can be used to gift wrap a way in the door.

Of additional critical importance is *Bag the Elephant!*'s emphasis on rebounding from customer catastrophes. Harking back to the old joke "Where does an elephant sit?" (answer: anywhere it wants!), Kaplan recognizes large corporate clients' low tolerance for mistakes and the expectation that they be accommodated in every situation. His advice on how to handle the inevitable errors that occur in all vendor/client relationships is essential for keeping a small business in the good graces of an elephant. Kaplan's advice on five killer mistakes that lead to the destruction of small companies is not to be missed.

The success of *Bag the Elephant!* led Kaplan to write a follow-up, *Be the Elephant,* a book on building one's business to new heights. However, before any salesperson can know what it's like at the apex of the food chain, he or she must master the skills of taming the titans of the corporate jungle. *Bag the Elephant!* is an essential read in accomplishing this task.

BAG THE ELEPHANT!
How to Win and Keep Big Customers
by Steve Kaplan

CONTENTS

THE SUMMARY IN BRIEF

Have you ever dreamed of landing that huge account—the monster contract that dwarfs any deals you've made previously, dramatically increasing your profits? "Bagging the Elephant" brings you new, deeper streams of revenue, and keeping that Elephant happy ensures profits for years to come.

If you are the owner of a small or medium-sized business, this summary will show you how to find the right Elephant for your business and business needs, navigate your way through huge companies, identify and secure internal champions, build strong alliances, and position your selling approach for maximum effectiveness. Are you afraid that your company's culture won't be a good match for an Elephant's culture? This summary explains how to align them to get the most out of your relationship. Are you having trouble finding the right decision maker in a prospect's company? This summary also shows you how to use the Elephant's inherent bureaucracy to your advantage.

The Elephant needs you. You might ask yourself, "What could I possibly have to sell that a big company would want?" The answer is, plenty, if you match your products and services to the company's needs.

There are six keys to thinking like an Elephant. In order to best develop and leverage your relationships with large firms, you need to know how they go about their business and how to anticipate needs before the Elephants even recognize them.

In addition, you will learn:

- How to embrace the bureaucracy. In large companies, bureaucracy is a given, and you can make it work for you by aligning your outputs and processes to make life easier for your client and, by extension, yourself.
- How to draw up your hit list. Don't be afraid to think outside the box to come up with the Elephants you will hunt. Ultimately, however, the business you pursue must make sense for your organization and your prospects.
- How to recruit great champions. Your attempts to bag Elephants will only prove successful if you have the right people on your side—people on the inside of the prospective organization who will speak up for you and influence decision makers on your behalf. These are the champions of your organization in more ways than one.

THE COMPLETE SUMMARY

Part One: Your Elephant Is Waiting

The Elephants Need You

Why are giant companies referred to as "Elephants"? Because they are huge, slow-moving, ponderous, strong, slow to react, often lovable, and sometimes stubborn—and because they require enormous amounts of input, which, if you can make it your job to supply, can bring you great financial rewards. Elephants are also smart, sometimes dangerous, uniquely individual, and equipped with long memories—all reasons for you to be supercautious and respectful when dealing with them.

Small Firm Thinks Big Paula Westman owned a small CPA firm that specialized in tax returns. Over the course of fifteen years, she had built a successful practice, preparing about 250 tax returns per year for individuals and smaller businesses, billing just over $300,000 annually. But the pressures of being a one-woman operation were burning her out. She lived with the concern that her business would collapse should she happen to become ill during peak tax season. She desperately wanted to expand her business so that she could hire other CPAs to help carry the load.

Clearly, Paula needed to bag an Elephant, but being in the service industry posed some unique challenges. Not the least of these was the fact that she couldn't imagine large companies needing her services. After some research, however, she found that there were large companies that provided tax planning and financial services to middle and senior management as perks managed by the organizations' employee benefits department.

Paula put in a solid year of hard work to get her first big-company client. She worked out a deal with her Elephant that guaranteed her 225 returns per year for the next five years. This allowed her to hire three full-time junior CPAs to shoulder some of the load.

Paula's firm now handles only corporate clients, preparing one thousand returns annually.

Answer Your Doubts You may have doubts about pursuing business with big companies—"bagging the Elephant." You may be saying one or all of the following things to yourself:

- "My business doesn't lend itself to big customers." One of the first things to learn is that almost any business in any industry can get big customers—it's just a matter of knowing where to look.

- "I wouldn't even know where to begin." Beginning is the toughest part. Once you've made the commitment, it gets easier.
- "I've tried to get big customers, but it just didn't work out." Chances are at the time you didn't know what you needed to succeed. You may have gone after the wrong customer or mischaracterized your pitch. Try again. These are things that can be corrected.

The Elephant Really Does Need You Perhaps the first barrier to overcome in achieving success with big companies is the belief that those companies have no use for your goods or services. You must get over the assumption that no large company could possibly be interested in what you have to offer. The truth is, the Elephant needs you almost as much as you need the Elephant. As you'll see, after you've been together awhile—after the Elephant has come to rely on your products and services, and you've become a larger, more powerful enterprise with other big clients—the Elephant may end up needing you more than you need the Elephant.

Part Two: The Secret Life of the Elephant

Six Keys to Thinking Like an Elephant

There are many things you have to do in order to pursue, capture, and hold on to your Elephant. First among these is to change your outlook. You must stop thinking like a business your size and begin to think like an Elephant. You must do this in order to get inside your Elephant's head. It is important that you see things from the Elephant's point of view.

Everyone who will be engaged in hunting your Elephant must be engaged in this manner—every executive, manager, accountant, service representative, delivery person, mechanic, marketing person, and board member with whom your Elephant might come into contact. Everyone in your business has a part and a stake in bagging your Elephant and keeping it happy.

To ensure your best chance for success, you must get everyone working together toward a common goal. All decisions about the customer; the way your employees or associates approach prospective customer requests; and the speed, priority, and accuracy with which work gets done—all affect your chances for success.

The Right Mind-set To help you focus on getting inside the mind of an Elephant, consider these six keys to achieving the right mind-set—the attitudes and habits you should cultivate (or, in some cases, avoid) in yourself and your business if you're serious about bagging and keeping that big, rich customer:

1. *One and Done.* This principle is simple—you're going to be working very hard with the hope of getting one shot at a potential client, and if you blow it, it's over. You're done. This means everything from the initial contact forward, including quotes, presentations, sales pitches, client requests, and—even after you've signed a deal—delivery and further sales, must be perfect. Though your business may be the best thing around, the big company may never find out if it doesn't hire you. Don't give your prospect any reason to doubt you or look elsewhere, not even for a moment.

2. *Priority One.* Everyone wants to feel special. Big customers are no different. Lavish plenty of attention on your Elephant. Make that big company feel looked after and cherished. Return calls speedily. Answer questions quickly. Address problems immediately. Be kind to your Elephant, and it will be kind to you.

3. *Whatever It Takes.* If you've looked after your client, your reputation for high-quality work will have spread throughout the company, where new opportunities await. Some of these opportunities may seem removed from your core business. Be flexible in this case. Even if your current product line keeps you hopping, be grateful for the chance to grow. If you can, adjust your business plans on the fly to adapt.

Flexibility comes in many forms. It might be as simple as invoicing early or late to work within a client's budget restrictions and time frame. It might mean setting meeting times to suit the prospect's schedule, pushing a delivery date up or back, or inventorying specified items. It might also mean the opportunity to expand your services. Never put limits on what can or cannot be done for your Elephant.

4. *Long-Term Vision.* You must view your big customer as a partner in a long-term relationship. Once you've established this relationship out of mutual trust, there will be plenty of revenue available to you. However, there are many short-sighted business owners and salespeople who try to break the bank on their first big score and end up paying the price. An Elephant that feels it is being gouged can depart in a hurry—and do much damage on the way out.

Think of your big customers as stepping-stones to success. If you want to get to the top, you might need several stones, and each one should be as high as possible but not out of reach of the one before. Go slow and enjoy the ride. If you get greedy, you can easily price yourself right out of the opportunity.

5. *Breath of Fresh Air.* Work should be fun. This is important for two reasons:

• Having fun is good for business. People work better when they're having fun. Look at Southwest Airlines, Seattle's Pike Place Fish Market,

Business Network International (BNI), and other thriving businesses that emphasize fun.

- Potential clients should feel that working with your business will be a pleasant experience. It strengthens the relationship.

Having fun—and showing it—is a great way to distinguish yourself from your competitors, most of whom will be so focused on getting the dollars that they'll forget about the relationship. If prospects or customers call your business and speak to anyone—receptionist, salesperson, customer service rep, etc.—they should have a favorable experience. The best compliment you can ever receive from a big customer is to be described as professional, knowledgeable, and great to work with.

6. *Partners.* A partnership is a two-way street—and that is how you should approach your relationship with your big customer. Yes, your Elephant can do enormous favors for you. Your relationship can bear much fruit in revenues and profits for many years, if you nurture it. But on the other side, you're in a position to do great favors for your Elephant, too. You can even make yourself an indispensable partner. Seek ways to help your Elephant. Look for processes and methods for streamlining its operations. Look for ways to save it money. Approach the relationship with the goal of finding the best deal that can both fill your client's needs and keep your business healthy and growing. Never underestimate what you can bring to the table.

What to Know About Elephants

Large companies are mysterious entities. Decisions to buy a product or service typically come about through a series of meetings during which a company representative collects information from you. Then, depending on the circumstances, this information is meshed with company policies and other criteria to determine whether you are the ideal supplier for the company's needs. Here are four things you must take into account in order to navigate this process effectively:

1. *Know Who Does What.* Seek to identify all your constituents at the company and what each needs and expects from you. Consider each of the following:

- Who influences? The people you're most likely to meet in the company are probably information gatherers and influencers, not decision makers.
- Who buys? These are the people who make the final decisions. Learn what they value and how you can make them more inclined to give you their business.

TOUCHING MEMORIES ADJUSTS AND REAPS REWARD

*W*hen the custom stationery supplier Touching Memories was asked by a corporate client to include calendars in its offerings, the company's owners were hesitant. They were, after all, up to their ears in notepad and letterhead jobs. After much consideration, however, they acquiesced. The corporate client agreed to fund start-up costs by placing a large order up front, enabling Touching Memories to develop the new product at a profit. Calendars are now the company's biggest sellers, thanks in no small part to the owners' flexibility.

• Who kills? Always remember that whatever the merits of your business, someone at the client company can kill the deal without your ever knowing why or who. Listen for comments your contact may make about the people with whom he or she is dealing internally.

2. Know How to Get on the List. More and more companies try to contract only with vendors on a preferred vendor list. They do this to optimize their cost savings, avoid unreliable vendors, make their purchasing process more efficient, and/or weed out fraudulent or unstable vendors.

As a rule, if your potential client has an approved vendor program or something comparable, embrace it as a way to separate yourself from your competitors.

3. Know the Company's Lingo and Quirks. Every company speaks its own language—unique acronyms; report names; buzzwords; clichés; and nicknames for people, positions, and facilities. Your job is to learn this language, because it distinguishes insiders from outsiders.

The only way to learn this internal language is to keep your ears open. For example, if you're sitting in a meeting and hear someone use an unfamiliar term, take note and make sure to follow up with your client contact to find out what the term means.

Likewise, every company has its own policies, processes, practices, and idiosyncrasies. Studying them can only work to your advantage.

4. Know the Budget Season. Every large company—your client base—develops an annual budget. This process can take up to three months and sap the energy of the company's departments. Most of the time, a budget earmarks monies for certain functions but doesn't get into specifics. To learn those specifics, you need to know when to step on the merry-go-round—that is, to know the start and stop dates of each phase and the other details of the company's budget cycle.

Embracing the Bureaucracy

Fighting your way through the red tape of a typical corporation's floor-to-ceiling organizational chart maze can be one of the most frustrating aspects of running a business. You can, however, turn a big prospect's bureaucracy to your advantage. The key is to figure out how it works.

A bureaucracy, in all its complexity, is the software that keeps a giant company running, a control system with built-in fail-safe routines designed to avoid catastrophe. It funnels every decision through a gauntlet of decision makers to ensure that prescribed standards of quality and cost are maintained. By its very nature and purpose, it slows things down and lowers operating efficiency—but it's a necessary evil. When you approach a big company with an eye toward doing business with it, get an early start on understanding its bureaucracy. Study it, map it, and look for its hidden connections and patterns.

Perfect Your Processes Quite often, you will see that your Elephant's bureaucratic processes are not suitable for your business—they add cost, unnecessarily complicate your business activities, or even threaten the quality of your product or service. In these cases, you must fight process with process. When selling to decision makers in a bureaucracy, don't make vague promises about how you will meet their needs. Explain your processes in detail. This will reassure them that the activity will occur.

Your potential client probably doesn't like dealing with the internal bureaucracy any more than you do. Help your client. When your client takes your information to fill out his or her own company's forms, ask your client how his or her company plans to use your data so you can give it to him or her in a useful format.

Part Three: Romancing Your Elephant

Drawing Up Your Hit List

Once your entire business has a big-customer focus, you're ready to go out and bag an Elephant. Now is the time to decide which Elephant to bag. Although your business could potentially sell to many big customers, not all big customers are right for you. You must focus your efforts on the Elephants you are most likely to bag—and to develop a mutually beneficial, long-term relationship with them. There are three steps to this endeavor:

1. Position your product or service for the big customer.

2. Develop a hit list of big companies you believe would make great customers and partners.

3. Whittle down that list to the best of the best.

Positioning Your Business When you think of big customers, look beyond the obvious contenders. If you usually target the general public, consider adapting your product offering for businesses, thinking broadly about your potential clients. This broad thinking will not only expand your hit list but will give you ideas for increasing revenues as well.

Compiling Your Hit List Make a long list of all potential big customers you can think of. Be as outrageous as you can, but match the companies with the need they might have for what you offer. In other words, list exactly how you might be able to help them. Never overlook the obvious prospects—sometimes the best ones are right under your nose. Also, don't ignore smaller companies that are growing fast and showing signs of becoming true Elephants. A friend made on the way up the ladder together can be a friend for life.

Selecting the Best Target Once you've scoured the business landscape for the obvious prospects, the less obvious ones, and the downright imaginative possibilities, carve out a realistic list of the most promising. To help you identify these, answer the following questions:

- **Which prospects have the most to spend on your product or services?** In other words, who has the big bucks?
- **Does the prospect's business philosophy dovetail with your strengths?** Relationships will fail if there is a poor match.
- **How does the prospect reward the employees who would be buying your product or services?** Consider how buyers at your prospective client receive bonuses and promotions. Are they evaluated according to their ability to bring innovative ideas to the table, to buy at the lowest possible price, or to enhance the company image? The answer can help you determine whether your company fits the client's incentive structure.
- **How much does the company really need you?** Can you help the company achieve competitive advantage?
- **How far afield will the association lead you**? Consider whether the prospect's logistical factors are a good fit for your business.

Knocking on Doors

After you've identified target companies and understand generally how large companies operate and the best ways to approach them, it's time to get to work. The goal isn't just to set meetings—it's to land that big client. Here are the eight steps you should follow:

1. *Build your prospect database.* Generate a list of specific people to contact at your prospective client companies. You can develop that list even when you're starting with a blank slate. Be prepared to make many calls. Be imaginative, resourceful, and tenacious—you have nothing to lose. As you get new prospects, divide them into three categories: hot leads (the company buys what you sell and your contact is a good one), great fits (the company isn't buying what you're selling but should be), and secondary leads (the prospect isn't in the market for your product right now, but you want to introduce your business to him or her anyway).

2. *Create an introductory mailing* to quickly introduce yourself and your business. Write a cover letter that explains what you do, in order to build credibility and awareness and to set the stage for a phone call and later mailings.

3. *Make the first phone call* to gather information necessary for future contacts and to set up a meeting. Do this two or three days after your prospect has received your mailing. Prepare well for the call and try to determine what the prospect might expect to see in your product or service, whether your contact is the decision maker or someone with influence, whether the company already buys from your competitors (and, if so, whether it's happy), and what unique opportunities there might be with this prospect.

4. *Send a detailed mailing* to give the prospect information about your product and to set up a presentation. Do this immediately after contacting the prospect. Really showcase your business and appeal to the prospect with testimonials, brochures, samples, and the like.

5. *Make the second phone call* two days after the prospect has received your detailed mailing. Do this to set up a presentation and further develop your relationship. Feel out the contact, but never ask whether he or she wants to meet—communicate the assumption that he or she does and that it's just a matter of setting up a convenient time.

6. *Send a creative mailing* two weeks after the second call to prospects who have not yet agreed to meet with you. This enables you to reengage the prospect in a creative way and advertise your business rather than hard-sell your product.

7. *Make the third phone call* to prospects with whom you have not set up a meeting, one week after they receive the creative mailing, to attempt once again to set up a presentation.

8. *Stay at the top of the prospect's mind,* even if, after the first seven steps, you still have not met face-to-face with the prospect. Send out an inexpensive mailing to update prospects on your achievements, new clients, press notices, etc.

Reevaluate your prospect list regularly, but be patient. Some client relationships take time to gestate.

Matching the Prospector to the Prospect

Putting the wrong personality type in the wrong selling situation is an easy mistake to make. Fortunately, matching a salesperson with a company is not hard to master and can easily mean the difference between success and failure in a sale. In fact, it's merely a two-step process. Here are the two steps to follow:

Step 1: Profile Your Sales Personnel. Salespeople fall into the following three basic types, based on their personalities, styles, and approaches:

- *The Sage.* The Sage cites his or her own experience to make the buyer comfortable with him or her and the product. The Sage succeeds by capitalizing on his or her experience and knowledge, not from being warm and fuzzy. The Sage thrives when he or she is selling to a conscientious or skeptical customer who is concerned about some aspect of the purchasing decision. To succeed, the Sage needs useful information; proof of your product's best features; and timely, accurate responses to the customer's questions.
- *The Pal.* The Pal is a great relationship builder—very outgoing and friendly. Customers will buy from the Pal simply because they like him or her. The main attribute of the Pal is his or her uncanny ability to build relationships. In fact, the Pal thrives when his or her customer wants more from a salesperson than business and when he or she can use entertainment as a sales tool. To succeed, give the Pal clear, simple, and detailed materials that explain your product or service. Pair the Pal up with a Sage—they can have a positive effect on each other and the customer. And give the Pal your consent to spend money on entertainment for the customer.
- *The Pit Bull.* The Pit Bull is all business, churning through prospects until he or she maximizes the sale. It's all a numbers game to the Pit Bull, and he or she is typically poor at customer service, often losing repeat business as a result. His or her tenacity breeds success, but it also makes enemies. Pit Bulls prosper when they're let off the leash. They appreciate having the latitude they need to clinch deals on the spot. To succeed, Pit Bulls need independence, latitude in pricing (enabling them to close deals quickly), customer-service support, and a simplified closing process.

Step 2: Make the Match. For each selling situation match the client or customer with the right salesperson. Read between the lines. You'll have to draw your own inferences about some of your customers' needs. Assess your sales force. Once you've identified the type of salesperson you need for each target customer, review your current sales team to see how it stacks up.

Matching the right salesperson with the right situation benefits not only you, but the salesperson as well. People thrive in a job setting that suits their needs and personality.

Face-to-Face with Your Prospect

In face-to-face interactions with prospects, first impressions are crucial. You want to come across as perceptive, experienced, and confident—a professional who works with big companies every day. In order to do that, you need to make sure you get your act together. Don't prepare a one-size-fits-all sales presentation that can be rattled off in any meeting. Go into the meeting with a discussion plan tailored to that particular Elephant. Set priorities by making a list of specifics you hope to accomplish. That will help you stay focused.

You should also be able to anticipate your prospect's concerns—what he or she is likely to ask—and answer them. Better yet, prepare documents that can help answer those questions, as well as others that can clarify your answers. In short, go in prepared—never let a prospect think you're not taking the meeting seriously. During the meeting, focus on the prospect. Establish rapport by using a pleasant, conversational tone. Get the prospect to tell you something about his or her own business and its needs.

After the meeting, prepare to engage in some follow-up activities. Take a minute to write up a quick recap and to-do list, then get whatever information your prospect needs right away. Of course, all your speed and anticipation mean nothing if you can't close the deal. Establish time lines for closing and apply whatever legitimate pressure you can muster to gain commitment from the prospect.

Standing Up to Your Elephant in Negotiations

Sometimes large companies use their enormous financial power as a bargaining tool, demanding a rock-bottom price in return for volume sales. You can neutralize much of that leverage by following a few key guidelines when negotiating with an Elephant:

- **Negotiate with a person, not a company.** You're not talking to a faceless entity who has no choice but to play hardball, as he or she would like you to believe. You're talking to a person—a person who has the power to make choices and decisions. Negotiate accordingly.

- **Prioritize what you're willing to give up.** Decide beforehand what really matters and what doesn't—and which points you can concede in order to appear magnanimous. If you reach the end of your price-cutting tether, look for throw-ins you can add to the deal to make the client feel the company is getting more value for its money.
- **Don't surrender too quickly.** Rather than agreeing to all points upfront, tell your prospect that you must check with your management. This will give the impression that he or she is doing a good job and that you're working to get your management to give in.
- **Don't sell yourself short.** If you didn't offer some promise of benefit to the prospect's company, he or she wouldn't waste his or her time talking with you.
- **Mitigate all pricing concessions.** Once you lower your prices, it's virtually impossible to raise them again. If you must do so anyway, have the company commit in writing to a volume buy or reduced service levels so you can still make a profit. In general, look for a long-term deal in exchange for a lower price.
- **Create a pricing strategy and stick to it.** Decide on a price that is fair and reasonable for everyone, then stick to that price when negotiating. Either you'll get the business or you won't. If you commoditize your offerings, it will be tough to get your full price again.

Recruiting Great Champions

A champion is someone inside the prospective company who goes to bat for you by trying to get his or her company to use your services. He or she speaks on your behalf during closed-door meetings and passes your name around to co-workers. As you spend more time communicating with your prospects, keep your eyes open for a champion, bearing in mind that your best champion is:

- **Motivated by what's best for the business.** He or she makes decisions based on what's good for his or her employer, not on politics.
- **Respected by superiors.** Management looks to him or her for solid business recommendations.
- **Socially networked.** People like a champion, so his or her endorsement carries extra weight and cachet.
- **Able to navigate the company to get things done.** He or she knows how to sell ideas internally.
- **Cut from the same cloth as you.** You have chemistry because you share the same business philosophy, work ethic, or background.

- **Willing to give credit rather than protect turf**. He or she must feel that your success and the success of the deal reflect well upon him or her.

Building Strong Alliances

Once you're booking sales, know your way around the client, and have at least one in-house champion backing you, it's time to seek and form alliances. Alliances will result in your getting business from a company in exchange for things your ally needs—power, information, or better work experience. In order to develop alliances, you must first identify which of those needs applies, then develop a plan to fulfill it.

Most large companies have many departments, which typically can be sorted into three categories. **Profit-Holder** departments are the keepers of the budget, monitoring income and outflow. They are the most powerful of the departments and are thus ultimately responsible for whether products make a buck. Because these departments hold the purse strings, they can be the most powerful and rewarding allies. Keep in mind that they are judged solely on bottom line—people working for them are on the upper-management track and need to perform. For that reason, you should emphasize your own efficiency and effectiveness at providing the best return for the money.

Necessity departments are crucial to the client's core business—they are the shippers, purchasers, manufacturers, and the like. Their daily tasks typically fall on the cost side of the budget, within the limits set by the Profit-Holder departments. Employees in Necessity departments tend to value comfort and working conditions over stellar performance; you need to make life easier for them—it's as simple as that.

Resource departments support the Profit-Holder and Necessity departments, often operating without a budget, as they are seen as nonessential areas—customer service, market research, new business development, etc. Whenever appropriate, consider inviting Resource employees to client meetings, if your client contact approves. This shows them you're in the know and looking out for them.

Putting Your Elephant to Work

Aside from making you wealthy, a strong client can do a great deal for you, your business, and your employees. If you're smart, your relationship with your Elephant should be all you need to catapult your business to success.

One area of business in which an Elephant can provide significant funding is in new business development. If you're selling one item, look for the need to buy others, then use your relationship to sell more. Once big clients begin to

---

KEEP YOUR CHAMPIONS CHEERING

*O*nce you have relationships with solid champions working your cause from the inside, you'll need to foster the relationships to keep getting the most out of them over time. Some ways to do this include:

Share the limelight. If you share credit with champions, you'll acquire a reputation as someone who is easy to work with and useful.

Share the knowledge. Keep champions informed of your latest plans and work with them, not around them.

Know when to back off. Don't exploit their generosity.

Make a happy family. Look for new champions as you move up the company ladder. You can never have too many, and you need them at all levels.

Express gratitude. A simple "thank you" goes a long way.

---

rely on you and you deliver for them, they'll want to use you in other parts of the business and will help you develop the capacity to meet these other needs. Your ability to use your relationship with these clients to identify such opportunities can provide a huge boost to your business.

Training and Expertise Another significant area of growth is in training and expertise. Look for ways to grow and learn from your client's knowledge base. If the client company needs an additional service from you or has a department that performs a service you can integrate with your other services, see if you can get the client to train your employees. Tell the client that its training your staff will help you support it. Many large companies also bring in national speakers to give presentations to their employees—some of the best speakers you will ever hear can be heard courtesy of a client. Make certain, however, that the client doesn't perceive you as taking advantage or moving into unauthorized areas.

A SEAT AT THE TABLE

by Marc Miller

I s Velcro the secret to more sales? According to Marc Miller, founder and CEO of Sogistics Corporation, the famous hook-and-loop fasteners are the perfect metaphor for the need to stick your solutions to your client's initiatives. The old method of straight-line sales has no place in today's marketplace. This type of bold statement is no surprise when one considers it comes from the author of *Selling Is Dead*, a book that examined the changing role of the salesperson from client conduit to growth engineer.

Miller's much-anticipated follow-up, *A Seat at the Table*, continues the author's technique of breaking the sales process down to its essence before giving sales professionals a new outlook. Value is at the heart of Miller's mission in this book. He plainly states that value is the customer's lone goal and the critical element on which a sales professional's company will be judged. This requires a transformation on the part of the sales representative. He or she is no longer a person with a product and a pitch. The sales professional is attempting to become part of the company's process to achieve its strategic goals.

The seat to which Miller refers in his book's title is firmly planted next to the lead decision maker in the prospect's company. This individual garners a good deal of attention in Miller's work. Sales professionals are taught how to quickly connect with this person. Miller gives readers one of the more effective methods of solidifying a relationship to come along in recent years. He artfully merges the schema presented by W. Chan Kim and Renée Mauborgne in their 2005 release *Blue Ocean Strategy* with the decision-making categories from Geoffrey A. Moore's best-selling innovation guide, *Dealing with Darwin*. The result is a matrix that allows a sales representative to construct the ideal solutions to match the prospect's urgent and important decisions. By targeting the key areas in which a client needs help, the salesperson removes the time-wasting process of random discovery that often leads a sale nowhere.

Miller reminds sales professionals to treat every sale as a unique situation. What's astounding is how often this advice is acknowledged by sales professionals yet immediately ignored as the call volume piles up. *A Seat at the Table* is a book whose emphasis on strategy demonstrates that Miller believes as much in the application of his ideas as in the ideas themselves. He provides readers with a detailed set of questioning techniques that are a critical component in the process of gaining a seat at the prospect's table. Upon achieving that seat, salespeople may find a feast awaiting them. The generation of value proves itself time and again to be the distinguishing factor when a decision maker examines his or her business plan and the role the salesperson will play in it. With Miller's strategies, sales professionals increase the likelihood of featuring heavily in the customer's plans.

A SEAT AT THE TABLE
How Top Salespeople Connect and Drive Decisions at the Executive Level
by Marc Miller

CONTENTS
1. Game Change
2. Velcro Value
3. The Great Game of Strategy
4. Connection Mastery
5. Conversations That Connect
6. FOCAS on Building a Case for Change
7. On the Same Side of the Table

THE SUMMARY IN BRIEF

To close more sales, stop selling.

Sales expert Marc Miller offers a new sales approach designed to help you earn "a seat at the table"—the place reserved for those select people who set the direction and the budget of an enterprise.

In today's commoditized business world, customers care about only one thing: value. To offer real value, you must stop being a salesperson and become a businessperson who sells. Only then can you help your customers increase productivity and profitability, which are the key factors of growth—and your continued success.

This summary explains how to connect with executives and decision makers from the very first point of contact—psychologically, strategically, and financially—to prove your value. When you can do this, you will be able to create demand for your products and services, protect your core business, and close more sales. Building on his experiences identifying best practices of thousands of salespeople, Miller offers all the tools you need to close more and bigger deals.

In addition, you will learn

- How to use a simple, analytical matrix for illuminating customer strategies.
- How to use a methodology that will have every contact offering up the information that you need to make the sale.
- How to generate recommendations that are perfectly aligned with customer strategic needs.
- How to close more and bigger deals—and help your customers succeed.

THE COMPLETE SUMMARY

Game Change

All of the difficulties companies are facing in our turbulent, constantly shifting economy are actually creating the opportunity of a lifetime for salespeople— specifically, the opportunity to play a far more important role in the lives of the customers on whom they call. For those special salespeople who embrace this new role, the world will be one of endless opportunity. Their customers will see them as difference makers, champions who deliver value far surpassing that of any single product or service.

There is new evidence to suggest that salespeople can transcend their current "brand" as product peddlers to achieve record levels of productivity. But to do this they must accept one simple truth:

The Only Thing Your Customer Cares About Is Value

To achieve radically better sales results, you must become radically more valuable to customers—strategically valuable. The game has changed, and new research suggests customers are pleading for a new and different type of value from salespeople. And when this new value is created, captured, and delivered, customers no longer view salespeople as salespeople at all. They now see "businesspeople who sell"—those worthy of a seat at their table.

Earning a Seat at the Table

Customers today are looking for value in the form of help—specifically, strategic help. Corporations are under pressure as never before—business failure and executive turnover are at an all-time high, and business models need adjusting not once every year, but seemingly every week. And executives often get lost in this rapid pace of change. They need to focus on the future, but the day-to-day running of a business is like gravity, a force that continually drags them down into the daily muck, battling the fires as necessary to drive short-term results. As a result, senior executives often get off track, becoming disconnected from the real purpose of their organizations—to sustain profitable growth.

And this is where you come in. You have an opportunity to play a new role, and that new role has two distinct parts. First, you have to help executives reconnect to their strategies. When you help customers reconnect to what's important, you connect to them. Second, you need to devise solutions that will help them achieve or expand their master strategic plan.

Quit talking about expenses (products and services) and start having discussions about investments (productivity and differentiation). From the perspective of the executives you will be calling, these are polar opposites. Comprehend your customer's strategies and connect your products and services to them. This is how you will earn a seat at the table—that lofty position that executives reserve for those special businesspeople who add strategic value, who make a profound impact on their results, their enterprises, and their people.

A New Role, a New Mind-set

To successfully engage at senior levels, salespeople need to abandon the old ways—in effect, unlearn to sell. This means letting go of the "sell something to someone" mind-set so pervasive among product-myopic sellers who cannot see the big picture of customer value beyond their products. Instead, the salesperson's focus must shift—uncompromisingly—to connecting and adding value to client strategy.

For sales revenues to lift, selling must end and helping must begin. No doubt helping a client achieve radically better results often requires a different sales mind-set. You will need to

- focus less on how you influence clients and more on how you impact their businesses;
- shift from competing with other vendors to creating value for your client;
- concentrate less on making a sale and more on making a difference.

In other words, the mind-set must be on helping the client. This means listening, understanding, and, on occasion, telling the customer that change might not be in his or her best interest. It means delivering a new kind of help that is more about expertise and know-how than about products and services, a kind of help that touches every facet of a business.

Strategic Value

All salespeople believe they are strategically valuable to customers. They believe they are already helping. Unfortunately, the evidence proves otherwise, as shown by a landmark survey conducted by MasterCard.

Looking for ways to differentiate itself in a crowded sphere, MasterCard asked more than one thousand of its key business customers an important question: What value would they like to receive more of from their MasterCard salesperson? In a resounding vote of need, customers requested that Master-Card salespeople help in more strategic ways: competitive strategy, strategic thinking, innovation, and alignment.

When the final numbers were tabulated, corporate customers rated Master-Card salespeople a paltry 4.1 on a scale of 1 to 10 on their ability to deliver strategic value. In other words, what customers felt was lacking was the ability of MasterCard salespeople to drive the customers' businesses. Master-Card executives asked MasterCard salespeople to rate themselves in the very same category. The salespeople gave their own strategic value-creation abilities a 9.9!

Upon seeing the results, MasterCard leaders realized they had just encountered a new enemy—the distorted belief system of their sales and account-management teams.

Flawed Self-Assessment Until salespeople understand that they can be an actual barrier to delivering new, more strategic value to customers, the organizations that employ them will never realize their true potential. Salespeople who do not understand how to add strategic value negatively impact both the sustainability efforts of their organizations and the customers on whom they call.

Velcro Value

You will need to "make like Velcro" to ensure that your complex solutions stick with your customers. Think of a fuzzy Velcro surface that has hundreds of loops representing all of the client strategies—a few big ones along with dozens to hundreds of substrategies.

The other Velcro surface—the coarse one with the hooks—is your value proposition. A single value proposition adds many, many different types of customer value. It removes a variety of problems, helps different departments in very different ways, and enables the accomplishments of multiple strategies. Now think of each single Velcro hook as representing these many individual value elements.

RAISING SALES PRODUCTIVITY

*W*hen you gain a seat at the table, sales productivity will rise significantly because of your ability to do the following:

1. *Protect the core:* Customer executives who consider you to be strategically valuable will not let their internal procurement people reduce the relationship to the lowest common denominator—that is, a cheaper price.
2. *Gain access:* When you have earned a seat at the table, you will be able to connect with more senior executives—the ones who can make big-bet, discretionary, risk/reward decisions that affect your offerings.
3. *Create demand:* Creating demand for new products and solutions requires building a case for change with multiple executives and decision makers.
4. *Get the best of both worlds:* When you successfully add value to the strategies of executives, you are able both to protect your core and to sell the new, without having to sacrifice one opportunity for the other.

Your job is to simply bring the two together, making sure the proper "value connections" are made with those people who have an important voice in the decision. When this happens—instant connection!

The more client strategies you can put your value hooks into, the better.

But before you can "make like Velcro," you're going to have to learn how to align your side with the client's side: how to make the connections in a way that will stick. To do this you need to learn a little bit more about what generates the Velcro surface with all the loops—the fuzzy client strategies.

New Customer Realities

The real takeaway of the MasterCard research is that today's customer not only needs but also is actively requesting a different kind of help. Customers and prospects are looking for the salespeople who call on them to connect and add value to their strategies.

Discovering the drivers of this common need is the first step salespeople must take in becoming strategically valuable and connecting with executives.

Customers, especially senior executives, are under enormous pressure today to deliver on two fronts:

1. The Province of Productivity, where senior executives must deliver the quarterly and annual numbers that satisfy all of the stakeholders—not an easy task. Productivity is about generating more with less.

2. The Domain of Differentiation, where senior executives must ensure that the enterprise is well positioned for the future—an even more daunting challenge. Differentiation means creating new offerings, entering different markets, or devising any new strategy that leads to competitive separation, higher growth, and the ultimate reward, premium profit margins.

Productivity and differentiation are the two major executive decision categories that drive scores of subdecisions within an enterprise.

Bridging the Divide

One cannot underscore the difficulty inherent in selling divergent or complex offerings, especially in scenarios where demand must be created. A wonderful vignette on the difficulty of change comes from Machiavelli's *The Prince*:

> There is nothing . . . more doubtful of success than an attempt to introduce a new order of things. The innovator has for enemies all those who derived advantages from the old order of things, while those who expect to benefit by the new order will be but lukewarm defenders. This indifference arises in part from fear of their adversaries and partly from the incredulity of established experience.

In other words, serious change that requires major commitment will necessitate building bridges that take executives beyond mere curiosity and that eliminate the divide between adversaries and supporters of the new order.

We call this process "bridging the divide," a process that requires salespeople to build a bedrock foundation for change—with change-resistant organizations. To do this requires a sound knowledge of an organization's master strategies and a different FOCAS (an acronym defined later in this summary).

Set Sail The first step in improving sales effectiveness lies in understanding that "not all sales are created equal." This is especially true for those faced with selling divergent, complex offerings that customer executives perceive as high reward but equally high risk. In these cases, demand is best created by attaching the offering to a ship that has already set sail—that vessel being customer strategy.

The Great Game of Strategy

Strategy is pretty simple stuff—as long as you have the proper schema to act as a road map. A schema is a mental model that serves as a visual reference point. For example, a blueprint of a new home is a schema. Schemas help you quickly make sense of a complicated situation, essentially helping you reach—in the words of Oliver Wendell Holmes—the simplicity on the other side of complexity.

FIGURE 5.1: THE MASTER STRATEGIC PLAN MATRIX

	Important Decisions	Urgent Decisions
Blue Ocean Strategies	I Innovation Decisions	II Implementation Decisions
Red Ocean Strategies	IV Outsourcing Decisions	III Optimization Decisions

The schema presented here—the Master Strategic Plan Matrix—is based on two distinct schools of thought about strategy and decision making. The first is the concept of Blue Ocean and Red Ocean strategies, developed by W. Chan Kim and Renée Mauborgne in their popular business book *Blue Ocean Strategy*, a treatise on how to create new forms of customer value. The second is an analysis of the two types of decisions high-level executives make almost every day that dictate how they allocate funds: important decisions and urgent decisions. This distinction was made by Geoffrey A. Moore, author of many books on marketing, in his book *Dealing with Darwin*.

Oceans Two

The first component of the schema is represented by two very large oceans—one red and the other blue. Each ocean represents a different category of strategy, and the two are diametrically opposed.

A Red Ocean strategy is any strategy that supports the "core business" of the enterprise. This is the domain of mature, competitive categories—products, services, or markets on which a company has relied for past growth and profits. Unfortunately, competition has gradually swooped in and commoditized offerings that were once new and unique.

A Blue Ocean strategy is any strategy that supports the new products, services, or markets that represent higher margins and faster growth. This is the place where the company sees its best opportunities for future growth. The goal in this space is to separate from the competitive herd through significant differentiation.

Moore delineates the decisions that executives make as important decisions or urgent decisions. Important decisions are decisions the executive considers important in the long run. Important decisions are typically about tomorrow, the future. That makes them less "edgy," or less critical, than urgent decisions, which require immediate attention.

An urgent decision is critical—it must be taken care of immediately. Since every organization must survive today—or there will be no tomorrow—urgent decisions often take precedence over important decisions.

The Master Strategic Plan Matrix

To understand how senior executives attempt to sustain growth requires classifying decisions into four quadrants. The Master Strategic Plan Matrix helps you visualize how the Blue and Red Oceans overlap with the important and urgent decisions.

The matrix (to be read clockwise from the top left-hand quadrant) is divided into two rows (the two oceans) and two columns (the two types of decisions) that intersect to create four quadrants. The top row of the matrix is Blue Ocean decisions; the bottom row is Red Ocean decisions. The left column is for important decisions; the right column is for urgent decisions.

Based on these elements, the Master Strategic Plan Matrix shows how executives make the risk/reward decisions that sustain profitable growth.

The Big Four Decisions

Categorizing organizational spending is a good first step in your quest to better understand client strategy. Next, you'll need to learn the big four decisions made by all senior executives in their quest to sustain the growth of their companies. The Master Strategic Plan Matrix will help you understand and analyze these decisions.

- **Quadrant I: Innovation Decisions (Blue Ocean, Important).** Decisions in this quadrant revolve around the future; new markets, value, or offerings must be created for positive differentiation—the driver of Blue Ocean strategies. The "urgent-less" nature of this quadrant means that these decisions tend to be less of a priority in many organizations.

- **Quadrant II: Implementation Decisions (Blue Ocean, Urgent).** These decisions are about deploying the Blue Ocean strategies that have been created in Quadrant I. New products and services have been created. Now it is time to turn the potential into the actual. Speed is critical in this quadrant—the organization must move quickly to capture new opportunities.

- **Quadrant III: Optimization Decisions (Red Ocean, Urgent).** In this quadrant, offerings and markets have now matured. Competition has entered the fray, squeezing margins and slowing growth—problems Red Ocean strategies are designed to combat. The primary focus of this quadrant is maintaining the legacy cash cow that still accounts for the majority of revenues—urgent dollars that pay the bills and enable the organization to survive for another day.

- **Quadrant IV: Outsourcing Decisions (Red Ocean, Important).** In this final quadrant, leadership must answer the question What should we not be doing? Valuable people and money need to be freed from the Red Ocean and redirected to the Blue Ocean for new differentiation strategies to succeed.

Connection Mastery

Prepare, capture, and feedback—this is the cycle required to gain mastery in any complex process, skill, or methodology.

Preparing for the Call

Cheat sheets are a key transformative tool for great preparation. Cheat sheets allow you to prepare for complex opportunities by highlighting critical information that you feel is essential to grasp for an upcoming call. Cheat sheets ultimately enable you to better prepare for critical sales calls—no easy task when calling on executives who run complex organizations.

Cheat sheet categories can be many and varied. All vastly improve sales call preparation. They include sales effectiveness cheat sheets, technical cheat sheets, industry cheat sheets, functional title/department cheat sheets, customer cheat sheets, and internal best practices cheat sheets.

Capturing the Call

Experts recommend that you record important sales calls using capture technology. But the technology needs to be unobtrusive so as not to inhibit open dialogue with the customer you're calling on. You need to ask for his or her permission, of course, but rest assured that most clients are open to capture technology for one simple reason—it adds value to their strategy.

Call Feedback

Once a call is captured, you must actually do something with the recording to ensure that this final step of mastery is accomplished. Make sure you're either self-coaching or using a third-party coach to ensure that you're both maximizing your potential and optimizing each of your valuable selling opportunities.

For savvy sales leaders and managers, this feedback capability is indeed the Holy Grail of sales-force effectiveness. Since selected customer conversations conducted in the field can now be immediately assessed with capture technology, the opportunity to quickly coach salespeople to higher performance is finally available. This moves training from the classroom to the field—the place of execution, where real accountability and change occur.

Conversations That Connect

Making a connection with a senior executive will require the combination of two important ingredients:

1. *A strategic blueprint:* The Master Strategic Plan Matrix tells you how organizations sustain profitable growth.

2. *A questioning structure:* The FOCAS questioning model enables you to quickly connect to executive strategy.

Discovery

Gaining an in-depth understanding of the customer does not happen on just one call. Discovery is where the process begins. This makes discovery the most important sales call of all.

Following are the four parts of discovery:

1. *Approach:* A one- to two-minute high-level overview that gives the prospect some important background information on your company.

2. *Questioning:* A twenty-minute to two-hour discussion to learn as much relevant information about the prospect as possible.

3. *Summary:* A quick "Here's what I heard" recap.

4. *Progression:* A recommendation of next steps.

Approach and Questioning

In the approach, you will cover two important pieces of information: what you do and the purpose of your call. "What you do" is your strategic positioning statement—something with which you probably grapple. This is a statement spoken in simple language that helps the customer understand what you do best. The important point here is to not describe your company as a "product" company, a very easy and common mistake. Remember, you are in the results business—high-impact results—and if you don't communicate this quickly to a senior executive you immediately risk misalignment and loss of interest.

The next step—and the most important part of discovery—is the questioning process. To help you, here is how to FOCAS.

FOCAS

"FOCAS" is an acronym, with each letter signifying a type of question. Each type of question is unique in its intent and function. Broken into its components, the FOCAS questioning model is as follows:

- **F**act Questions
- **O**bjective Questions
- **C**oncern Questions
- **A**nchor Questions
- **S**olution Questions

The FOCAS model allows you to transcend negative, pain-based questioning, helping you learn what an organization is attempting to create. This dialogue is much more positive in tone, and it will generate valuable information to help you build your case for change.

FOCAS on Customer Strategy

FOCAS is a questioning structure that leads to very dynamic customer conversations. What keeps FOCAS on track is its strategic intent—to uncover strategy, objectives, and challenges of the customer in a systematic way. This strategy is the glue that keeps the conversation coming back to common ground and keeps your queries high payoff for both parties.

Fact Questions

Fact Questions are the easiest type of questions in the FOCAS model. Fact Questions are used to collect data, facts, and information about the buyer's current situation. Here are two examples of common Fact Questions:

- Could you give me a little more background on this division?
- In which markets do you generate most of your revenue?

Fact Questions are necessary to capture vital information that you are unable to acquire through precall research. However, they are also low-payoff questions for both buyer and seller. You need to limit the number of Fact Questions you ask, spending five to ten minutes on them at most, and move quickly to questions that you and the buyer find more meaningful.

Objective Questions

Objective Questions are questions used to identify and investigate the buyer's objectives.

Objective Questions are critical to helping you understand the master strategic plan of the customer, the driving goal of the questioning process. Once you learn this plan, you can drill down into each quadrant, uncovering which objectives are most critical from both a differentiation (Blue Ocean) and a productivity (Red Ocean) perspective. The following are examples of Objective Questions:

- How do you see the organization needing to change over the next few years to retain its competitive edge?
- Where do you see your best future opportunities for profitable growth?

Once you feel you've learned the critical goals that relate to this organization and individual, it is time to move on.

Concern Questions

Concern Questions explore the dissatisfaction, difficulties, concerns, and problems that the executive or prospect may be experiencing. Therefore, the strategic intent of Concern Questions is to find buyer dissatisfaction—especially strategic discontent.

Following are two examples of Concern Questions:

- Could you share with me some of the more interesting challenges you are facing in the accomplishment of your core strategies?
- Have you had any issues with losing market share to overseas competition?

Concern Questions serve as an excellent foundation on which to build a case for change for your solutions.

Anchor Questions

Anchor Questions explore the seriousness of problems already identified. Anchor Questions are designed to broaden the discussion of these issues, helping an executive see that narrow problems often have systemic consequences. For this reason, Anchor Questions are extremely high payoff because they help executives see the broader—or enterprise—implications of a problem.

Examples of Anchor Questions include:

- Do you feel that your bottlenecking problem is affecting your reputation in the market?

• How is that void in hiring quality people affecting your ability to make faster inroads into the new market?

Anchor Questions resonate because they represent the reasoning process of an executive.

Solution Questions

The last type of question in the FOCAS model is Solution Questions. Solution Questions are unique in that they develop the executive's recognition of the value or usefulness of your solution. Unlike Concern or Anchor Questions, they do not explore dissatisfaction areas. Rather, these are value-focused questions that help you understand the interest level of an executive in potential solutions.

Following are two examples of Solution Questions:

• In what ways might it help your organization to solve that bottleneck issue?
• How would it help you if we could free up valuable resources in that area?

Solution Questions help you learn whether the executive sees value in the removal of problems. Solution Questions get the buyer to think about potential solutions and determine whether or not his or her problems or dissatisfactions are serious enough to justify action.

They also help the buyer see your potential role in the achievement of his or her objectives and opportunities and help you get feedback on the value of helping in important strategic areas.

On the Same Side of the Table

Good strategy is always based on sound objectives, so let's start by examining some important goals you'll ideally want to accomplish on the next visit:

1. *The case for change*: You need to demonstrate that change might be in the best interest of the client—or at least worthy of further investigation.

2. *Same side of the table*: At some point during this second meeting, those in attendance must begin seeing you as a consultant.

3. *Shock absorber*: You need a shock-absorber mechanism between needs analysis (the discovery call) and your eventual specific proposal (in the future).

4. *Conceptual agreement*: The sooner you can conceptually agree on direction, the better.

Ultimately, you want to paint a vision for the prospect—a powerful vision that adds significant value to his or her current strategy. This happens *after* you've demonstrated that you understand his or her objectives and constraints but *before* you show ideas and options. In other words, a vision is introduced only after one has *connected to strategy*.

General Recommendations

The General Recommendations tool will enable you to connect to customer strategy, build a case for change, and achieve your other goals for this second meeting. The purpose of this tool is to establish a business argument that change is in the customer's best interest. Done properly, this mechanism not only accomplishes this goal but also offers a range of options for how to move forward at appropriate—but varying—risk levels.

General Recommendations are presented in a document that you will walk through with the buyer, page by page. This can be done in a visual presentation format for a larger group, but since your second meeting usually will have only a handful of individuals, a paper document is more appropriate. The process of delivering the document is critical, and the delivery should become a disciplined skill.

A General Recommendations document consists of five parts:

1. *Situation summary.* This first section contains factual information learned via your Fact Questions during discovery.

2. *Goals and objectives.* Ideally, this portion of the document captures the critical objectives of the enterprise at two levels: organizational and departmental.

3. *Constraints, issues, and challenges.* This section reveals the problems—and the systemic consequences of those problems—originally uncovered in your discovery visit.

4. *Vision.* This should be a fairly simple but powerful depiction of the better future you are espousing for this particular client.

5. *Options.* By offering fundamentally different types of value at this point, you can better—and more quickly—determine the true quality of this opportunity.

No Closing

Encourage the group to talk things through before they make a decision. In other words, please do not implode your entire effort by attempting to close on one or all of the options. Slow down the process by encouraging the key decision base to discuss your suggestions to determine the best course of action.

Then simply agree on a date in the (near) future when they can give you commitment or direction.

Difference Maker

When executives who lead companies say that you really made a big impact, they are indirectly telling you that you have gained a seat at their table. This table is reserved for those special businesspeople who have made a profound impact on both the executives' personnel and their enterprises.

Helping your clients in new and different ways is really your ultimate reward, and there could be no better or higher reward. Remember, you can make a huge difference in their lives.

A Businessperson Who Sells

Until you become a businessperson who sells, the client will never see you as being different. You will be viewed as a salesperson, a strategic account manager, a sales engineer, a technical specialist, or even a sales consultant—all traditional roles played by traditional people who deliver traditional results. You will be uninteresting, underwhelming, and unnecessary. An expense. Nothing could be worse.

On the flip side, when you help a client achieve a differentiated position, you will be viewed as something entirely different—a change agent, a strategic consultant, or a client adviser. You will be interesting, important, and impactful. Not only will you be sought out, but you will also stand out. An investment. Nothing could be better. You will be seen as a difference maker, and the difference is profound.

EXCEPTIONAL SELLING

by Jeff Thull

Jeff Thull understands the barriers that prevent salespeople from reaching the next level of success. He points to limited access to prospects, mishandling of intense negotiations, verbal ambiguity, and pointless objections as the most common problems. Many of these roadblocks begin and end with poor communication. Thull's expertise as a communicator makes him an excellent resource to overcome this critical issue for sales professionals. Thull has delivered more than 2,500 speeches and seminars, the majority of which have addressed the topic of complex sales. In addition, he has worked with clients such as Shell Global Systems, 3M, and Georgia-Pacific in the area of executive strategy.

Thull brings this expertise to the individual sales professional through his writings. Coming on the heels of his earlier success, *Mastering the Complex Sale*, Thull's 2006 release, *Exceptional Selling,* is a course in communication taught by a master of the art. Like a few of his contemporaries, Thull recognizes the need to make the sales process resemble amicable partnering for a common good, rather than two combatants sitting down to negotiate terms of surrender. Where Thull differs, to the benefit of salespeople who read *Exceptional Selling*, is in his in-depth evaluation of the psychology behind the process.

Not content to pin the lost sale on the customer, Thull begins *Exceptional Selling* by forcing sales professionals to look inward. A professional's mental attitude is probably the single greatest factor in determining whether or not he or she will be able to sell the product or service to the client. Price, aggression, and negativity can all be overcome if the salesperson is willing to let go of what Thull refers to as the Old Brain emotional mind-set. He leads salespeople to a better understanding of what drives their actions in the heat of the moment. The salesperson can then take this information and use it as an emergency brake when the emotions of the sales call cause him or her to lurch into instinctive reactions.

Exceptional Selling is a step-by-step walk through the sales process with dozens of insights at each turn. Thull explodes the traditional notion of a sales presentation and instead instructs sales representatives to work on diagnosing the prospect's organization. He points out that sales professionals too often present the prospect with a solution before truly understanding the organization's problem. Not only does this smack of a certain level of presumption, but it does nothing to open the customer's mind to the salesperson's ideas. Thull helps salespeople to see the value in journeying with the customer on a path he calls the Progression to Change. This key concept helps set *Exceptional Selling* apart from other sales titles that push an agenda of door-busting power moves.

Punctuating the book with answers to what he calls the Cynic's Sidebar, Thull is unafraid to tackle the questions that underperforming sales professionals are likely to ask. He offers no excuses for poor performance and guides salespeople through the twists and turns that commonly derail a sale, even when everything seems to be going perfectly well. Perhaps the greatest lesson a salesperson can learn from *Exceptional Selling* is to walk away from each sale as a partner with the customer in creating a solution instead of merely serving as an order filler. It's not just about selling a product, and Thull captures this sentiment in an effective, applicable manner.

EXCEPTIONAL SELLING
How the Best Connect and Win in High Stakes Sales
by Jeff Thull

CONTENTS

THE SUMMARY IN BRIEF

Exceptional Selling is a practical guide to sales success that shows sales professionals how to avoid the many traps of self-sabotage brought about by pressure and traditional sales approaches. It shows sales professionals how to create a different kind of relationship with the customer and use powerful diagnostic principles to reframe the typical sales conversation into open, honest, and straightforward communication.

Even today, with so much sales experience in the world, the marketplace is cluttered with seminars, consultants, trainers, and books that espouse antiquated approaches to selling. The goal of *Exceptional Selling* is to show you that by replicating the practices of top-performing professionals, you'll learn new, exceptional ways to sell that can set you apart and pull you ahead of the pack. Those of you looking to notch up your skills in order to compete effectively in an ever-evolving market will see that fine-tuning some areas of your approach can have a major impact on your results.

Sales professionals and entrepreneurs will also be warned about the pitfalls that can get them into trouble, such as creating "dangling insults" that can shut down conversations with both customers and best-qualified prospects. Sales conversations are rife with such traps. *Exceptional Selling* exposes those traps and offers logical and proven alternatives that enhance the clarity, relevancy, credibility, and trust that sales professionals are trying to create in conversations with customers.

In addition, you'll learn the following:

- Three root causes of failure that can prevent you from succeeding
- How ingrained reactions and traditional selling strategies and techniques combine to create an atmosphere of confrontation between salespeople and their customers
- How preprogrammed behaviors and reactions get both salespeople and their customers into trouble
- How salespeople consistently overestimate both the customer's comprehension of the problem to be solved and the solutions proposed and the customer's readiness to make decisions

THE COMPLETE SUMMARY

Part I: "What We Got Here Is a Failure to Communicate"

No sales professional in his right mind would sabotage his own efforts; nevertheless, salespeople all too often undermine their credibility and alienate the very customers and prospects they count on for their livelihoods.

Salespeople can't look to customers to clue them in. Customers aren't going to rationally discuss how they were insulted or alienated. Instead, successful professionals win customer loyalty and trust through respectful, honest, and diagnostic-based communications.

The More You Sweat, the Less You Sell

The most common forms of sales sabotage are stylistic. How salespeople talk with customers can easily undermine the ability to succeed and win business. If you don't know how to effectively structure and conduct customer conversations, what you talk about doesn't make much difference. How you speak with your customers has an equally powerful impact on your career. When customers are engaged, they learn. When what they learn is compelling enough to make them want to change and take action, they will buy. It might be difficult to accept that you may be sabotaging your own career, but consider the evidence:

- Most people, and that includes sales, service, and support professionals, are not naturally effective communicators.
- The techniques promoted in the majority of sales-training programs exacerbate our innate communication shortcomings.
- When salespeople get emotionally involved in the outcome of a customer engagement and start to try to drag the customer into compliance using outdated techniques, they are confirming the customer's negative assumptions and stereotypes about the sales profession.

The Emotional Mind-set—the Root of Miscommunication Your emotional mind-set can either provide the foundation on which all successful communications are built or be the primary instrument sabotaging your credibility.

One effective way to recognize the sources and effects of mind-set in conversation and relationships is by looking at patterns of adopted beliefs and observed behaviors, like the pattern of parent and child. A very common scenario occurs when salespeople unwittingly play the parent with customers and alienate them at the very beginning of the sale. Many customers hear a parent or superior insinuating that they don't know their own business.

Once the parent and the child manifest themselves in a business conversation, old patterns of reacting often kick in, and what's left of your connection and credibility with the customer quickly deteriorates.

The Amazing Old Brain Another hidden element of an emotional mind-set that negatively impacts salespeople resides in what scientists define as the Old Brain. Think about how quickly a customer's gesture or tone of voice can trigger a negative perception, or worse, a negative reaction in you. There is a good chance you are seeing the Old Brain and the adaptive unconscious at work in these situations.

Stress can also close salespeople down. They start thinking about the consequences of not closing this sale, worrying about how they are going to salvage it and what they are going to say next. They are so involved in their own problems that they aren't paying attention to the customer and they stop listening.

Presentations Commoditize Solutions The solutions salespeople sell are often more confusing to customers than the problems that are solved. First, they transform salespeople into professors giving lectures, one of the least effective ways to transmit knowledge. The second flaw is the concept of the salesperson as persuader. The problem here is that we rarely stop to think about how customers perceive the tactics of persuasion that salespeople are taught and encouraged to use. Suddenly, the meeting between salesperson and customer has turned into a debate, or worse, an outright argument.

Customer Expectations—Snake Oil and the Hard Sell Just as it takes two to tango, salespeople and customers enter conversations with preconceived perceptions and expectations and distinct mind-sets. Customers tend to paint all salespeople with the same brush. To them, salespeople—no matter whether they sell advanced avionics or used cars—all come out of the same mold. And customers' negative perception of salespeople is often based on direct experience.

Solving the Style Challenge To break these patterns and establish credibility and trust with customers

- salespeople need to be professionally involved and emotionally detached in conversations with customers;
- salespeople must retrain themselves and learn new conversational processes and skills;
- salespeople have to confront their conditioning and establish themselves as valued business advisers.

Nobody Buys a Value Proposition

The overwhelming abundance of information in today's world secures the issue of substance as the second major challenge in credible conversations. What is the one and only thing your customers really want to know? Value.

Commoditization of the Value Proposition Companies create value propositions to articulate the value they plan to offer customers. These statements become the basis and guiding force of the collateral materials that marketers develop for the sales organization: sales messaging, brochures, PowerPoint decks, and so on. The sales force dutifully takes all of this collateral and presents it to the prospect. However, the salesperson has no idea if the value has relevance for the customer. Often, the customer doesn't, either.

SALESPEOPLE PLAY THE "CHILD" ROLE, TOO

*I*n the dialogue that follows, you'll see that salespeople often respond as the child to their customer-parents:

Prospect: Our company is planning to purchase an integrated CRM software package for our marketing, sales, and service staff. We would like you to demonstrate your solution to our management team by the end of the month.

Salesperson: First, I need to get a better understanding of your company's needs and budget. I'd like to meet with several of the executives at your company.

Prospect: We'd rather not take the time for that. We'd like to start with an overview first, and if things look good, we can progress from there.

Salesperson: It's very difficult to present such a complex solution without understanding more about your situation and budget constraints.

Prospect: We don't have time to waste on meetings. Do you want to work with us or not?

Salesperson: Certainly. When would be the most convenient time for the demo?

What happened here was driven by emotion. The customer says he wants a product demonstration, a normal and often costly part of the complex sales process. The salesperson responds as an adult and seeks to ensure that a demonstration of his product can be tailored and is appropriate for the customer and his own company. The customer responds like a parent; it's going to be his way or the highway. The salesperson, overly anxious to please and scared to lose the sale, responds like a child by complying, and, in doing so, commits to an expensive course of action that may very well have no chance of yielding a sale.

This problem is magnified when value propositions are poorly conceived. When you communicate value with phrases like "rapid response" and "limited breakdowns," you are using the same words that all of your competitors are using. Customers don't buy them, rightly or wrongly; they dismiss value propositions as empty words.

At the same time, salespeople usually act mystified by customer pressure on price. They don't understand why their customer doesn't "get it."

The Burden of Proof You can't count on customers to recognize on their own the value you bring to the table, to calculate what it's worth, or to accurately determine if they should pay its price. You must help the customer connect the dots. The customer is the judge and jury in the sale, but you are the expert, the guide. The value proposition is nothing more than a capability, and your primary responsibility is to make it relevant. Once you know how to translate value, you are on your way to regular and predictable success in sales. When a value translation is done properly, the pieces of the customer's puzzle come together and you get the credit.

Sources and Uses of Value Sources of value encompass the ability of the elements of your solution (its features and functions) to create value for customers or enable customers to create value for themselves.

Value can be delivered anywhere along a spectrum—at the product level, the process level, or the performance level. Knowing where and how to position your offering on the value spectrum has a lot to do with the job responsibilities and concerns of each person you are talking with. When salespeople neglect the customer's perspective, they put both their credibility and relevancy at risk.

You've Got to Get Your Mind Right

In studies of exceptional sales professionals, the number one characteristic they have in common is that they think differently from their less successful colleagues. Their thought processes have far more in common with those of successful professionals in other disciplines who depend on credible communication than they do with those of other salespeople. They run a close parallel with the qualities of top leaders: creativity, insight, change management, integrity, and respect.

Awareness is the first step in the process of selling. For example, the compulsion to have an immediate answer for everything creates a significant barrier to listening and understanding customers' situations. The more effective you become as a decision-process guide, the more likely customers are to reveal the privileged information you need to execute successfully.

Diagnosis: The Mind-set of Success The diagnostic mind-set is the antithesis of a presentation mind-set. Diagnosis is more effective than presentation because

- it is always focused on the customer;
- it is about the observable symptoms of problems and the parameters of solution, not blame;
- it engages the customer as a collaborative partner;
- it promotes ownership;
- it differentiates you from your competition;
- it is something you do with your customer; selling is something you do to your customer.

The mind-set that supports value diagnosis is characterized by five traits and capabilities:

- Value relevancy
- Change leadership
- Mutual self-esteem
- Mutual self-interest
- Emotional maturity

Creating value with customers is like helping them work a connect-the-dots puzzle. The more value elements you can help your customer understand and connect, the more linked you and your solutions become to the customer's organization. When you think about sales from this perspective, it immediately becomes clear that successful selling is also about managing the customer's emotional acceptance of change.

Mutual Self-esteem Successful sales professionals maintain and protect their self-esteem and their customer's self-esteem at all times. What does self-esteem have to do with sales? When salespeople inadvertently damage their customer's self-esteem, they risk losing the cooperation and participation that are so important to the sales process.

Some salespeople ask the customer questions like "What's keeping you awake at night?" and "What types of pain are you feeling in your manufacturing process?" The danger is that you are insinuating that the customer doesn't know what he is doing. If you "get to the pain" without being sensitive to self-esteem, you can easily alienate the customer and destroy the relationship.

Mutual Self-interest Mutual self-interest, the next quality of the diagnostic mind-set, flows naturally from mutual self-esteem. It enables us to reconcile and serve the dual responsibilities that every sales professional eventually struggles with, that is, the responsibility to serve your customer and your employer while simultaneously looking out for yourself.

Cool, Calm, Collected The final element of the diagnostic mind-set is emotional maturity. A sales engagement is not the right place to get our emotional needs met or give our emotions free rein. Salespeople should be professionally involved but emotionally detached.

Part II: Taking It to the Street

The sequence and phrasing of credible conversations are determined by your system or process. We know three things about this system:

- It must be your system.
- It can't be the traditional prospect-qualify-present-close system.
- It must support the twin imperatives of conversational substance and style.

The salesperson's goals are discover, diagnose, design, and deliver. This is called the Prime Process. This process provides a much-needed structure and synchronization for our sales conversations. Too often, salespeople approach conversations with customers in a scripted manner that is closer to presentation than conversation. The results are usually disastrous.

Earning the Keys to the Elevator

The initial contact with a prospective customer is the most critical and no doubt the least forgiving stage of the sale. The goal is to earn the "keys to the elevator." This elevator will take you to the top floor of the organization where the decision makers are located. As you enter this situation, you are considered guilty until proven innocent, and you must strike the relevancy and credibility chords simultaneously and instantly (within fifteen seconds) out of the box. In many cases, the real problem is the sales process, not the salesperson.

The Research Conversation Effective preparation and credible initial conversations lead to successful sales, and they start with symptoms, not solutions. The best way to sound like everyone else is to start your sales process by talking about your solutions. That's a prescription for a suboptimal sales engagement. The first conversations we should be having with customers are not sales conversations; they are discovery conversations.

These discovery conversations are not sales calls. You need to learn about this company's reality—its internal characteristics, what it is experiencing, the potential consequences, and the customer's viewpoint on those consequences. Think like a lawyer during the discovery phase of a case. This same purpose should be reflected in the questions you ask and don't ask during these calls. You should be solely focused on the existence of the symptoms of the absence of your value. You shouldn't be asking about who buys your offerings or who might be interested in learning more about them.

Invoke the Twenty-Second Rule It's common for customers to ask questions as they become involved in the engagement conversation or throughout the entire process. You must answer these questions, particularly early in the sales engagement. Honest, open, straightforward—that's the mind-set. If you refuse, customers will see you as a stereotypical salesperson. When you answer, invoke the twenty-second rule—answer the question succinctly and follow it immediately with a continuation of the diagnostic conversation with your next diagnostic question.

Diagnosis Trumps Presentation Every Time

When you give your customer a presentation/proposal, being optimistic, you are expecting him to make a decision. A customer's awareness that he might have a problem is a state of mind that can earn a salesperson the keys to the elevator, but it is not compelling enough to create a decision to change/buy.

There is a major risk here. When the sales engagement is focused mainly on your solution—solution bias—most customers are not going to be able to find enough compelling reasons to undertake the degree of change that the sale represents. How do you move a customer to the crisis stage? You must focus on the customer's present situation, not your solutions or the future state the customer will be able to attain with the help of these solutions.

Diagnosis Requires an Expert When salespeople ask customers to define their own problems, they fall prey to the implicit and erroneous assumption that customers understand the scope and severity of all their problems and all the opportunities they are not acting on. The irony is that customers very likely do recognize the merits of your solution, so there are no objections to handle. This is the danger of encouraging and accepting self-diagnosis.

The Diagnostic Conversation There is one fundamental format for the diagnostic conversation. It's a dialogue with the customer that progresses from job responsibility to indicator to cause to priority. This dialogue is driven by questions. Questions are the levers for change. Every time the diagnostic conversation begins with a new cast member, relevancy must be established and credibility must be built once again.

There are five important parts to this process:

- Focus the field of inquiry on a job process the manager is responsible for.
- Have the customer begin a review of the process.
- Describe the optimal outcome of the process.
- Protect the customer's self-esteem by acknowledging his achievements.
- Harvest the thought process you have just guided your customer through. It is the springboard into an in-depth diagnosis.

Probing the Symptoms When you and your customer have reached the level of process where the detailed symptoms of the absence of value exist, it's time to begin asking indicator questions to check the customer's experience and/or knowledge of problem symptoms. These questions enable you to drill down into an issue to confirm that symptoms exist and determine their causes, consequences, and priorities.

Ask a series of indicator questions, such as:

- Could you tell me more about . . . ?
- Could you tell me more about the behaviors you are looking for?
- Could you give me an example of . . . ?
- When did you first notice . . . ?

- What seem to be the key contributing factors to . . . ?
- How has this affected . . . ?
- Have you had a chance to look at what this might be costing the business in terms of . . . ?

Cutting Through the Smoke and Mirrors

Customers face a new and equally daunting challenge when they must decide on the solution that will best resolve their situation. As sales professionals, our job becomes one that is best characterized as orchestrating the design of that solution. It's ironic. Salespeople tend to depend too heavily on the customer's view when it comes to problem diagnosis and not enough when it comes to solution design. The best way to prepare customers to purchase your solution is to work with customers to define a solution that can best solve their problem.

There are important advantages to this strategy, including:

- Customers can provide important insights regarding the optimal solution.
- Design parameters supply customers with the questions that need to be asked in order to cut through competitive smoke and mirrors.
- Salespeople capture an unparalleled opportunity to set themselves apart from their competitors and gain an inside track to winning the sale by taking a leading role in the creation of rules on which the solution decision will be made.

The Design Conversation The design conversation enables customers to achieve a positive future by

- clarifying expected outcomes;
- choosing the optimal solution alternative;
- identifying the resources required to implement the solution and achieve its value;
- establishing the time frame in which the outcomes will be achieved.

Great Expectations Aren't Always Realistic One of the more common complaints from salespeople is that they have a difficult time managing their customers' expectations. The simple reason this problem occurs so often is that the conventional sales process mistakes needs for expectations. Needs do not equal expectations.

Introduce Critical Outcomes as Necessary While we should always start by asking customers to define their expectations, we also have to recognize that they may not know enough to cover all outcomes themselves. Then we have to introduce additional outcomes.

We also need to recognize that outcome expectations vary with perspective. When we are working with multiple individuals within the customer organization, we will discover contradictory expectations.

Resources and Timing Resources and timing are critical issues with regard to winning the sale, successful implementation, and the establishment of a positive long-term relationship with the customer. Yet salespeople tend to avoid or underestimate these issues because they are afraid that by acknowledging the often difficult realities of these issues they might lose the sale.

It Doesn't Pay to Surprise a Corporation Closing has long been looked at as the be-all and end-all, the final element in the conventional sales process. It becomes a focus of training because conventional selling quickly moves to the presentation/proposal stage and positions the proposal as a document for consideration. This misguided focus insists that salespeople first propose solutions for the customer's consideration and then deal with the ensuing questions and objections. As we've already seen, when customers have not had the opportunity to thoroughly understand their situation and participate in the design of a solution, they don't have the foundation they need to make a sound decision.

How do businesspeople naturally react in such circumstances? At best, they are cautious and noncommittal. They might be complimentary about the merits of the solutions, but again, they don't know why they should buy it. So salespeople call on their "closing skills" to push customers into making a decision. At worst, customers actively resist when they are surprised by new, unconsidered information. They raise objections. Now salespeople struggle to overcome the objections. No matter how delicately they respond to their customers, these reactions are inherently confrontational and counterproductive. They are jeopardizing their credibility and their relationship with the customer, and certainly they are putting the sale at risk.

There are only two reasons why customers don't buy:

1. They don't believe they have a problem, so they don't have incentive to change.

2. They don't believe the solution proposed will work.

We should be managing these issues. Our process should be front-loaded in terms of customer consideration. The last thing we would want to do now is surprise the customer with previously unconsidered issues. Business customers do not look kindly on surprises.

We also need to adopt a broader perspective and a sales process that can support multiple goals. These include short-term goals, such as winning the sale and ensuring the value that the customer is expecting is actually delivered, and long-term goals, such as creating new value-delivery opportunities and positioning yourself to enlarge the customer relationship.

Proposals and Presentations A sales proposal shouldn't be a document of consideration but a document of confirmation, to document the series of decisions that have already been made. Here are some guidelines for creating and delivering your proposal:

1. No surprises.

2. Use the customer's fingerprints.

3. Solicit feedback.

4. Customers should continue to take an active role in the process.

5. Anchor the larger solution in the presentation.

When Things Go Wrong Today's high-stakes sales environment requires that salespeople remain accountable to the customer after the sale is concluded and during the solution implementation. It's tempting to sidestep potential problems, but you will save yourself an awful lot of grief by being straightforward with the customer. One valuable dividend of the proactive discussion of potential problems is that it can often become an expectation that sets you apart from the competition.

Confirming and Communicating Value Delivery Many traditional salespeople use feedback as a thinly veiled excuse for up-selling, so customers usually try to avoid feedback conversations. But there are several important reasons for having them:

- Ensuring customer awareness of the "value delivered"
- Protecting the customer relationship from competitive threats
- Expanding the customer relationship
- Gaining new customers

At the end of the feedback conversation, now's the time to ask one or both of two questions: "Is there anyone else in the organization who is experiencing similar symptoms to what you had?" and "Is there anyone you know from another company who may be experiencing these same symptoms?"

Part III: Breaking Away with Exceptional Credibility

Most salespeople are meeting the standard of expected credibility, but that's only the table stakes in the world of sales. If you want to earn exceptional credibility and exceptional results, you must master financial conversations and executive conversations.

Show Me the Money

In business, money talks. But just as customers typically do not have a quality decision process, they even more frequently cannot accurately determine the financial impact of a situation and its proposed resolution.

Barriers to Financial Conversations The conventional sales paradigm is responsible for the lion's share of the blame for the inability of salespeople to guide customers through effective financial conversations. Other barriers include the mind-set of salespeople and customers who are reluctant to share financial data.

Financial Conversations Never be afraid or unwilling to tell a customer your price the moment the question is asked. The right question is not whether the price is reasonable or not. The right question is "Does the customer's situation warrant our level of solution in financial terms?"

The most important financial conversation, providing the basis for all that follows, is the cost of the problem. If you can't establish the cost, you don't have a problem. Ignoring the cost or asking the customer to establish the cost is risky business. If you don't establish a credible cost of the problem, customers are far less likely to buy.

Financial Return on Solution The second integral financial conversation defines the financial impact that the customer expects from the solution. The best way to counter this situation is the return-on-solution conversation. Customers participate in the calculation of return-on-solution, and it is built on numbers that they can verify. The return-on-solution conversation tallies the gains (cost savings and/or new revenues) that will be generated by the solution and the total cost of the solution in order to estimate the net financial impact of the solution on the customer's business.

It's also important to define the level of investment that the customer can appropriately make to obtain the full value of the solution. The goal of the investment conversation is to establish the threshold at which it makes sense for the customer to buy a solution.

Monetized Results Lead to Executive Conversations The final issue in financial conversations is reporting the results. We want to begin our engagement with higher-level executives who have financial and operational accountability for the aspects of the business that are most affected by the absence of our solutions.

Connecting at the Level of Power and Decision

The nature of high-stakes sales has always required sales professionals to connect with operating managers and functional executives within their customers' organizations. There are two primary trends driving sales professionals up the elevator. The first is the increasing complexity of the products and services that are being sold. The second trend is the changing nature of customers' organizations. They are growing leaner as their leaders are driven to increase productivity, cut costs, and outsource everything except core competencies. Salespeople and their managers are quickly discovering that selling up the ladder is a major challenge. This realization hits with full force when sales executives tell their sales forces, "Start selling to the C suite." Unfortunately, all too many salespeople use this trend to abdicate their responsibility and introduce high-level executives into poorly prepared engagements.

Barriers to Executive Conversations The systemic barrier to executive conversations is that most salespeople have not been properly trained to deal with the higher levels of the customer's corporate hierarchy. Senior executives simply do not see or, for the most part, care about the lower-level implications of solutions. Senior executives are responsible for the big picture, not the details. Typically, salespeople become less and less confident and more and more uncomfortable as they travel up the elevator.

The Executive Conversation—Rules for Engaging Rulers

1. *The issues we propose to address must be relevant in the larger context of the business.* When we move up to the customer's executive suite, we can't describe problems in the same terms as we do at the operational level. The rule of relevancy requires that we identify the business issues on the executive's dashboard and translate our value capabilities into those terms.

2. *The statement of value assumption must be valid.* We must demonstrate to executives that the situation or problem that our solution addresses exists.

3. *The problem and solution must be attainable.* We must address whether and how the customer's situation can be viably resolved.

4. *The solution's value must be measurable.* The ability to measure and quantify issues, allocate funds accordingly, and track the returns is a constant concern.

5. *There must be consensus and alignment around the findings, conclusions, and final decision.* A working majority of the cast of characters must agree about the relevance, validity, actionability, and measurability of the problem and solution before the salesperson arrives at the executive suite.

A Final Word on the Sequence of Executive Conversations Most often, executives play two roles in high-stakes sales. First, they act as cast members, with their own job responsibilities and personal perspective. At the same time, they act as sponsors. In this role, they are only indirectly involved in the mechanics of the sale; their direct participation is required only at key milestones.

The best way to master these sponsoring-executive conversations is to approach them as if you had accepted a senior staff position for a specific project. If you picture yourself in this new role and mind-set, you can begin to evolve into a trusted adviser and valuable business partner. In response, your executive customers will begin to treat you as a prime resource and your sales success will multiply exponentially.

CUSTOMERCENTRIC SELLING

by Michael T. Bosworth and John R. Holland

Sales professionals are expected to serve as a company's expert when speaking to prospective clients. This expectation is reinforced through hours of training and the sales professional's own time spent studying marketing materials and preparing sales presentations. While this preparation is a necessary part of the job, it can occasionally have some negative results. Traditional sales training often leads a salesperson to feel that the "company line" is the only way to go about pitching a product. There's also the problem of what happens when a sales representative combines his or her natural self-confidence with a vast amount of product knowledge. The customer can occasionally feel overwhelmed as a take-no-prisoners salesperson pipes up with "expert" opinions about what's best for the prospect's company.

On the opposite end of the spectrum, companies that have a revolving door of salespeople tend to need warm bodies in the field ASAP. In this environment, sales training is condensed and the representative is left to him- or herself to fill in the gaps about a product's benefits. Companies that are quick to move sales professionals into the field also frequently suffer disconnect between the sales and marketing departments. This can be fatal to a sale when the salesperson's message doesn't match up with the message the prospect finds on the company's Web site.

In either of the above cases, the salesperson is left to his or her own devices to make the sale. Michael T. Bosworth and John R. Holland saw more than a few doors slammed in the faces of salespeople during the course of their own careers in sales management and consulting. What they noticed is that the emphasis in the selling situation was in entirely the wrong place. The customer became an afterthought, someone whose job title popped up on a list of leads from a trade show. Bosworth and Holland knew that the biggest mistake salespeople made was forcing the prospect into a solution rather than allowing the prospect to find his or her own way.

CustomerCentric Selling is a handbook for turning the spotlight on the customer and his or her needs. A salesperson is intended to be the conduit between the problems at a prospect's company and their resolution via a product. Bosworth and Holland help sales professionals change their approach to customers and give much-needed softening to the traditionally hard-edged work of selling. Readers will particularly note the pair's efforts in breaking down the standards of the sales process. They encourage salespeople to put away their PowerPoint presentations and focus on delving into the root of the customer's problem. Once the sales representative gains a basic understanding of a customer's need, he or she can use the tips provided by Bosworth and Holland to lead customers to their own decision to use the product.

A key element that makes *CustomerCentric Selling* an essential read for any salesperson is the notion of needing to completely understand the prospect's situation. Bosworth and Holland point out that doctors wouldn't prescribe medication without first asking a variety of questions to understand the illness. Sales is too often dismissed as a profession of blunt force and fast talk. There is a clinical side to sales of which the best practitioners are true masters. *CustomerCentric Selling* is intended to help sales professionals take the next step toward the highest level of customer interaction.

CUSTOMERCENTRIC SELLING
Integrate Sales and Marketing, Develop Sales-Ready Messaging, and "Clone" Your Top Salespeople
by Michael T. Bosworth and John R. Holland

CONTENTS
1. What Is CustomerCentric Selling?
2. Opinions—the Fuel That Drives Corporations
3. Sales-Ready Messaging
4. Core Concepts of CustomerCentric Selling
5. Qualifying Buyers
6. Negotiation: The Final Hurdle
7. Getting Forecasting Right
8. Upgrading Sales Activity

THE SUMMARY IN BRIEF

Even if you are the best salesperson in your company, you could be even better. Forget everything you think you know about selling products to buyers—the rules are changing, and it's about time.

In *CustomerCentric Selling*, sales experts Michael T. Bosworth and John R. Holland lay out a new approach to sales, one in which salespeople stop forcing products on buyers and start listening to their goals, problems, and needs. Stop giving your "expert" opinion on why a buyer should snap up your products, and start engaging decision makers in business conversations that yield results. *CustomerCentric Selling* will help you stop working inefficiently and start moving toward better, longer, more mutually beneficial relationships with your customers.

In addition, you'll learn:

- **Sales are conversations.** Selling at its best consists of a series of conversations with buyers, during which the seller uncovers and understands the buyer's needs, problems, desires, and goals.
- **Selling is most effective when the seller uses consistent messages**. The most successful customercentric organizations use Sales-Ready Messaging—a way of approaching a sales conversation that greatly increases the chances of success.
- **Pipelines need to be flushed now and then.** Organizations must qualify buyers, disqualify others, and develop a smoother, more efficient pipeline.
- **You should negotiate from a position of strength.** Negotiation is the logical conclusion to a well-planned, well-executed sales cycle, one for which salespeople and their managers must prepare well.
- **Forecasting should be a science.** Sales managers must remove subjectivity from forecasting to more accurately reflect business opportunities.

THE COMPLETE SUMMARY

What Is CustomerCentric Selling?

Customercentric behavior has the following seven basic tenets that set it apart from more traditional selling behavior:

1. *Having situational conversations versus making presentations.* Traditional salespeople rely on making presentations because they believe this approach gives them the opportunity to add excitement to an offering with snazzy visuals and the supposedly innovative use of such presentation tools as PowerPoint. Such dramatics, however, are unnecessary. In order to be effective, a salesperson must be able to relate his or her offering to the buyer in a way that will enable the buyer to visualize using the offering to satisfy his or her needs. The most effective way to determine those needs is through honest conversations with the buyer.

2. *Asking relevant questions versus offering opinions.* People love to buy but hate feeling sold to. Most salespeople come to a vision of the buyer's problem before the buyer does, usually to the buyer's chagrin. Customercentric salespeople use their expertise to frame interesting and helpful questions rather than to deliver opinions, drawing out of the buyer a realization of his or her needs and building toward a more useful solution.

Earn the Buyer's Respect

3. *Solution-focused versus relationship-focused.* Salespeople who are not trained to converse with decision makers about product usage gravitate toward focusing on their relationship with their buyers, which can be fleeting, depending on the product and market. In situations where the buyer is attempting to satisfy a need, the successful seller must first earn the buyer's respect by knowing how his or her wares can provide a solution to that need.

4. *Targeting businesspeople versus gravitating toward users.* Traditional salespeople gravitate toward the users of their products, while customercentric salespeople target business decision makers. Most traditional salespeople can talk a great deal about a product's features but very little about how it is used in day-to-day applications. Customercentric sellers, conversely, focus on how to use a product, what results can be expected, and how much it costs versus the benefits it presents.

5. *Relating product usage versus relying on product.* Traditional salespeople educate buyers about a product and assume buyers will know how to apply the product's features to meet their needs. Customercentric sellers are able to relate conversationally with buyers about product usage.

Monitor Progress When Necessary

6. *Managing managers versus needing to be managed.* Traditional sales managers monitor activity rather than progress; they are promoted to management positions in part because they were good salespeople—management skills are rarely used as criteria for promotion. Managers of customercentric salespeople, on the other hand, must only monitor their charges' progress and, when necessary, provide company resources to help them make a sale.

7. *Empowering buyers versus attempting to sell them.* Selling is not about persuasion, pressure, or coercion; it is about empowerment. A seller's objective, going into a new customer relationship, should be to help the buyer solve a problem, satisfy a need, or achieve a goal. The difference between the two sales approaches is fundamental.

Opinions—the Fuel That Drives Corporations

Opinions play an important role in our personal and professional lives. When organizations need to make important decisions, most hire experts who become familiar with their situation and make suggestions on how to remedy their problems. Not everyone's opinion is of equal value; as you look further down the corporate food chain or line of command, the power of individual opinions to shape policy drops off sharply.

The exception to this rule is often the sales function. Without necessarily understanding that they're doing so, companies tend to rely on the opinions of traditional salespeople to build pipelines, create forecasts, and deliver revenue. This can spell disaster for firms whose sales departments cannot deliver according to plan.

Sales Versus "Tactical Marketing"

In many cases, the job of positioning offerings is, by default, the job of the individual salesperson, a situation that often results in inconsistency of message from one salesperson to another, regardless of how much a company has invested in "tactical marketing" (literature, brochures, advertising, Web sites, and so forth). Indeed, companies that cannot bridge the gap between tactical marketing and sales are often at the mercy of the opinions of their salespeople. Very few of these salespeople are capable of overcoming the lack of marketing support and taking a genuinely customercentric approach to each sale—positioning offerings according to buyers' needs.

Consider, then, how much the opinions of underprepared, underwhelming salespeople are responsible for how businesses predict their future incomes. After a brief, often misdirected training effort, new salespeople are asked to immediately begin volunteering opinions. They must first condense their understanding of the company's offerings into a coherent message for buyers. They must provide their opinions of what accounts and titles to call once in a given territory; which accounts should be in their pipelines; what accounts will close, when, and why; what prospects will be lost and why; and what enhancements to offerings are needed to improve win rates.

That's a lot to require of anyone's opinions, particularly those of traditional salespeople. Reports are only as good as the quality of the input that goes into them. When the sales process is flawed, sales forecasting is virtually meaningless. Allowing salespeople to forecast sales abdicates control to people whose mission is to justify their jobs, not to predict which opportunities will actually close. Without a good process, opinions rule.

Some companies succeed anyway, without a workable structure, but often not for long. Traditional salespeople tend to "wing it" in one-on-one meetings with prospective customers, launching into a "here's what you need" product pitch, regardless of what the prospect tells them. This creates problems on several levels:

Most people do not like to be told what to do or think.

When assaulted by a so-called spray-and-pray sales pitch, buyers will realize there are features of the product they do not need.

The salesperson in question displays a lack of understanding of the buyer's current environment and future needs.

"Winging It" in Management

As if this were not bad enough, those who manage sales forces are often ill suited for the job. Companies tend to promote their top-performing sellers into these positions, regardless of whether these people possess the skills required to teach customercentricity to others. These managers have often "winged it" much of their careers and don't know what has made them successful: It was intuitive. They've never broken down their success into teachable components.

Sales-Ready Messaging

Selling at its best and most customercentric consists of a series of conversations with buyers, during which the seller uncovers and understands the buyer's needs, problems, desires, and goals. As the salesperson learns about the buyer's circumstances, he or she also begins to position the company's offerings.

Selling organizations want to influence and steer these conversations. To converse effectively with a buyer, these three conditions must be known by the seller:

• The buyer's title and vertical industry

• The willingness of a buyer to articulate a business goal or admit a problem that can be addressed

- The capability of the seller's offerings to help the targeted buyer achieve a goal, solve a problem, or satisfy a need

Given these three conditions, organizations can create Sales-Ready Messaging—a way of approaching a sales conversation that greatly increases the chances of success. The most effective way of creating Sales-Ready Messaging can be broken down into four major steps:

1. *Document titles and goals.* Make a list of your vertical industries, and for each industry jot down the titles or functions a salesperson is likely to call on to get your offering sold, funded, and implemented. For each of the job titles listed, write down what goals or business objectives those in that function should have, and note which goals are addressable through the use of your product or service. Each goal listed should be a business variable that your company's offering can help a particular title achieve. Creating this list sets the stage for Targeted Conversations the seller will have with potential buyers as the relationship moves forward.

2. *Create Solution Development Prompters.* The next step is to develop questioning templates, called Solution Development Prompters (SDPs). These templates are the core content of a company's Sales-Ready Messaging, constituting a kind of road map for a salesperson—a tool he or she can use to lead a specific job title to a specific vision of using the company's offering to achieve a specific goal. If, in a Targeted Conversation, a seller can approach a call with a clear idea of whom he or she is talking to and where he or she hopes the conversation will wind up, the chances of success increase considerably.

The role of the salesperson is to become a buying facilitator by leading the buyer with questions that are biased toward a particular offering. SDPs help develop "buyer visions" that are biased in favor of your offering.

3. *Create your Sales-Ready Messaging.* Once you create your Targeted Conversations list for a given offering, you are ready to create Sales-Ready Messaging in the form of SDPs by assembling four components:

- Offering. A specific product or service.
- Industry. The industry category (for example, Fortune 500 company) to which the buyer belongs.
- Title. The title of the contact with whom you will engage in a Targeted Conversation.
- Goal. The overall outcome you want to communicate to the buyer.

4. Position your offerings. With the goal you have identified in mind, you can present all the features of your product or service that can be used to achieve this goal. As you do, keep in mind the perspective of the contact—a CEO, for example, will have different interests than a lower-level executive. The detail with which you discuss specific features of your offering must be adjusted according to audience. You can use SDPs to create "real world" examples that illustrate how your offering will help the buyer achieve a goal.

If properly prepared, SDPs provide a more consistent positioning of offerings by all salespeople and should help your sales effort overall.

ADDITIONAL CONSIDERATIONS FOR SDPS

There are a few additional things to consider when creating Solution Development Prompters (SDPs).

They get easier to prepare after you have created your first few, because some usage scenarios can be recycled for multiple Targeted Conversations.

The true test of an SDP is whether it can be used in making a call. If it can't, it must be modified.

At executive levels, anticipate that a salesperson has fifteen to twenty minutes, or less, to have a discussion, which limits the number of usage scenarios you can use in the conversation.

SDPs are dynamic, not static, and must be updated over time. Sales-Ready Messaging is a journey, not a destination.

Core Concepts of CustomerCentric Selling

CustomerCentric Selling reframes the concept of selling, empowering sellers to execute Sales-Ready Messaging to help buyers visualize using their offerings to achieve a goal, solve a problem, or satisfy a need. This reframing is accomplished via a set of core concepts of the CustomerCentric Selling approach.

The first concept is that you get delegated to the people you sound like. If a traditional salesperson proves capable enough to get an audience with a decision maker, and he or she merely presents product features and functions to someone with no interest in those things, the salesperson will get delegated to someone else in the company who has a similar interest in features and functions but who has no authority to make a purchase. The objective is to present the prospect with the product or service as the means to a solution. The salesperson will then get delegated to a decision maker whose job it is to implement the solution to the problem.

Diagnose Before You Prescribe

Take the time to diagnose before offering a prescription. Physicians will ask patients a series of questions and put them through a diagnostic process before offering medication. Why should selling be any different? The ability to ask intelligent diagnostic questions of a buyer is a key differentiator between great salespeople and traditional ones.

In today's competitive environment, a salesperson must be sincere and competent just to get the opportunity to compete. Customercentric salespeople ensure that buyers retain ownership of their goals, problems, and needs—this helps the seller maintain credibility that would be lost if he or she were to give a "here's what you need" speech without asking the buyer any questions.

Don't give without getting. Negotiation is not an event—it's a process, and nearly every sale involves some sort of negotiation. Each side should take a "quid pro quo" approach—getting something in return for giving something. When this is established early in the selling relationship, sellers can become more effective negotiators and deliver more profitable business.

Bad News Can Be Good News

You can't sell to someone who can't buy. Sellers must get to the person who can spend budgeted funds. Ideally, your prospect is both a user of your product and the head of a department that has money budgeted to make a purchase.

Bad news early is good news. Some salespeople engage in extraordinarily long sales cycles, in part because the buyer is merely going through the motions, practicing due diligence on multiple vendors even though he or she already has a vendor in mind. If you are not the predetermined vendor, however, bad news early is good news—finding out quickly that you have no real shot at the business gives you the chance to pull up stakes and pursue other winnable opportunities.

No goal means no prospect. When first meeting a buyer, the salesperson's focus should be on building rapport and trust—without these things, a buyer is less likely to share goals or admit problems. A sales cycle cannot begin until the buyer shares a goal with the seller, at which time the seller can ask questions and empower the buyer with scenarios to understand what can be achieved with the product. Without a goal, there can be no solution development and therefore no prospect.

People are best convinced by reasons they discover themselves. When the selling process is strong, sellers can let buyers reach their own conclusions. In the process of answering the seller's questions, buyers are able to discover their own reasons that prevent them from achieving a specific business result.

When selling, your expertise can become your enemy. Once you know something, it is difficult to have patience with or empathy for people who don't know what you know. If a salesperson is tempted to use his or her expertise without consulting the buyer about his or her goals or problems, the seller would be better off not having that expertise. Without it, he or she would ask more questions and spend less time pontificating or trying to convince the buyer to make a purchase.

It's Not a Solution Until the Buyer Says It Is

The only person who can call it a solution is the buyer. The seller cannot and should not define a solution—that is up to the buyer only. The seller can help the buyer get there, but he or she can't get there first.

Make yourself equal, then make yourself different—or you'll just be different. When asked to differentiate a product from a competitor's offering, sellers need to respond with the question, "What do you hope to accomplish?" If the buyer responds with a goal, the sale can proceed from there. Before differentiating an offering, sellers must get on equal footing with a prospect from a personal, competence, and capability standpoint.

JUSTIFYING EMOTIONAL DECISIONS

A man bought a very expensive, beautiful, fun-to-drive German car. When asked why he purchased it, he used several different points as his rationale: It will be a classic, it will go up in value, and it has an aluminum body that will never rust. These were all logical reasons, but the truth is, he bought the car because he loved it at first sight, wanted to drive it, and felt he looked more handsome driving it. If a close friend asked him why he bought the car, the emotional reason would flow along with the question, "Don't I look good in it?" If a stranger asked, most likely the logical reasons would be offered.

If a buyer answers to no one and doesn't care what others think, he or she can buy strictly on emotion. Most people, however, need some kind of logic to explain to peers, superiors, subordinates, and friends why they made a given purchase. Salespeople need to be ready to sell to both logic and emotion.

Emotional decisions are justified by value and logic. Buying is an emotional act but one that must be entered into with logic and thought. Salespeople need to be prepared to deal with both logic and emotion. A buyer might make an emotional decision to purchase a product but should be armed with the logical reasons behind that purchase so he or she can defend it to a superior.

Don't close before the buyer is ready. Once a seller closes a deal with a buyer, their relationship will never be the same. Sellers should make sure they understand the buyer's goals and how they can be achieved through the use of the product. The seller must understand the buyer's current situation and how he or she can help the buyer justify the cost of the purchasing decision.

Qualifying Buyers

Many organizations are slowed down or otherwise hampered by inefficiencies in their sales pipelines. Basically, they have no standard way of accurately assessing which prospects are likely to buy. Sales managers need to work with their salespeople to qualify buyers, disqualify others, and develop a smoother, more efficient pipeline. Sellers need to identify and qualify the Key Players whom a seller must access in order to sell, fund, and implement a product or service offering.

Foremost among Key Players are Champions, who provide access to other Key Players as requested by the salesperson and who can be found at any level within the prospect organization. Ideally, the Champion is also a decision maker who is willing to provide access to those below him or her in the organizational hierarchy. Such top-down access is always preferred.

Qualifying a Champion

One key element of CustomerCentric Selling is the identification and qualification of a Champion, often by a letter, fax, or e-mail composed by both the salesperson and his or her manager. This Champion letter should

- provide a sanity check for salespeople to verify they understand the buyer's goals, situation, and vision;
- serve as a reminder to the buyer of a previous conversation with the salesperson;
- facilitate internal selling by providing the Champion with prospect-ready messaging.

Following Up

Once a Champion letter has been sent, the salesperson must follow up on that communication in order to get the buyer's agreement to the following points:

- The letter accurately summarizes their conversation(s).
- The buyer is willing and able to provide access to the appropriate Key Players.
- After interviewing all Key Players, there will be a chance to gain consensus that further evaluation is warranted.

Phone conversations or face-to-face sales calls can commence once the Champion has agreed to provide access to Key Players. When meeting with Key Players, the salesperson should make sure everyone understands the potential benefits to the organization should they agree to buy. Spreading the word to several Key Players provides the seller with multiple points of contact in the organization, which can be helpful if one of those players leaves the prospective company. If there is a strong Adversary, he or she will be identified early enough for the seller to determine how to best circumnavigate him

---

DEFINING THE KEY PLAYERS

*A*side from Champions, salespeople and their managers must also be aware of these other Key Players with important roles in a client relationship:

Coaches want the seller to win the business and are willing to assist with information and inside selling, but they have limited authority within the organization.

Decision makers can make the vendor selection and free up unbudgeted funds. They can commit internal resources to evaluate a seller's offerings.

Financial approvers are those who must sign off on expenditures—either by rubber-stamping a purchase or by being actively involved in the purchasing process.

Users and managers of users can provide a groundswell of support from the rank-and-file members of a given organization.

Implementers are responsible for migrating from the current method or environment to the new offering. They often prefer to work with vendors who offer professional services and ongoing support.

Adversaries are individuals who either do not want to change, want to control change internally, or want to do business with a competitor.

or her. If the Adversary is strong enough to withstand these efforts, the seller may make the decision to withdraw from the sale rather than go the distance and lose.

Walking Away

Sellers must always be willing to walk away from a sales opportunity if it becomes clear that that opportunity is not winnable. This fact is anathema to most traditional salespeople, whose focus is to keep a full pipeline. If that pipeline is clogged with business that will never reach fruition, however, it is of little use to an efficient sales organization.

Some salespeople are afraid to withdraw a proposal and walk away from an opportunity. However, the two most likely results are:

1. *The buyer does not call back.* Ultimately, it is better to get rid of blockages in your pipeline, have a realistic view of what winnable opportunities exist, and arrive at the appropriate business plan to develop those winnable opportunities.

2. *The buyer calls back and asks why the proposal has been withdrawn.* This is an opportunity to determine whether the buyer wants to buy or would be interested in making changes to the proposal and trying to see if a favorable decision can be reached. If given a second chance, the seller can now focus on helping the buyer understand how to use the offering to achieve goals or solve problems.

Negotiation: The Final Hurdle

Most sellers will tell you they are outstanding negotiators—even if their approach to "negotiating" is to keep discounting until the buyer says yes. If a sales cycle has been executed properly, though, the close should be a logical conclusion rather than an arm-wrestling contest or a fire sale. When it comes to negotiating, there are no magic bullets; salespeople must be prepared and must stick to their game plans. That preparation includes these key components:

- **You must verify that you are the vendor of choice and that price is the only obstacle to doing business.** Sellers, on their own, often have trouble verifying that they are the top choice. This is just how the buyer wants it—to put the seller in a perceived competition with other sellers.
- **You must make certain you are negotiating with a decision maker.** If you are not, you can consider any concessions you make to be

mere starting points for when the real decision maker comes into the picture.

Getting to Yes Through No

• **You must posture by using polite "no" questions to respond to requests for better pricing.** Some examples of these questions might be "Is there anything you would like to take out of the agreement?" or perhaps "We've spent a lot of time discussing how to [remedy a problem or help achieve a goal]. Has anything changed?" Some buyers will agree to go forward after one, two, or three of these polite "no" questions. This posturing provides artificial patience during a stressful point, maximizing the possibility of a profitable transaction.

Giving and Getting

• **You should ask the buyer whether the "get" you want is possible.** Establish an atmosphere of quid pro quo. Prior to giving, the seller should first ask for something from the buyer. If the seller offers a concession, the buyer will take it and still want a lower price. Also, the psychology is to convince the buyer that he or she is getting the best possible deal. If the buyer makes the first concession, the seller's concessions appear even more valuable.

• **You should offer your conditional "give" and be prepared to walk if the offer does not close at that point.** You should, of course, also leave the door open for further rounds, but only after taking your concession off the table. There are many things a seller can ask for— money up front, a larger transaction or a longer commitment, and even an introduction to another department, enabling the seller to pursue more business.

Getting Forecasting Right

Salespeople tend to dislike forecasting, because, in most cases, they are being asked to lie in writing. They know all too well that their forecasts will bear little or no resemblance to the numbers they really generate. In fact, the major value of forecasting is that it gives underperforming salespeople a wake-up call every month that there are inadequate opportunities in their pipelines, encouraging them to increase their business-development activities.

Where sales managers often err is in not removing salespeople from the

REFERRALS—QUALIFICATION VIA CUSTOMERS

Satisfied customers represent an enormous untapped asset for customercentric sales organizations. People who have made a buying decision have a tendency to conclude they've made a wise choice and are willing to tell others about it—thus providing sellers with a potential source of new prospective buyers. Why do vendors not take advantage of customer referrals often enough?

They neglect to ask for referrals.

They fail to ask for a "warm" referral—one in which the customer acts as a conduit between the seller and a new prospect.

They make no attempt to find out from customers what specific business goals or problems the prospect might be facing.

They fail to share with the prospect the success story involving their customer—the one that helped bring them together in the first place.

forecasting process—it simply must be done. To make forecasting more accurately reflective of business opportunities, a number of complementary components are necessary:

1. Sales-Ready Messaging designed to position offerings specific to title, vertical industry, and goal, providing less subjective input into the pipeline.

2. Auditable correspondence between seller and buyer.

3. Sequences of events containing estimated close dates, as negotiated with the buyer.

4. Company-wide milestones, with defined ways to achieve and document them.

5. Sales managers who are willing and able to audit milestones, grade pipelines, disqualify low-probability opportunities, and predict what will close.

6. Senior executive commitment to ride through potential "push back" from salespeople and sales managers who prefer less visibility and accountability.

Grading Opportunities

To provide the kind of analyses required to maintain healthy pipelines, sales managers must have a system in place to grade opportunities. Consider these categories:

- **Inactive.** The account fits a target market and is assigned to a salesperson, but there's no current activity.

- **Active.** Contact has been made and some interest from the customer or prospect has been expressed.
- **Goal shared.** This is the initiation of the sales cycle, when a targeted Key Player has shared a desire to achieve at least one goal that the seller can help address.
- **Champion.** This status can be granted only by the sales manager, and only after the prospect has been thoroughly qualified.
- **Evaluating.** This status is determined by the sales manager, but only after the salesperson has gained consensus from Key Players that further investigation of the salesperson's offering is called for. Opportunities remain in this status until the buyer withdraws, the seller withdraws, or the seller asks for the business after all events in the sales sequence have been completed.

Wins, Losses, Verbals, and Proposals

Once the seller has asked for the business, the opportunity registers one of four grades:

- **Win.** An order with all necessary documents signed.
- **Loss.** The buyer informs you that he or she will not be moving forward with you.

WHY DO SALESPEOPLE FAIL TO CLOSE?

So many salespeople view the sales cycle as a mystery, just as they view selling opportunities as mysteries when they don't lead to a closed sale. There are a number of reasons individual sellers have trouble closing. Among them are the following:

Most closing is driven by the agenda of the sales organization, with little or no regard for the buyer. Under pressure to meet targets, many organizations resort to business "blitzes" to close sales.

The vast majority of closing occurs before the salesperson has earned the right to ask for the buyer's business. When sellers make this error, they run the risk of being perceived as a pushy traditional salesperson or scaring the buyer off entirely.

If a salesperson closes before a buyer is ready, he or she has likely discounted the products in an effort to earn an early signing. In some instances, the discount offered to non–decision makers becomes the starting point for the real negotiations.

• **Verbal.** The buyer has given you a verbal commitment to go forward.

• **Proposal.** A proposal is provided to the prospect with a decision due.

By implementing this system, managers can detect early warning signs that a given opportunity is stalled or in trouble. They can forecast by reading each salesperson's report on the sequence of events for each opportunity. With this system in place, forecasting becomes a monthly review of the pipeline, with sales managers selecting opportunities that are likely to close and affording themselves the opportunity to be proactive with procrastinating sales reps.

Upgrading Sales Activity

As sales managers are increasingly proactive in analyzing pipelines, they can also influence and upgrade the quality of activity. To do so, they must break down selling into seven essential skills: (1) new business development, (2) solution development, (3) opportunity qualification and control, (4) proof management, (5) access to Key Players, (6) negotiation and closing, and (7) monitoring success metrics. These are skills that come into play at different times in the buying cycle.

For example, if a salesperson has an insufficient number of new business opportunities flowing into his or her pipeline, his or her manager will recognize the problem as one of business development. In response, a proactive, customercentric manager could do the following:

• Ask to see the letters, faxes, and e-mails that the salesperson uses to generate interest. The manager can help design more effective documents and/or strategy.

• Ask the seller to spend some time with a more successful peer. It may be appropriate for the struggling rep to listen to successful phone calls, witness successful lead development practices, and see successful approaches to the sales cycle.

• Role-play being a buyer taking a prospective call from the sales rep.

• If blockages in getting prospects from Active status to Champion status indicate a lack of skill in getting buyers to share goals, spend time reviewing the following things:

  ○ The goals for each Key Player the seller is using

  ○ The success stories used to take a buyer from latent need to sharing a goal

○ The approaches used to get the buyer to share goals or admit problems

By using such techniques, sales managers can contribute to the improvement of their sales staff, all the while keeping their pipelines visible and predictable.

SECRETS OF
QUESTION-BASED SELLING

by Thomas A. Freese

Salespeople inevitably come across a prospect that is the buying equivalent of a brick wall. There's no going over it and no going around it, and trying to go through it will only lead to pain. Generally, this prospect suffers from a common problem: He or she is used to dealing with traditional sales methods. The old-fashioned sales professional schedules a meeting with the prospect, bombards him or her with a straightforward sales pitch, then attempts to coerce the prospect into signing a purchase order. Combine this with the natural tendency toward overriding the prospect's objections and it creates a set of instincts that generate hostility toward any sales professional who walks through the door.

Author Thomas A. Freese saw enough of this type of behavior, on the part of both seller and potential buyer, during his years as a sales professional. He noticed that there are two major risks for sales professionals in any selling situation: the risk of rejection and the risk of automatically countering the words of the customer. Freese began to develop a method for honing his presentation skills, one that would see him gain credibility with the customer while uncovering the customer's most urgent needs. He put the results of his years of effort into the compelling book *Secrets of Question-Based Selling: How the Most Powerful Tool in Business Can Double Your Sales Results*.

This summary provides a framework for sales professionals to increase their close rates by getting to the heart of the customer's issue. Questions are the key to Freese's theory, and sales professionals may be surprised at the way in which the structure and delivery of a few key questions can break down traditionally difficult barriers. Using techniques such as "reversing the positive," where a question is framed negatively to ensure a positive reply, salespeople will begin to train themselves in the art of advancing the sales process beyond tense negotiations.

Human relationships are another essential element of chiseling a doorway in a brick-wall type of prospect. *Secrets of Question-Based Selling* presents insight into the method of conversational layering, a technique Freese uses to generate intense curiosity on the part of the prospect. Freese guides readers through the best way to structure their questions so that the prospect's own motivations prevent him or her from interrupting or disconnecting from the conversation. Examples of creating questions to work with both general types of motivation, fear based and reward based, appear. The book is careful to point out that the salesperson's objective is to create a mutual agenda with the prospect. This plays directly into the natural human tendency toward bonding and sharing effort.

Freese's writing style allows readers to move effortlessly through his concepts. His examples prove invaluable in helping distinguish his book from other question-oriented sales books that lack the practical applications found in *Secrets of Question-Based Selling*. Of particular interest is Freese's demonstration of using publicly available information to make a cold call that a prospect is unlikely to forget or ignore. Creativity is an essential element of a sales professional's distinguishing him- or herself from the pack. The book's subtitle states that use of the question-based method can double one's sales results. While results may vary, the tools necessary to accomplish this goal are present throughout Freese's method.

SECRETS OF QUESTION-BASED SELLING
How the Most Powerful Tool in Business Can Double Your Sales Results
by Thomas A. Freese

CONTENTS
1. Questions Can Reduce Risks
2. How to Disarm the "Mismatching" Reflex
3. Conversational Layering: The Key to Building Effective Relationships
4. Create Curiosity with QBS
5. Establish Your Credibility
6. Uncover Buyers' Needs
7. Present Solutions
8. Commitment: Close the Sale
9. Putting It All Together: Using QBS from Start to Finish

THE SUMMARY IN BRIEF

Despite the claims of many sales trainers and consultants hawking their methodologies, there is no single "right" way to sell. Every sales call is a unique, creative process. People you call on have different needs, biases, and experiences. They also will respond differently in different situations. And what's right for one prospect may not be right for another.

Question-Based Selling (QBS), therefore, is not an ironclad formula for selling. Instead, QBS offers a systematic framework, using questions as its primary tool, that strives to increase your probability of success—and, just as important, decrease your risk of failure.

The first part of this summary shows how QBS can anticipate and reduce two of the major risks involved in the sales process: the risk of rejection and the risk of what author Thomas A. Freese calls "mismatching"—the automatic tendency of people to counter what someone says.

The second part of the summary introduces Freese's Conversational Layering framework. With Conversational Layering, you'll learn how to use questions to

- spark prospects' curiosity about your product or service;
- earn credibility;
- build relationships;
- uncover needs;
- make effective sales presentations;
- secure a commitment to buy.

The sales process has one goal: to close the sale. If what you do causes the prospect to respond favorably, you are moving closer to your goal. If what you do causes the prospect to respond unfavorably, you are moving further from your goal. Through the power of questions, QBS will help you elicit favorable responses from your prospects, leading them to become, eventually, satisfied buyers.

THE COMPLETE SUMMARY

Questions Can Reduce Risks

The dominant "smile and dial" approach to selling is not very successful—between 95 percent and 98 percent of all such sales calls do not result in a sale.

To overcome such daunting statistics, salespeople must find ways to increase their probability of success and decrease their risk of failure. The skillful use of questions will help them achieve their goals.

This summary introduces a methodology, called Conversational Layering, that uses the power of questions. First, however, we will examine how questions can be used to reduce two of the greatest risks in sales: rejection and "mismatching."

The Greatest Risk in Sales: Rejection

Rejection isn't pleasant. Most people will do anything in their power to avoid such personal humiliation and defeat. In the sales arena, the threat of hang-ups and abrupt "no thank yous" is constantly present.

One way to reduce the risk of rejection is to use the "single ping" theory—sending out feelers and seeing what kind of response you get in return.

An example of this theory is offered in the movie *The Hunt for Red October*. In one scene, a nuclear catastrophe is averted when the CIA officer on board a U.S. sub tells the captain to send out a signal to the just-discovered Soviet sub fewer than one hundred yards from it in the deep, dark waters of the North Atlantic. All indications are that the Soviets are ready to attack the Americans. Then the American captain sends out a brief sonar message, which the Soviets answer with a single ping, the underwater equivalent of a white flag. Once the Americans know where the Soviets stand—that they wish to defect rather than engage—they have greatly reduced the risk of making a mistake (in this case, firing nuclear weapons).

In the sales process, you should also send out signals and see what kind of response you receive. Those signals are often best framed in the form of a question. For example, rather than approach prospects with a direct "Let me tell you about our product," first show basic courtesy by asking, "Did I catch you at a bad time?" Even if you have caught them when they're busy, you've left the door open for your next question, "When should I call you back?" Few people will say, "Never!"

Another single ping to send out might be the question, "Can I ask you a question?" Since most people will say, "Sure," you have the prospect's permission to proceed.

Let's take an example at the other end of the sales process—when you are trying to close the sale. Instead of demanding a yes-or-no answer to the proposal—which could push prospects to respond with a "no"—you might say: "Mr. Prospect, you've been considering our proposal for some time now. Does it make sense for us to think about sitting down and wrapping up the details?"

In sum, the single ping method uses questions to advance the sales process while reducing the risk of failure.

How to Disarm the "Mismatching" Reflex

Rejection is not the only risk that salespeople face during the sales process. Mismatching—the tendency of people to automatically contradict what someone says—is another barrier to success. In this case, both the prospect and the salesperson can be guilty of mismatching, with equally disastrous results.

The Need to Be a Contrarian

The human body has certain natural reflexes. Blinking is a physical reflex. Mismatching—which author Freese defines as "the instinctive tendency of individuals to resist, push back, or respond in a contrarian manner"—seems to be an almost universal emotional reflex.

Freese describes how one day he lamented to his neighbor that yard work was cruel and unusual punishment. His neighbor insisted that he found yard work relaxing and enjoyable. Out of curiosity, Freese later told another neighbor that he found yard work relaxing. The other neighbor immediately took the other position, describing how working in the yard was depressing. Each neighbor took the opposing viewpoint, which may have been a coincidence but was more likely an example of mismatching.

Mismatching also occurs in the sales process. If you ask someone, "Did I catch you at a good time?" they will most likely respond cautiously with something like, "That depends on what you need." By anticipating mismatching, however, you will know to frame the question as, "Did I catch you at a bad time?" which is far more likely to yield a response such as "No, that's okay. What can I do for you?"

This is a technique known as "reversing the positive." By framing the question negatively, you put mismatchers in the position of responding in a positive manner. To take another example, it is better to ask, "Will the pricing in this proposal make your boss nervous?" than "Is this price okay?"

Other strategies for disarming the mismatching reflex include:

- **Asking more questions and making fewer statements.** Questions are much harder to mismatch than statements because they invite people to contribute to the conversation. This reduces your risk by helping to expand your dialogue with the client.
- **Building your credibility.** Prospects will naturally be cautious with salespeople they don't know. As you build your credibility with them, you will reduce their need to resist.
- **Leveraging curiosity.** If someone is curious, he or she will want to know more. Curiosity neutralizes the mismatching reflex.

As shown in the following articles, credibility and curiosity are key elements of a successful sales process.

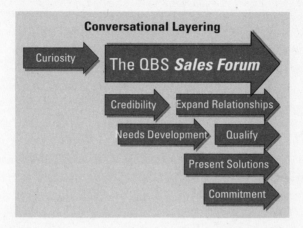

Conversational Layering: The Key to Building Effective Relationships

Most salespeople now recognize that the key to successful selling is to build a relationship with prospects. Prospects must believe in the salesperson's honesty and credibility. The question is how to create this type of relationship.

The **Conversational Layering** methodology is designed to help salespeople ask the right questions at the right time to slowly build up the relationship.

The first challenge of the relationship-building process is to establish the conversation. Most prospects are deluged with calls from salespeople. How can you differentiate yourself from other salespeople and capture the prospect's time and attention?

The answer: Use questions to elicit the prospect's curiosity.

Create Curiosity with QBS

QBS differentiates itself from other sales methods by trying to create a mutually beneficial discussion between buyer and seller. If you take the time to make prospects curious, even the standard sales pitch will have much more impact.

Five ways to build curiosity are:

1. *Provocative Questions.* Don't underestimate the power of simple declarative statements or pointed questions, such as "Guess what?" Such provocative questions or statements by nature make people stop and wonder why you said or asked them that.

2. *Partial Information.* Share just enough information with prospects so that they'll want to ask you more questions.

3. *Glimpses of Value.* If your product or service could be used to help a prospect save money or reduce downtime, suggest this solution without too many details.

4. *Newness and Exclusivity.* Dangling something new and shiny in front of a prospect has a tremendous appeal.

5. *Leveraging Momentum.* Use your sales to other companies in the same industry as a starting point by showing how you've solved similar problems for another organization.

The Herd Theory

One effective method for creating curiosity uses what Freese calls the Herd Theory. This theory is based on the basic human fear of being left out.

If most companies in an industry appear to be interested in a certain product or service, other companies will also become interested. Rather than rely on traditional "happy customer" testimonials, QBS creates a sense of momentum by implying that since so many others are interested in your product, there must be a good reason for it.

Freese first tested the Herd Theory when he was transferred to a new city by his employer, KnowledgeWare, and told to start selling. He soon saw that the old "smile and dial" approach was not working. He was desperate as his quota deadline neared. So he tried something new.

Knowing that KnowledgeWare offered a packaged "road show" presentation, he booked a hall at the headquarters of one of KnowledgeWare's biggest business partners in that city and sent out invitations to his prospect list. He quickly followed up that mailing with phone calls, but the first few responses were noncommittal, and he knew he needed to change his tactics. He came up with the following script for his remaining follow-up calls. It was such a successful maneuver that not only did he meet his sales quota, but by the end of the year, his territory had finished number one in sales. Here's his sales script:

> "Hello, Mr. Prospect, my name is Tom Freese and I'm the regional manager for KnowledgeWare in your city. I wanted to contact you about the CASE application development seminar we are hosting. Do you remember seeing the invitation we sent you?

"Frankly, we are expecting a record turnout—over one hundred people, including development managers from [name several companies], just to name a few.

"I wanted to follow up because we haven't yet received an RSVP from your company, and I wanted to make sure you didn't get left out."

As Freese discovered, when you say to someone, "I just wanted to make sure you didn't get left out," the next four words that person will say are, "Left out of what?" When prospects become curious about what they might miss, they always ask for more information.

Effective Voice-Mail Messages

Your prospect spent his morning in back-to-back meetings, and when he gets back to his office he learns he has sixteen voice-mail messages, including yours. Some sales programs suggest hanging up on message machines or voice mail and encourage you to keep trying until you reach the person. But with caller ID, many businesspeople are reluctant to answer calls from unknown phone numbers.

A better strategy is to leave voice-mail messages that make prospects curious—and thus willing to call back. Here are three suggestions:

- **"A Question Only You Can Answer."** Think of ways to personalize a message, such as "I'm calling because I have a question that only you can answer. If you would, please call me back. I'll be in my office until 4 p.m. today." Of course, you will need to have a question in mind to ask the prospect when he or she calls back. By setting up your call by asking the prospect a question, you are giving him or her a chance to feel important and valued.
- **"Something Made Me Think of You."** This is a more personal approach. Maybe you and a client talked about fishing or golfing once, and you happen to hear a good fish story or just played a great game of golf. Then you could leave a message such as "Hi, Prospect. I decided to pick up the phone and call because something happened today that made me think of you. When you get a minute, call me back. I'll be in the office until five today."
- **Associative References.** When you are entering a new account and don't know anyone in the firm, QBS suggests creating and leveraging an associative reference. Even if you really need to speak with the CEO of a company, you might start with the actual end user of your service or product, typically someone in the purchasing department.

I HAVE YOUR TAX RECORDS!

*F*reese shows how one commercial real estate agent differentiated his cold calls from those of other commercial real estate salespeople. Simply by getting copies of readily available county tax records, this salesman came up with the following cold-call script:

"Hi, Mr. Jones. My name is Dave Brown and I'm with ABC Realty. I'm holding a copy of your county tax record, and I have a question. Could you please call me back?"

Contrast this with his previous cold-call phone message script:

"My name is Dave Brown and I'm with ABC Realty, the leading commercial real estate brokerage firm in Atlanta. Our firm specializes in getting landowners the highest value for their property. I would like to have an opportunity to talk with you about the possibility of listing your property. Could you please call me back?"

After listening to the first message, most people will want to know, at the very least, why this person had a copy of their tax record. The original script did not create any curiosity.

Here's a sample script: "Hi, my name is XYZ and I'm with ABC Corporation. I've got a little problem that I was hoping you could help me with. Did I catch you at a bad time?" You're empowering this person to help you solve a problem and creating a mismatching scenario that works in your favor. If he or she is truly not busy, he or she will usually be eager to help you. This is a good time to ask about the purchasing process for your type of products and whom you should talk to about presenting your product.

Now you have an associative reference and can leave a much more interesting voice mail for the key decision maker in the firm. Here's a sample: "Hi, decision maker, this is XYZ with ABC Corporation. I just got off the phone with so-and-so in purchasing . . . and I have a question. Could you call me back . . . ?"

Curiosity is the driving force behind the entire QBS strategy. By constantly piquing the prospect's interest, you build up the credibility you need to ask more probing questions and to offer solutions, and finally, a sale.

Establish Your Credibility

Once you have engaged a prospect's curiosity to get his or her time and attention, you are able to set up a QBS sales forum—a time and a place for you to meet the prospect and begin the actual selling of your product or service. The QBS sales forum, in other words, is where the action takes place.

In this forum, your first priority is to establish your credibility—that is, to convey a favorable impression to the prospect about your trustworthiness, believability, and competence. Credibility is key to your success as a salesperson, for if you are unable to establish credibility early in the process, you are unlikely to successfully close a sale.

QBS shows you how to establish credibility by narrowing the scope of your questions early in the relationship, then broadening the scope of your questions once you have gained the prospect's confidence.

Ask Diagnostic Questions

First, narrow the scope of your questions.

Many salespeople make the mistake of asking broad, open-ended questions that they have not earned the right to ask. For example, financial planners may start a phone call with, "Hi, Mr. Smith, my name is John Doe, and I'm with Financial Planners of America. What are your financial goals and objectives for the next five years?"

Mr. Smith, of course, is not very likely to engage in a conversation about his financial goals and objectives with a person he has never met or talked with.

Salespeople will have more success if they begin with targeted, diagnostic questions. Diagnostic questions are closed-ended and very specific and only require a short answer from the prospect. These questions establish your competence and experience while slowly building a conversation with the prospect.

The first question should always be "Can I ask you a question?" If the prospect says yes, you can then start to fire your diagnostic questions.

Here's the start of a sample conversation between a prospect and a seller:

SELLER: "How many file servers do you currently have installed?"
PROSPECT: "We have twenty-two servers downtown and seven in the annex."
SELLER: "Is your network topology Ethernet or Token Ring?"
PROSPECT: "Ethernet."
SELLER: "Are you using Microsoft NT or Novell?"
PROSPECT: "Microsoft."
SELLER: "Version 3.X or 4.X?"

The conversation is now engaged.

Diagnostic questions address the disadvantages of both closed- and open-ended questions. Many prospects, as described above, are not likely to open up to open-ended questions from people they don't know. On the other hand, closed-ended questions can quickly close down a conversation, especially if they are answered with a simple no.

Diagnostic questions allow the conversation to continue without pushing prospects to divulge more than they are ready to.

Uncover Buyers' Needs

By starting off asking short-answer, diagnostic questions, you earn the right to ask more focused, probing questions that will enable you to uncover the needs of your prospects. People will buy your product because they see it as a solution to their needs. It's your job to uncover those needs.

There are four types of questions that help to focus your conversation: Status, Issue, Implication, and Solution. As you move from the general status questions to the specific solution questions, you escalate the focus of your questions, thus zeroing in on prospects' needs.

From Basic Information to Specific Solutions

Status and Issue questions are analytical and are helpful for garnering basic information. Two examples of status questions are "How many file servers do you currently have installed?" and "Is your network topology Ethernet or Token Ring?" Two examples of issue questions are "What's the most significant business issue you currently face?" and "What would you like to accomplish with this type of product?"

Once you've found out what is important to the customer, you need to find out why it is important, and this is where implication questions play a role.

Probe and discover the implications of each issue, both for the buyer personally and for his company, by asking implication questions. If the customer said that the biggest issue facing his company was downtime, then a follow-up implication question would be "How does your downtime affect your customers?" or "What would happen if your data were lost completely?"

One way to elicit more information is to use "global questions," which show prospects that you are eager to hear more from them. If a prospect tells you that security is very important to his business, an effective global question for you to ask next would be "How do you mean?" A word of caution: Using the question "What do you mean?" can cause some people to go on the defensive by making them think their opinion is being challenged.

Finally, once you have learned what is important to the prospect, you need to phrase solution questions to move the sales process to the next step. An example of a solution question is "Mr. Prospect, if I could show you how to solve each of the issues we just discussed, would you be willing to take the next step?"

Create a Sense of Urgency

To successfully identify buyer needs, you must understand the difference between latent and active needs. Active needs occur when prospects realize that they are no longer satisfied with the status quo; latent needs are those that the prospect hasn't yet recognized.

Freese once informed a cold-calling septic system maintenance salesperson that he didn't need a maintenance system. However, after Freese had hung up from that sales call, he began to think about the maintenance and upkeep of his home's septic system and eventually did purchase a service agreement—but not with that initial salesperson's company.

The original salesperson, in other words, failed to uncover Freese's latent need for a better maintenance system and then failed to transform that latent need into an active need by convincing Freese of the urgency of the situation.

If you can uncover latent needs and transform them into active needs, you will increase your probability of success. The septic maintenance salesperson skipped the stage of creating a sense of urgency by uncovering Freese's latent needs and went right into the boilerplate sales pitch.

Present Solutions

Once you've made prospects curious, established your credibility, and uncovered buyers' needs, the next step is to present solutions.

This is a pivotal point in the sales process, where you educate the prospect about the value of your product's or service's solution. Most sales training programs focus almost exclusively on this point in the sales process, but QBS recognizes that it is only the midpoint of a sale.

The Mutual Agenda

When you give your sales presentation, QBS suggests you use the audience to help define problems. You do this by asking them an issue question: "To what extent is _____ important?" If they agree that this issue is important, write it down on your flip chart. After a few more issue questions, you have written down not just an agenda, but your prospects' agenda (what they need) as well as your agenda (what needs must be filled by the solutions your product or service offers).

DISPOSITION: THE THIRD ATTRIBUTE

*A*ccording to Freese, there are three attributes to strategic questions: scope, focus, and disposition. "Scope" refers to the broadness of a question. Beginning the sales process with narrow rather than broad questions helps establish your credibility. "Focus" refers to the specific purpose of the question. Status questions, for example, are designed to uncover the status of a sales opportunity. Issue questions are designed to reveal issues that prospects may be dealing with.

"Disposition" refers to the tone of your question. Many salespeople try asking questions with a positive spin, such as "Our solution looks really good, doesn't it?" The underlying message, though, is that the salesperson is trying to avoid hearing bad news by encouraging the other person to respond positively. But because of the natural tendency to mismatch, prospects may automatically counter your positive spin with a negative answer. Furthermore, if there are problems with a client or a deal, questions posed with a positive spin are not going to uncover those problems. While it is more comfortable to avoid difficult issues or problems, to bring a sale to a close all problems must be dealt with. By neutralizing the disposition of your questions, you invite open and honest sharing with your client. One way to do this is to offer the prospect a choice, such as "Mr. Prospect, would it be possible to meet later this week . . . or would that put a burden on your schedule?"

Presentation Strategies

QBS suggests five strategies for creating a more effective sales presentation:

1. *Divide and Conquer.* After you have created the mutual agenda, realize that different people in your audience will react to different parts of the agenda, because buyers are motivated differently. The mutual agenda will also help you because it breaks down the bigger selling decision into its smaller component parts. It is easier to educate prospects on the individual components of your product.

2. *Use Stories.* Not only do stories break the ice, but people will remember a funny story better than they will the specs on a new computer system.

3. *Gold Medals and German Shepherds.* Because buyers can be motivated by either rewards (gold medals) or fear (German shepherds), remember to position your product both as providing positive rewards and as a defense against negative consequences.

4. *Use Confirmation Questions.* Don't let the audience doze off on you. Interject short confirmation questions, such as "Are you with me?" or "Does that make sense?" during your presentation.

5. *Say and Explain.* Don't assume everybody knows as much about your product as you do. If you are using technical jargon, make sure you explain it or at least ask the audience if they've heard of the term.

TWO KINDS OF BUYERS

*W*hat motivates people to buy something? According to Freese, buyers are either running toward gold medals (having the latest and greatest) or running from German shepherds (avoiding potential problems). If you can learn to phrase your product's attributes as providing positives and avoiding negatives, you will have doubled your chances of a sales success.

For example, you might say to a buyer: "Ms. Prospect, our reliability features will increase your productivity [gold medal] and reduce all those pesky interruptions that would otherwise handcuff your business [German shepherds]."

Here's another example: "Because our systems use advanced technology, you can access more information than ever before [gold medal] without any risk of overloading the system with excess network traffic [German shepherd]."

Remember that your beliefs about what the prospect should do are unimportant. It is the buyer's motivations that are important. As Dale Carnegie once said, "Personally, I am very fond of strawberries and cream, but I find that for some strange reason, fish prefer worms."

Commitment: Close the Sale

This is one of the riskiest stages in the sales process, because most salespeople ask for a commitment too early in the sales process.

QBS doesn't believe in using high-pressure tactics to get customers to buy something they don't really want. Customers are smarter and more sophisticated than ever and will walk away if they feel in any way pushed or hassled. The focus in QBS selling is to get the customer to keep moving the process forward, rather than the salesperson dragging the customer along.

Closing Strategies

To reduce the risk in this stage of the sales process, QBS offers a four-point checklist:

1. *Know the Status of the Opportunity.* If you don't ask for the sale, the prospect can't say no. And if the prospect does say no, then you can learn what is preventing the sale from closing and work from there. Find out what the prospect expects from the sale. For instance, if a client tells you, "The price in your proposal seems a little high," QBS encourages you to elicit his or her expectations by saying, "How much did you expect to pay?" Getting your client's insights and expectations gives you more information with which to navigate the sales process further.

2. *Tit for Tat.* QBS recognizes each sale as a mutual exchange of value. Don't bend over backward giving prospects more and more without expecting a commitment from them, because they will come to expect the moon and the stars with every order they place with you. Again, use a strategic question that gives the prospect a few options, such as "Mr. Prospect, if we do this or that, would you be willing to agree to move forward with a purchase?"

3. *Reiterate Your Value.* Since the sales process can take anywhere from two weeks to two years, you will need to keep your product's value fresh in the minds of your prospects. Remember that they have many other duties, and just

---

FIVE PREREQUISITES TO CLOSING SUCCESSFULLY

There are five prerequisites that must be satisfied before a prospect will buy your product or service:

1. *A recognized need. Recognizing a need sets prospects on the hunt for a solution.*
2. *A viable solution. The benefits of your product or service must match the needs of the prospect.*
3. *Value justifying the cost. The value of the solution must exceed its cost.*
4. *A sense of urgency. Prospects must be emotionally ready to make the purchase. It's far easier to accept the status quo.*
5. *The authority to buy. Are you dealing with the right people? If not, the other four prerequisites won't do you any good.*

because you've already covered the mutual agenda at your sales presentation doesn't mean everyone will remember every part of it.

4. *Emotional Reassurance.* All decisions, especially large-purchase decisions, are highly emotional and full of uncertainty and risk. Sellers need to offer not just analytical support (to justify the cost of the decision) but also emotional reassurance to make the prospect feel more comfortable. Empathy (as long as it is sincere) will go a long way not only in the deal at hand but in helping build a long-term relationship.

Putting It All Together: Using QBS from Start to Finish

Every successful sale is the result of a multistage process. QBS divides the sales process into three stages: Interest Generation, Presentation, and Closing Steps. While most sales training programs stress the importance of the presentation aspect, QBS recognizes that most of the salesperson's time is spent generating interest and moving prospects toward closure.

The Interest Generation phase of the sales process involves the initial sales calls and other prospecting initiatives—attending trade shows, holding seminars and special promotions, and sending out mass mailings—designed to get the attention of potential customers. As described in the Conversational Layering framework, making the prospect curious and establishing your own

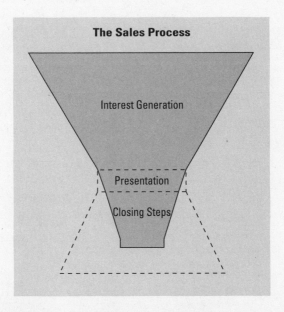

The Sales Process

Interest Generation

Presentation

Closing Steps

credibility while uncovering client needs are part of the Interest Generation phase.

The Conversational Layering framework uses both broad and focused strategic questions to lead prospects through these three phases, resulting in a successful sale.

Question-Based Selling: The Key to Control

By being the one posing the questions, you place yourself in a position of power because you are controlling the subject of the conversation. Here's an example:

> SALESPERSON: Mr. Prospect, several people on the committee were not able to attend last week's presentation. Does it make sense for us to educate those people—so they will be up to speed when it's time to review the details of our proposal?
>
> PROSPECT: Yes, that probably would make sense.
>
> SALESPERSON: Could we schedule a follow-up event to include everyone who was unable to attend the first presentation?

In sum, by asking the right questions at the right time, you will control the sales process from beginning to end. That is the power of Question-Based Selling.

THE POWER PRESENTER

by Jerry Weissman

I t's one of the oft-quoted statistics when discussions of fear arise. In many surveys on the topic, the fear of public speaking outranks fears of heights, confined spaces, and, depending on the source, death itself. Few things can inspire so much terror in some individuals as the thought of standing before an audience of any size and delivering a speech. It would be natural to assume that individuals who work in sales love the spotlight of the profession's frequent presentations. Surprisingly, this is not the case. Many sales professionals count themselves among the masses who would rather stand on the edge of a high cliff than stand before a microphone.

When it comes to taking the fear out of presentations, Jerry Weissman knows how to use psychology to conquer biology. The "fight or flight" instinct that causes one's stomach to churn and pulse to pound can be reduced to the point of nonexistence. In *The Power Presenter: Technique, Style, and Strategy from America's Top Speaking Coach*, Weissman provides the techniques necessary to relieve much of the tension created by public speaking. His goal is to prove that the amount of sweat you put in *before* the presentation, via careful, rigorous preparation, will figuratively reduce the amount of perspiring you do once you have your audience's attention.

Weissman's self-proclaimed status as "America's top speaking coach" comes with laudable accomplishments behind it. He has coached executives on the finer points of presentations for more than two decades. He separates himself from other speaking coaches by putting as much emphasis on structuring one's presentation as he does on getting past the fear of giving the speech. The tips provided by Weissman are essential for salespeople who are looking to go beyond the basics of clicking through a PowerPoint presentation. *The Power Presenter* helps speakers understand how an audience perceives a presenter and teaches the steps necessary to master the vocal and visual cues that win an audience's attention and comprehension.

This summary includes Weissman's updated analysis of the secrets behind President Barack Obama's public-speaking abilities. Obama's ability to command an audience and convey his message is recognized even by his critics. Weissman, not one to play partisan politics, acknowledges that one of Obama's strengths as a speaker, the ability to control his speech cadence, likely came from a study of President Ronald Reagan. Politicians have a similar task to salespeople in that they are required to make frequent speeches in hopes of convincing a group of people of the validity of an idea. This may be why Weissman includes mentions of Winston Churchill, along with Presidents John F. Kennedy and Bill Clinton, as people who have mastered the art of presentations.

Clinton, in particular, is used to demonstrate a point to those who quiver during speeches. His early forays into public speaking were less than successful. Weissman even references a speech Clinton gave that the latter referred to as "thirty-two minutes of total disaster." The point, for presidents as well as salespeople, is that public speaking is not an ability with which everyone is born. However, that does not mean that the skills to make someone a captivating speaker cannot be learned. *The Power Presenter* is an excellent tutor to guide you along the path to the podium.

THE POWER PRESENTER
Technique, Style, and Strategy from America's Top Speaking Coach
by Jerry Weissman

CONTENTS
1. **Your Actions Speak Louder Than Your Words**
2. **The Butterflies in Your Stomach**
3. **How to Prepare Your Content**
4. **The Mental Method of Presenting**
5. **Learn to Speak with Your Body Language**
6. **Masters of the Game**
7. **Graphics Synchronization**

THE SUMMARY IN BRIEF

Presentation coach Jerry Weissman has spent twenty years teaching CEOs and other executives how to deliver successful, profitable IPO road shows. Weissman's strategies have worked for dozens of top business leaders, including former Yahoo! CEO Tim Koogle, Intuit founder Scott Cook, and Netflix founder Reed Hastings.

The Power Presenter introduces the same effective technique, style, and strategy that executive teams from more than one thousand companies have used to raise financing, sell products, propose partnerships, or seek approval for projects. Supported by examples of famous presentations, this summary describes how to deliver a winning speech or presentation that will engage your audience from beginning to end.

Weissman offers a seven-step plan for crafting your content into a compelling story as well as advice on how to conquer your fear of public speaking and to present naturally with force and conviction. You'll also learn how to speak with your body language, create empathy with your audience, and integrate your graphics and animation with your delivery.

For anyone who has to stand up and deliver, *The Power Presenter* is a master resource filled with proven techniques, practical tools, insightful wisdom, and inspiring examples.

In addition, you will learn

- how to handle the Moment of Truth, when the presentation begins;
- how to strengthen your presentation with the correct way to organize, develop, and think through your content;
- how to take charge of your content with the Seven Steps of Story Development;
- what every speaker can learn from Barack Obama;
- how to integrate presentation skills, tools, and slides with a unique new skill called Graphics Synchronization;
- the five essential elements of every presentation.

THE COMPLETE SUMMARY

Introduction

> Cisco originally expected to get $13.50 to $15.50 per share for its stock. But during the road show the company was so well-received that it managed to sell 2.8 million shares at $18.00 apiece, Don Valentine, chairman of the Board of Cisco Systems, said. He attributed at least $2 to $3 of the increase to Weissman's coaching.
> —San Francisco Chronicle, July 9, 1990

When a business offers shares of its stock to the public for the first time, the company's senior management team develops a presentation that it takes on the road to potential investors. It's the most demanding and high-stakes presentation any executive will ever make.

Because only a few hundred companies go public in any given year, you are more likely to win a national lottery than to launch an IPO. But you'll almost certainly have to give a presentation or make an important speech at some point during your lifetime. And whether you are a businessperson or an ordinary citizen, your challenge is to be as well received as the Cisco Systems IPO road show.

Your Actions Speak Louder Than Your Words

Audience Advocacy is a viewpoint that asks you, the presenter, to become an advocate for your audience. Put yourself into your audience's place and think about their hopes, fears, and passions. Consider what your audience knows about you and your message or cause and what they need to know in order to respond favorably to you.

Think of the presenter and the audience as the beginning and ending points of all interpersonal communications; then think of the presenter as a transmitter and the audience as a receiver. The presenter transmits a set of dynamics—human dynamics—that can be summed up in three Vs:

Verbal. The story you tell.

Vocal. Your voice, or how you tell your story.

Visual. Your body language and what you do when you tell your story.

Your audiences are affected by these dynamics to varying degrees. Interestingly, body language has the greatest impact, the voice next, while the story has the least impact.

Surprised? You're not alone. Given the amount of time and effort that most presenters and speakers expend scribbling on yellow legal pads, pounding away at their computers, or shuffling their slides in preparation for their mission-critical presentations, they assume that content is paramount; but at the moment of truth, the story takes third place behind the body language and the voice.

The Crucial Task: Creating Audience Empathy

In addition to the visual, vocal, and verbal forces that influence your audience, they are also impacted by another dynamic: empathy. Evolved from the Greek word for emotion or affection, empathy refers to shared or vicarious feelings. In the presentation environment, empathy is the shared feelings between the audience and the presenter, but the sharing on the audience's part is involuntary.

To illustrate, let's consider the example of the presenter who stands up and freezes like a deer in the headlights. Although you may not know this stressed presenter, when you are in the audience and see that person's nervousness, you are most likely to feel similar, vicarious feelings. That is the power of empathy.

Empathy also works positively. For a case in point, let's go back to July 27, 2004, at the Democratic National Convention. Barack Obama, a then-unknown forty-two-year-old state legislator from Illinois, stood and delivered a stirring keynote speech. Obama spoke of the energy, urgency, and passion that he felt for America, and he expressed it with great energy, urgency, and passion in his voice and body. What was the result?

- The delivery system lifted the payload into orbit, and the convention delegates at the packed Fleet Center in Boston rose in unison to give Obama an enthusiastic ovation.
- Three months later, he swept into office as a first-term U.S. senator with 70 percent of the vote, the widest margin ever in an Illinois Senate race.
- Four years later, his momentum unabated, Barack Obama became the forty-fourth president of the United States—all launched by just one sixteen-minute, twenty-five-second speech.

The Butterflies in Your Stomach

Every living being on the planet, from one-celled organisms to four-legged animals to two-legged humans, responds to imminent danger by standing its ground and fighting or fleeing for its life. To enable either of these reactions, the body releases a sudden spurt of adrenaline and activates the sympathetic nervous system. This vast internal emergency network then sets many parts of the body into accelerated motion:

- **Eyes:** Pupils dilate to increase the field of vision.
- **Heart:** Pumps faster to send blood to the extremities to flail in defense or to run to safety.
- **Blood pressure:** Elevates due to increased blood flow.
- **Blood sugar levels:** Elevate to generate more energy.
- **Lungs:** Increase respiration rate to put more oxygen into the blood.
- **Sweat glands:** Activate to avoid overheating.
- **Salivary glands:** Shut down to suspend digestion.
- **Limbs:** Primed for fight or flight.

When a two-legged presenting animal is faced with the daunting task of standing exposed before an audience, the solitary focus of attention for dozens, if not hundreds or thousands, of watchful eyes, it responds with the flight reaction: pacing the platform like a caged tiger.

1. The eyes sweep the room frantically in search of escape routes.

2. The heart pumps faster to rush blood to the extremities.

3. The hydraulic system screeches into reverse: The palms, usually dry, get clammy from perspiration, cooling the rush of warm blood, and the mouth, usually moistened by the salivary glands, goes bone dry.

4. The nerve synapses fire more rapidly to heighten alertness.

Audience Perception

All of the preceding involuntary presenter behavior gathers momentum in a rolling chain action that impacts audience perception.

Rapid eye movement makes you as the presenter appear shifty eyed or furtive. Sweeping your head back and forth makes you appear harried. Wrapping your body with your hands and arms appears defensive.

The defensiveness immobilizes your features, which makes you look fearful and also makes your posture rigid. Moreover, by pressing your arms against your rib cage, you constrict the air supply in your lungs, which in turn impacts your voice, creating low volume, which sounds weak, and narrow inflection, which sounds monotonous.

Your vital organs, affected by adrenaline, can also affect audience perception. The heart, lungs, and synapses accelerate into time warp, which increases your cadence so that the tempo of your presentation sounds rushed. Words are crammed into a steady flat-line pattern, which results in a data dump that makes it difficult for the audience to separate the ideas you are presenting. And the steady pattern also causes the repetition of unwords, such as "um" or "ah," which makes you sound uncertain.

The Moment of Truth

All these powerful forces surging around inside your body and your mind—and reverberating throughout your audience—occur at the critical juncture of the Moment of Truth. But that moment is preceded by many other moments that stretch all the way back to another important moment: when the date and time for your mission-critical presentation are set.

As the clock starts ticking down to D-day, you think, "How will I ever find the time to get it done?" Suddenly, you ignite a state of high anticipation that builds in intensity until the Moment of Truth; and then the sight of your live audience kicks your adrenaline flow even higher.

Diminish your anxiety by taking charge of your content in its preparation.

How to Prepare Your Content

Many presenters and speakers, pressured by the demands of business and daily life, beg, borrow, or steal a colleague's material or put off their own preparation until the eleventh hour. Your presentation will be much stronger if you spend enough time to organize, develop, and think through your content. During the preparation, clear your mind by eliminating all the superfluous material and identifying the essential.

The Seven Steps of Story Development

1. *Framework:* Define your objective. What is your call to action? What does your audience need to know in order to respond to your call to action?

2. *Brainstorming:* Consider all the possibilities. Distill all your ideas into a few main themes.

3. *Roman columns:* Find a mnemonic device for your main themes. If you visit Rome today and tour the ruins of the great Forum, you are likely to hear your guide talk about the classical Roman orators, who spoke in the Forum for hours on end without any notes. To help them remember what to say, the orators used the stately marble columns of the Forum as prompts. The object of your brainstorming is to develop the Roman columns of your own story; about five or six in all is optimal.

4. *Flow structure:* Provide a road map for your audience and for you. Give the individual components of your story a meaningful, orderly flow. Two of the simplest and most common flow structures are chronological (track your story along a timeline) and numerical (combine all your Roman columns and assign them a number, then count down for your audience as you discuss each column). Think of David Letterman's "Top Ten List."

5. *Graphics:* Use visual aids, but give your graphics their proper role as support for your narrative.

6. *Ownership:* Take charge of your own presentation. Become a hands-on presenter and supervise your presentation's development at pivotal points.

7. *Verbalization:* Practice the right way. In your rehearsals, speak the actual words of your presentation or speech aloud, just the way you will do it when you are in front of your intended audience. Verbalization crystallizes ideas.

Charisma Not Required

"Good speakers are born, not made," and its extended variation, "That person has natural charisma," are often said about a presenter's delivery skills.

The corollary implication of this view is that change is impossible. You either have it or you do not. For some unearthly reason, many people cling to this preconception and recite it, almost as a pledge of allegiance. Change is possible for anyone.

A Case in Point—President Bill Clinton Bill Clinton, with his usual rhetorical flair and an established reputation as a superstar of the keynote circuit, seemingly did not need any makeover. But Clinton was not born with this capability. He admits as much in his autobiography, calling his first speech effort while in high school "unremarkable." He was still far less than remarkable in 1988 when, as the governor of Arkansas, he gave a nominating speech for Michael Dukakis at the Democratic National Convention in Atlanta. Clinton rambled on for so long that the delegates began to chant, "We want Mike!" And when he finally said, "In closing . . ." the crowd roared its approval. In his autobiography, Clinton confessed, "It was thirty-two minutes of total disaster."

The Mental Method of Presenting

Control of the mind, or concentration, is essential in every activity in the human experience. Even relaxation requires you to clear your mind of extraneous thoughts and focus on one tranquil image. Think about your sport of choice, be it skiing, tennis, golf, swimming, basketball, or soccer; in each of them, concentration is fundamental. Well, it happens to be the very same mind and the very same body that you use when you stand in front of an audience to present or to make a speech. Use concentration to conquer your adrenaline rush—and your audience.

What Was Going Through Your Mind?

During coaching sessions at Power Presentations, each participant is asked to stand and deliver a brief presentation to the other participants in the room— their colleagues—while the presentations are recorded on a digital video camera, an intentionally adrenaline-inducing scenario. As each person concludes, he or she is asked, "What were you thinking? What was going through your mind as you were speaking?" All of their responses have a lowest common denominator: "How am I doing?" They were thinking, "Uh-oh! They're all looking at me! I'd better do well!" This mind-set serves only to heighten their—and your—fear of public speaking.

Do a sharp U-turn. Change the mind-set. Think instead, "How are you doing?" "How is your audience doing?" Shift the focus from yourself to your audience. This shift will not only reduce your anxiety, it will also heighten the effectiveness of your presentation or speech. That is the essence of the Mental Method of Presenting.

Concentration and Conversation

The pivotal factor in this shift is concentration. In sports, concentration ranks higher in importance than conditioning, muscle mass, nutrition, hydration, or stamina. Universally in sports, the mind is used to control the body. It is the very same mind and the very same body that you use in presentations and speeches, so use your mind to control your body when you stand in front of an audience.

The foundation of the Mental Method of Presenting is person-to-person conversation. The challenge when you are in front of an audience is to recreate the conversational mode, the very mode in which most human beings are comfortable. To do this, let's first analyze the key dynamics of conversation.

In any person-to-person exchange, the two parties

1. make eye contact;
2. use their hands and arms to express themselves;
3. use their voices to punctuate their words;
4. interact by asking questions and exchanging ideas.

In presentations and speeches, the adrenaline rush causes drastic changes in each of those core elements. But does the interaction really stop? If you see a person in your audience smiling at you in knowing appreciation, that's an interaction. So there is indeed interaction with your audience, but at the Moment of Truth, the interaction suddenly switches from verbal to nonverbal. The challenge then is to focus on that pivotal instant and make the nonverbal interaction work for you rather than against you. And the way to do this is to shift from presentation mode to person-to-person conversation.

Person to Person

Whenever you step up to the front of a room to present or speak, regardless of the size of the audience—four, forty, four hundred, or four thousand—pick one person. For an instant in time, set a new default: Presume that you and that individual are the only people present and, for that instant, disregard everyone else in the room. Make that person the object of your concentration. Then, as if the two of you were across a table or a desk, strike up a conversation. After a moment, move to another person and strike up another conversation; after another moment, another person and another conversation. Continue around the room in a series of person-to-person conversations.

THE FOUR STAGES OF LEARNING

*I*f you've ever taken up the study of a physical activity, such as a sport, you've gone through a process known as the Four Stages of Learning. The stages also hold true for the physical aspect of presenting or speaking before a group.

Stage One: Unaware of what to do, you perform poorly and are unconscious about your incompetence.

Stage Two: The instructor tells you what you did wrong and you become conscious of your incompetence.

Stage Three: The instructor tells you what to do and you become conscious of your competence. But the first time you try to follow the instructor's advice it feels unnatural. Your Stage Three, then, is actually self-consciousness about your competence.

Stage Four: You perform your skill without thinking about it; you are unconscious about your competence.

Learn to Speak with Your Body Language

Negative behavior, driven by the fear of public speaking and its attendant instinctive reaction, the fight-or-flight syndrome, creates negative perceptions in the audience.

How do we change the behavior to create a positive perception? The key is to approach our challenge from the 35,000-foot view. Accept that there is a difference between the way it feels to you as a presenter and the way it looks to your audience.

In the Power Presentations program, participants are asked to stand up in front of the room and gesture with their arms open wide. Because the new behavior feels uncomfortable to them, they inevitably resist. As soon as they are told that their discomfort will diminish over time, they accept and are able to make significant improvements.

Eventually, opening your arms will feel comfortable to you and look comfortable to your audience. You will appear poised, confident, and ready to take on the world. Whatever behavior you have been practicing until this point in your life is behavior you have been reinforcing. To develop new habits you need repetition. Repetition over time will move you from self-conscious to unconscious competence.

Qualitative Versus Quantitative

Each of the following instructions describes the quality of your engagement with the one person with whom you are having a conversation:

- Your eyes hold until they connect.
- Your features reflect your enthusiasm.
- Your head nods to create involuntary agreement.
- Your balanced posture appears poised.
- Your hand and arm reach out, replicating a handshake.
- Your voice conveys your message with conviction and punctuation.

All of the preceding is summed up by the acronym ERA: Eye Connect, Reach Out, and Animate. This single instruction brings all the elements of your delivery system into play. ERA also happens to be what you do when you have a conversation. So whenever you step up to the front of the room to present or speak, have a conversation with each person in the audience. As you do, use the Mental Method of Presenting. Read the reaction of each person you address and be prepared to adjust your content.

Control Your Cadence

Cadence in speech is the equivalent of rhythm in music. For our speech metric, we turn to our three presentation dynamics and focus now on the verbal, or the content. In text, the written form of the verbal, that metric is a sentence. Spoken language, however, is different. When we speak, we don't form full sentences; we speak in partial sentences or phrases. Therefore, use the phrase as the metric for your cadence. This will give your speech a clear rhythm. When you speak in a clear and coherent cadence, you will make it easy for your audience to follow you. Here's how it all works together in a presentation or speech: When you step up to the front of the room, pick one person in your audience, the one with whom you're going to have a conversation. Then:

- Deliver one phrase to that person.
- Pause.
- Move to another person and deliver one phrase to that person.
- Pause.
- Move to another person and deliver one phrase to that person.
- Pause.
- Continue around the room, delivering one phrase to one person at a time.
- Pause between each phrase and each person.

Complete the Arc

Stay with one person for the entire logic of the phrase—regardless of its length—and then drop your voice. Stay with that one person for the full trajectory of meaning. The length of each unit is measured logically rather than numerically. Dropping your voice at the end of every phrase is called Completing the Arc.

1. Stay in Eye Connect all the way through the full phrase "The key to winning presentations is the Mental Method," and then drop your voice at the end.

2. If you do not drop your voice at the end of your phrase, if you let it hang in midair, you convert your statement into a question.

The First Ten Seconds

The moment you stand up in front of that room, the adrenaline will start coursing through your body. It will cause your eyes to sweep the room in search of escape routes. You will not be able to hold back that sweep. You will barely be able to think of what to say. Your eyes will go into motion, searching for the exits.

- Go with it. Let the sweep happen. Let your eyes take in the entire room; but make the sweep work for you rather than against you.
- Accompany your continual eye movement with words directed to the entire group, and be gracious about it: "Good morning. Welcome. I appreciate the opportunity to speak with all of you." These simple amenities will make your rapid eye movement appear sincere rather than frantic.
- Once you have swept the room with your welcoming remarks, stop. Turn to one new person, set your eyes on both of that person's eyes, and get ready to speak the first phrase of your presentation.

Masters of the Game

The Great Communicator

Ronald Reagan was known as the Great Communicator, and deservedly so. To see what makes him so effective, let's look at his delivery of his final State of the Union message.

On January 25, 1988, in the House Chamber of the U.S. Capitol, Ronald Reagan stood poised on the historic dais, looking out at the sea of faces in a joint session of Congress. He spoke with—not at—the men and women of the Senate and House of Representatives, and he did so as if he were having individual conversations. The warm tone of his voice reflected the intimate human-interest words of the text. The vast, packed chamber watched and listened in hushed awe, drawn in by the hypnotic, long, looping rhythms of his cadence.

As the speech reached its climax, Reagan displayed all the dynamics once described by a Pulitzer Prize–winning television critic: "His physical presence begins to eclipse his words . . . when you begin watching more and hearing less . . . feeling more and thinking less. Look and mood completely take over. That presence on TV: just the sight of him cocking his head with his sincere grin and lopsided hair, is still worth a thousand words and millions of votes."

Conversation and Empathy

Contrast Ronald Reagan's conversational style with that of Winston Churchill, John F. Kennedy, Martin Luther King Jr., and Billy Graham. These orators used their hands and arms with dramatic gestures that approached choreography. They had rich, resonant, nearly operatic voices. Moreover, Churchill and Kennedy were national leaders who spoke from on high down to their audiences and asked them to come up to their lofty level. The latter two, King and Graham, were religious leaders who also spoke from on high and asked their audiences to go up to a higher authority.

Ronald Reagan, on the other hand, spoke to his audiences at their level. The essence of Reagan's style was his uncanny ability to be completely at one with his audience in every setting, across every dimension. He projected his gentle persona into the living rooms of America.

What Every Speaker Can Learn from Barack Obama

On October 2, 2002, at the very same time that President George W. Bush and Congress were announcing their joint resolution to authorize the invasion of Iraq, Obama, then an Illinois state senator, spoke at an antiwar rally in Federal Plaza in Chicago. *The New Republic* reported an eyewitness account.

> Jesse Jackson was to be the day's marquee speaker. But it was Obama, wearing a war-is-not-an-option lapel pin, who stole the show. Obama's 926-word speech denounced a "dumb war. A rash war. A war based not on reason but on passion, not on principle but on politics." The electrified crowd knew that a political star was born.

Barack Obama is, by any standard, a very good, if not great, speaker. But his talent did not spring from birth or from mystical, magical powers. Obama uses a set of accessible techniques that you, too, can use.

1. *Verbalization:* Obama practices verbalization. In a *Washington Post* story he was quoted as saying, "My general attitude is practice, practice, practice. . . . Besides campaigning, I have always said that one of the best places for me to learn public speaking was actually teaching—standing in a room full of thirty or forty kids and keeping them engaged, interested and challenged."

2. *Person to person:* You should attempt to connect with individual members of your audience by adjusting your content. A *New Yorker* magazine profile of Obama gave an example from his campaign for his Illinois senate seat where the candidate adjusted his content to address a potentially difficult audience. When speaking to a group of AFL-CIO building tradesmen who had supported his opponent in the state primary, Obama adjusted his content to include a prolabor message. The result: "Heads began nodding slowly, jaws set, as he drove home his points."

3. *Think "you":* Obama used that persuasive word, "you," strategically throughout his campaign for the Democratic nomination, on his Web site, and in his speeches.

4. *Speak with your body language:* Eye Contact: Obama's strong eye contact is apparent in every type of speaking situation. Reach Out: *Time* magazine reported, "Physically, he is uncommonly restrained: He keeps his hands close to his head, and his shoulders are always tight and squared." Animation: In all settings, large and small, Obama is always animated, his face expressive, breaking into a ready smile or expressing the meaning of his words with passionate emphasis.

5. *Control your cadence and complete the arc:* Emulating Reagan, Obama rolls out his words in long arcs, like a ship riding the waves on the high seas, completing each arc by dropping his voice and punctuating each point forcefully. The pauses between the arcs allow his listeners to absorb the meaning of his words, if not to become captivated by his compelling rhythm.

Graphics Synchronization

Graphics Synchronization is a close cousin of graphic design. Design is what you show, or what your audience sees displayed by your PowerPoint slideshow; synchronization is what you do (your eyes and body language) and say (your voice) when you show what you show. Graphics Synchronization is the integration of your slides with your visual and vocal components. All these factors exist in a teeterboard relationship. The classic skill set to adapt is: Tell 'em what you're gonna show 'em; show 'em; and tell 'em what you've shown 'em.

There are many tools of the presentation trade: screens, microphones, lecterns, projectors, computers, and remote-control devices. All six tools must be carefully integrated with each presenter's or speaker's Graphics Synchronization skills.

Presenter and Screen

Present with the screen at your left.

Present in the screen plane.

Present at the edge of the screen.

Avoid the projection beam.

Presenter and Audience

Face front.

Illuminate for Eye Connect.

Present at the eye level of the audience.

Check sight lines.

Graphics and Narrative

Start your discussion of every slide with a Title Plus. (When you look at a new slide, look at it in its entirety. This overview is called Title Plus. The title serves as the headline for the whole slide.) It will make the rest of your narrative flow more smoothly and enable your audience to stay with you. After the Title Plus, however, different types of slides have different narrative follow-throughs.

- Simple slides start with a Title Plus.
- Moderate slides also start with a Title Plus, but then you must help your audience understand your slide by guiding them through the image.
- Complex slides also start with a Title Plus, but then they become the exception to the rule. Certain slides require a level of detail that is irreducible: for example, financial charts, architectural diagrams, or flowcharts. You can build the slide in stages.

Alternatively, you can display all the information on the screen at once and then, rather than try to make Eye Connect, turn to the screen and become a voice-over narrator.

All the concepts must work together inseparably. Any one element can impact the others, as well as the fate of your entire presentation.

For example, you can develop a persuasive story, illustrate it with dazzling graphics, present it with poise and confidence in a presentation environment with all the trappings of a first-class, modern theater, and have your audience listen to you in hushed awe for the full length of your presentation. But if, when you open the floor to questions, you react to the first tough question defensively, evasively, or contentiously, everything that went before will be negated.

The Power Presentations Pyramid

The five essential elements of every presentation can be viewed as tiers of a pyramid, beginning with the base—story, graphics, delivery, tools, and Q&A. The foundation of the pyramid for every presentation is a solid story that is illustrated by the graphics of the slide show. In turn, these elements are delivered by the presenter's body language and voice, all supported by the tools of the presentation trade. The entire presentation is then subject to the scrutiny of the audience's questions, which the presenter must handle with complete assurance and credibility.

The ultimate conclusion is that a presentation does not exist on the screen alone, in the presenter alone, or in the audience alone. A Power Presentation combines all these dynamic elements into a living entity that changes every time you present.

As Cindy Burgdorf, former CFO of SanDisk Corporation, commented after concluding the last of four intensive days of the Power Presentations program, "This isn't just about presentations, is it? This is about communicating in any situation. It all applies everywhere."

SECRETS OF POWER NEGOTIATING FOR SALESPEOPLE

by Roger Dawson

When heading into a sales presentation, preparation can make the difference between walking away with a deal and walking away empty-handed. Negotiation is never an easy task, and for sales professionals, their entire livelihood rests on their ability to be masters of this essential skill. Prospective clients tend to view the negotiating process as combat in which they are the noble defenders of the budget seeking to repel the gluttonous desires of invading sales raiders. A prospect will use every tool at his or her disposal to make sure that he or she exits the deal as the victor.

Roger Dawson may have given prospects an unfair advantage with his first book *Roger Dawson's Secrets of Power Negotiating*. Building on years of in-the-field observation and experience, Dawson made his Power Negotiating Institute into one of the major negotiation training centers in the U.S., Canada, and Australia. There are enough Dawson disciples out in the business world to make the average salesperson quiver. Fortunately, Dawson decided to level the playing field by writing a sequel, *Secrets of Power Negotiating for Salespeople*. This book reshapes common perceptions of negotiation and gives salespeople the necessary tools to help move the discussion forward.

Secrets of Power Negotiating for Salespeople operates under the notion that a salesperson's objective should be to win a negotiation but leave the other person feeling like he or she has won. Dawson treats this process like the chess match that it truly is for many salespeople. The metaphor extends through his introduction of gambits for the opening, middle, and closing of a sale. Dawson makes it clear that negotiation should never be confused with confrontation and that the latter is something that should be studiously avoided because of its ability to bring an instant halt to any progress made during a negotiation.

The tactics discussed in *Secrets of Power Negotiating for Salespeople* are field-tested and cultivated from experiences that sales professionals will run across time and again during their careers. The explanation of four techniques to discover how much a buyer is willing to pay is a key passage for salespeople who have been spurned repeatedly when the negotiation gets down to price. Dawson has a deep understanding of the psychology of the sales situation. His recognition of the buyer's possible motives and explanation of how to bring a salesperson's strategy in line with the buyer are key tenets of the power-negotiation formula.

Dawson acknowledges that the negotiation skills of today's buyers are growing. He understands that businesses view negotiation as a key to keeping costs low when dealing with vendors and service providers. What's more, Dawson is quick to point out the overwhelming wealth of information buyers have at their fingertips. The us-versus-them attitude in the marketplace can sometimes even lead competitors to team up against a vendor. A better-informed buyer with better negotiation skills is a formidable opponent. Rather than raising a fist, *Secrets of Power Negotiating for Salespeople* teaches sales professionals to extend a hand to the prospect, one that the salesperson hopes will be shaken when the deal is made.

SECRETS OF POWER NEGOTIATING FOR SALES-PEOPLE
Inside Secrets from a Master Negotiator
by Roger Dawson

CONTENTS

THE SUMMARY IN BRIEF

Imagine that you had the tools to win every negotiation you were called upon to enter with buyers, while simultaneously making the person on the other side of the table feel like he or she had won as well. What tools would be in your tool kit? What, in other words, would you need to know?

You likely would need to know a bit of psychology to determine, identify, and engage in the dynamics of the negotiation. You would also need to analyze the personality of your buyer to understand how he or she would act and react, offer, and counter. Most important, you would need a strategy to tie it all together, a collection of instructions to guide you through every conceivable negotiating tactic.

Look no further—your tool kit is in your hands. In *Secrets of Power Negotiating for Salespeople*, master negotiator Roger Dawson gives you the tools you need to foster a win-win negotiation every time you sit down at the table. Among others, he provides the following tools:

- A detailed set of rules to guide you through the beginning of a negotiation, when your preparation and initial demands set the tone for everything that comes after.
- Six negotiating gambits to use and watch for in the middle of a negotiation, when you need to maintain momentum to keep the ball rolling in your direction.
- A set of closing gambits that help you seal the deal and get the buyer's final commitment on the terms you set, while also giving the buyer the impression that he or she has won.
- A strategy to downplay the importance of money in a negotiation by increasing the buyer's awareness of the value of your offers.
- A set of techniques to help you determine your buyer's negotiating range, in order to maximize your effectiveness in the bargaining process.
- Tips to help you recognize and understand what buyers are doing when they try to intimidate you.
- A unique, personality-driven approach to moving buyers from a firm position, in an effort to find a mutually beneficial solution.

THE COMPLETE SUMMARY

Three Trends: Challenges for Sales Negotiation

Only the best and brightest salespeople will be equipped to grow and prosper in the next millennium, in the face of constant shifts in the vocation (indeed, the life) of sales. Roger Dawson sees three major trends coming to fruition:

1. Buyers are becoming better negotiators. Customers seem intent on improving their bottom lines by taking away from yours. This is a trend that is certain to continue in the foreseeable future. Customers have three ways to improve profits:

Sell more by either going head to head with a competitor (to improve their own market share by taking a portion of someone else's) or creating a new market share through product innovation (a risky and expensive proposition).

Reduce operating expenses via employee attrition or by upgrading to more efficient (and expensive) equipment.

Do a better job negotiating with their suppliers. This is the easiest way to improve profits, and the one that affects you the most.

With an increased focus on negotiation in most companies, the buyers with whom you deal most often are better educated and more savvy than the buyers of ten or twenty years ago. They know that doing a better job of negotiating with you directly affects their bottom line.

2. Buyers are better informed than ever. Buyers used to need salespeople because they brought to the table a wealth of valuable information the buyer could not get elsewhere. That knowledge was power—power the salesperson could use to his or her advantage at any point in the negotiation or sale. Thanks to point-of-sale data collection, demographic analysis, and the Internet, buyers have all that information and more literally at their fingertips, and the power that accompanies that information is theirs to wield, not the salesperson's.

3. Salespeople are facing a role reversal. The once highly defined role of the salesperson has now blurred to include a host of other tasks, including buying for retailers, specialty stores, supermarkets, and the like—an intriguing role reversal. To meet this challenge, salespeople must be more intelligent, more versatile, and better trained than ever. And most of all, they must become better negotiators.

Beginning Sales Negotiating Gambits

Beginning gambits are critical in your negotiations, because every advance you make will stem from your early preparation and the demands you make in the initial stages of the negotiation. Your beginning gambits must reflect a careful evaluation of the buyer, your market, the buyer's organization, and other crucial conditions. These early moves can win or lose the negotiation for you.

In beginning sales negotiating gambits, several key rules apply.

Rule 1: Ask for More Than You Expect to Get

Henry Kissinger once said, "Effectiveness at the conference table depends upon overstating one's demands." In other words, why begin a negotiation with your target result when you know that in the normal give and take of bargaining you will have to make some concessions that move you further away from that ideal point? By making a high (even extreme) initial proposal, you both give yourself some negotiating room (you can always go down, but never back up) and set the stage for advancing your Maximum Plausible Position (MPP)—the most that you can ask for and still have the buyer see some plausibility in your position.

Going in high also raises the perceived value of your product or service, negates the deadlocks typically caused by conflicting egos, and creates a climate where the other side can also win. High initial demands provide plenty of "wiggle room," allowing negotiators to work their way toward the middle ground, to find a solution with which both sides can live.

Rule 2: Bracket Effectively

Your initial proposal should always be an equal distance on the other side of your objective as their proposal. If, for example, a buyer is offering $1.60 for your product, and you know you can live with $1.70, bracketing tells you that you should start negotiations at $1.80. Your proposal should be structured so that if you and your opponent end up splitting the difference, you still get what you want.

The trick is to get the buyer to state his or her position first; you cannot bracket effectively if you make the first offer. Once the offer is on the table, you can bracket the negotiation with your counteroffer, then continue bracketing until you have zeroed in on your objective.

Rule 3: Never Say Yes the First Time

Saying yes to the first offer or counteroffer from an opponent automatically raises two regrets.

"I could have done better." This reaction has little to do with price and everything to do with the reaction of the other person. When you ask for more than you expect to get and carefully bracket your offer to attain your objective, you naturally expect a counteroffer; when this does not materialize, you doubt the worth and veracity of your offer.

"Something must be wrong." When your opponent accepts an offer you did not think he or she would, the mental picture you have formed of how he or she would respond is shattered, catching you off guard. This is a big danger in negotiation, particularly if you have invested a lot of time in coming up with a proposal. Regardless of how difficult it may seem, turning down a first offer is a crucial step in Power Sales Negotiation.

Rule 4: Flinch

Body language is a critical part of negotiations. Thus, you should always flinch in surprise in reaction to a proposal from a buyer. The buyer may not expect to get what he or she is asking for; if you don't show surprise, however, you communicate that his or her most extreme offer is a possibility, and it makes him or her a tougher negotiator. It is important to remember that concessions often follow a flinch.

Of the people with whom you will deal in a negotiation, 70 percent are visual and will react when they see a flinch. Do not dismiss flinching as theatrical or childish until you have had an opportunity to see how effective it can be.

Rule 5: Play the Reluctant Seller

Power Sales Negotiators should always play the Reluctant Seller when they're selling to squeeze the negotiating range before the negotiation even starts. Showing reluctance usually feeds the desire of the opponent to strike a deal, so much so that he or she may give away his or her bargaining range immediately.

On the other hand, you must also be wary of the Reluctant Buyer, whose aim is to get you to divulge your lowest price. You must be wary of these individuals and learn to play the negotiation game better than they do.

Rule 6: Concentrate on Issues

Sometimes, intense negotiations can result in flashes of anger or upset on either or both sides. When this happens, maintain your cool. Never focus on personalities in the negotiation; focus instead on the issues at hand.

Imagine a top arms negotiator walking out on a treaty negotiation with Russia and telling the president, "Those guys are so unfair; I got upset, so I just walked out."

Staying calm and concentrating on the issues of the negotiation allows you to fend off distractions brought on by the actions of the other negotiator. To do so, keep a running tab of your progress in a negotiation—compare where you are presently to where you were an hour ago, a week ago, or a month ago. These are the only things that matter.

Rule 7: Use the Vise Gambit

The Vise gambit is a measured response to an offer or counteroffer, one that tells your opponent, "You'll have to do better than that." Of course, the next tactic after making this statement is to simply shut up—say nothing and let your opponent do the talking, make the next move, or alter his or her position.

When using this gambit, concentrate on the dollar amount being negotiated;

a negotiated dollar is a bottom-line dollar. Don't be distracted by the gross amount of the sale or by percentages. Be aware of what your time is worth and what the sale will mean in terms of your bottom line.

Middle Sales Negotiating Gambits

Middle gambits feed off your early work and keep momentum going in your direction. You'll be able to respond to the pressures that pull you and your opponent apart and use those pressures to master the negotiating game.

Appeal to a Higher Authority

A very popular negotiating tactic on both sides of the table is the Higher Authority gambit, in which one person claims he or she must appeal to a higher authority before making a final decision. This tactic is as powerful as it is popular; it shifts pressure off your shoulders without forcing a confrontation. The Higher Authority appeal sets aside the pressure of making a decision, but it also might cause some frustration, as your opponent may surmise from your appeal that in speaking with you, he or she is not speaking with the decision maker.

The gambit is a ruse; you might have the power to make a decision, but you do not allow your opponent to know that. Your Higher Authority should be vague—a "board" or "committee," rather than an actual title (the other person can always demand to meet your authority figure if he or she knows a title). If the gambit is played on you by buyers, attempt to get them to admit they have decision-making authority by countering their gambit with one of your own:

appeal to their ego;

get their commitment that they'll recommend you to their Higher Authority;

get them to commit to a decision, subject to some other consideration or time period.

Note the Declining Value of Services

When you make a concession, ask for a reciprocal concession immediately; the value of your concession will drop very quickly, in accordance with the Declining Value of Services principle. This principle states that, although the value of any given material object you buy may go up in value over time, the value of services (like a concession) will decline rapidly after those services are performed. Never trust the other side to "make it up to you later." Negotiate concessions or counteroffers immediately.

Never Offer to Split the Difference

In this country, we have a tremendous sense of fair play, which indicates that if both sides give equally, the eventual outcome is fair. What is rarely considered is that these "equal" concessions do not often reflect the opening negotiating positions of the opponents. For example, if a seller overvalues a property and an underinformed buyer negotiates from the seller's bracketing strategy, the results will rarely be equitable for the buyer, regardless of whether the two meet in an acceptable "middle ground" in their negotiation.

In a negotiation in which a middle ground is apparent and close, never offer to "split the difference" yourself; you should, however, encourage your opponent to do so. Stress both the time you have spent on the negotiation (preparation time, time spent at the bargaining table, and so forth) and the small amount of money that separates you from the other person. If he or she offers to split the difference, use that as the starting point for further negotiation, rebracketing your negotiating range each time. Splitting the difference doesn't mean splitting down the middle, because it can be done multiple times.

By getting the other person to offer a split, you put him or her in the position of suggesting a compromise, which you can then use to your benefit, either pushing for more concessions or agreeing to the proposal, however reluctantly. This makes your opponent feel victorious, even though you have actually subtly controlled the negotiation yourself.

Mind the "Hot Potato"

When buyers want to give you their problem and make it yours, it's like tossing you a hot potato at a barbecue. For example, if a buyer says, "I need that delivery tomorrow, or the line will come to a screeching halt," he is taking a problem that is his and trying to make it yours.

When the other party tries to toss you a hot potato, test the problem for validity immediately—is this the deal killer your opponent says it is, or is he or she trying to test you for your reaction? For example, if the buyer has a procedural problem, there is very likely someone in his or her organization who can override the procedure and let the deal progress. If the buyer is simply trying to get you to lower your price, recognize this and find a way to resolve the issue without giving him or her a better deal.

Watch Your Trade-offs

Like the Declining Value of Services principle, the Trading Off gambit requires you to immediately ask for something in return when a buyer asks for a concession in a negotiation. When you do this, one or all of three things will happen:

1. You just might get a significant concession.

2. You elevate the value of your concession by demanding something in return.

3. It stops the buyer from repeatedly coming back for more or "grinding away" in the negotiation.

An important point to remember is to refrain from asking for something specific in return—it usually forces a confrontation. Let the other party make the concession offer, then negotiate from that point forward, toward the concession you really want.

AVOID CONFRONTATION

*N*ever argue with a buyer who disputes what you say; argument forces a confrontation, which could have one of several negative effects:

The buyer might develop a personal stake in proving you wrong and him- or herself right.

Your argument will make him or her doubt your objectivity.

The more you argue, the more you'll force him or her to defend his or her position.

Use a countergambit to give yourself more time to think, regain composure, and turn any hostility to your advantage in the negotiation.

Ending Sales Negotiating Gambits

Ending gambits prepare you to get the buyer's final commitment in a negotiation. These strategies allow you to close the sale by getting what you want, while the buyer also feels victorious. As in horse racing, there's only one point that counts—the finish line.

Good Guy/Bad Guy

One of the best-known negotiating ploys is the Good Guy/Bad Guy gambit. Variations of the tactic have appeared in everything from Charles Dickens's *Great Expectations* to just about any television police drama you can name. One negotiator on the other side will hold firm to his or her offer, get emotional, and leave the table, where his or her partner, a much more friendly, amenable sort, will "buddy up" to you in an effort to entice you to make a concession in response to his or her pleasant demeanor.

Buyers use this gambit much more than you might believe; be on the lookout for it when you're dealing with two or more people. Good Guy/Bad Guy is usually defused when it is identified; buyers are so embarrassed to be caught using it, they will typically back off immediately.

Nibbling

The Nibbling principle dictates that you can accomplish things more easily with a "nibble" later in the negotiations, suggesting an additional concession after a decision is made. Nibbling enables you to sweeten the deal you have made with buyers and to get them to agree to something they would not have agreed to earlier. A terrific example of nibbling is the optional automobile warranty, which sellers only detail after the buyer makes the decision to buy the car; the seller nibbles in the closing room, getting the buyer to purchase additional coverage and spend more than he or she might have otherwise.

Don't ask for every concession up front; get the buyer to commit to a deal, then nibble for a little extra. Determine first which elements you are better off bringing up only as a nibble—concessions to which the other side would not agree the first time around but that you might successfully negotiate by nibbling. You also must be vigilant, recognizing that your opponent may nibble on you at the last moment. Try to counter this by tying up all loose ends and details and by using gambits that make the other party feel as though he or she won.

Pattern of Concessions

The way you make concessions is very important, because it can create a pattern of expectations in the buyer's mind. There are four errors to avoid when making concessions:

- **Making equal-sized concessions.** Buyers will keep pushing you if you concede an equal amount every time they push. If, for example, you lower your price by $250 the first time the buyers push and by $250 the second time they push, don't you think they would expect another $250 concession if they pushed you again?
- **Making the final concession a big one.** When you make a big concession in the middle of the negotiation to reach your lowest possible concession, you create an expectation of further large compromises. For example, if your first concession is six hundred dollars, and your second four hundred dollars, buyers may expect at least one more similar concession, perhaps of one hundred dollars. If you do not concede (having reached your lowest possible figure), you may create an atmosphere of hostility that could kill the negotiation.

- **Giving it all away up front.** Some buyers may try to entice you to reveal your entire negotiating range up front by asking for a "last and final bid," or by telling you, "We don't like to negotiate." This is a trap—the buyer is indeed negotiating with you; he or she is simply trying to get you to make all concessions before the negotiation even begins.
- **Testing the waters with a small initial concession.** If you make a small opening concession and it is rejected, the temptation may exist to increase the increment of money relinquished with each concession. A smarter approach would be to begin the negotiation with a modest concession, then decrease the increment with each concession, thus creating a decreased expectation with each compromise.

Withdrawing an Offer

When a buyer continuously grinds away at you for a lower price, you can sway the negotiation to your advantage by calling the buyer's bluff and withdrawing your offer from the table, either by backing off your previous price concession or by removing extended terms (training, installation, etc.) from consideration. This tactic is a gamble to be used only in extreme cases and only in combination with another gambit—the Higher Authority ploy, perhaps, or the Good Guy/Bad Guy gambit. Withdrawing an offer on your own authority creates a confrontational atmosphere when you want to appear to be on the buyer's side.

Position for Easy Acceptance

The best negotiation results occur when you win the concessions you want and need and the buyer walks away feeling as though he or she won also. In order to affect this ideal situation, it may be necessary for you to make one small, last-minute concession that allows the buyer to feel good about giving in to you. In these cases, the size of the concession is not as important as the timing of it; indeed, the concession can be small and still do the trick. Some positioning concessions may include the following:

1. A free training class for the buyer's operational staff.

2. A hold on the price for ninety days, in case the buyer wants to duplicate the order.

3. A three-year extended services warranty for the price of a two-year warranty.

The point to remember is that the concession, regardless of how token, allows the buyer to walk away happy with pride intact.

THINGS MORE IMPORTANT THAN MONEY

*T*wo decades of training salespeople have convinced Roger Dawson that price weighs more heavily on the minds of salespeople than it does on their customers. In fact, customers who ask you to cut your price are secretly wishing they could pay more for your product or service. To get them to do this, however, you need to accomplish two things:

You must give customers a reason for spending more.

You must convince customers that they cannot find a better deal than the one you are offering.

The second point is one of the central issues at work in Power Sales Negotiating, because the feeling of getting a great deal is more important than the dollar amount spent in the deal.

There are many other things that are probably more important to buyers than price. Among them are:

- *The quality of the product or service. If it were true that buyers only bought based on the lowest price, 90 percent of vendors would be out of business. When buyers admit that they see your product as a commodity only, you must recognize the tactic as a negotiating ploy and kick in your Power Sales Negotiating techniques from there.*

- *The terms you offer. Recognize that companies make more money on the financing of their product than they do on the products themselves (bought a car lately?). Pay attention to the full range of terms you negotiate; your buyers will definitely be doing the same.*

- *Credit. Extending a line of credit with your company can help a customer through a lean time or through the bottom levels of a cash-flow cycle. This offer may be more important to the buyer than price.*

- *Flexibility. If you are willing and able to tailor a product or service to the needs of a customer, that customer may be willing to pay a little extra for that product or service. Flexibility is key; if you can bend to meet your client's needs, the client is more likely to overlook a price differential between you and your closest competitor.*

Writing the Contract

Regardless of how long or detailed your verbal negotiation with a buyer, there will always be details that are overlooked until the actual written contract is created. Chances are, the person writing the agreement will think of at least a half dozen things that did not come up during the verbal negotiation; that person can then write the clarification of these points to his or her advantage, leaving the other side to negotiate the changes before signing.

This very fact should give you the impetus to position yourself to write the contract, from the briefest counterproposal to the final long agreement. Writing the agreement gives each party one last chance to reach true accord; up to that point, each side might have interpreted the agreement differently. The written contract is the final, official interpretation of the agreement. The side that writes it thus has the advantage of having its interpretation stand.

Find Out How Much a Buyer Will Pay: Four Techniques

The negotiating range of your buyers runs from the wish price (what they hope you will sell your product for) all the way up to the walk-away price (the highest price they are willing to pay). As a Power Sales Negotiator, your duty is to uncover their walk-away price, using one or more of a number of tactics, including the following:

- **Raise the buyer's top offer by hypothesizing what your Higher Authority might be willing to do.** If he or she is currently buying a similar product at $1.50 per unit and you are asking $2.00 per unit, you can make a comment along the lines of "If I could get my boss down to $1.75, would that work for you?" You do not necessarily have to sell your product for $1.75; getting the customer to acknowledge that $1.75 might be acceptable raises his or her negotiating range, so that you are now only twenty-five cents apart, not fifty cents.
- **Determine the buyer's quality standards by offering a stripped-down version of your product.** You can use his or her concerns about quality as a means to prove that price is not his or her sole concern. For example, use the line "I can get down to $1.50 if you don't care about this feature. Would that work for you?"
- **Establish the most the buyer can afford by offering a higher quality version.** Offer to add new features for a modest price increase. If the buyer shows interest, you'll know he or she could pay more; if he or she sticks to the original offer, you'll know that fitting the product into that price bracket is critical.
- **Remove yourself as a possible vendor.** It is a gamble, but offering to back away from the sale can disarm buyers enough to cause them to reveal some information they would not necessarily share if you were still in the game. For example, you might say, "We'd love to do

PERSONAL POWER

When you are face-to-face with a buyer, you automatically get a feel for how much power you have over that person. Perhaps you get a mild burst of confidence that you can close the deal, that it just might be your lucky day. Sometimes the power is overwhelming; you're certain that you possess all of the power in the sale. Sometimes you feel confident but you don't know why.

This personal power can be demystified by understanding where the power comes from; it can also be used as a tool that enables you to understand what buyers are doing when they seem to intimidate you. Take note of the different types of power you and your buyer may exert at the negotiating table:

Legitimate Power—the power of one's title or position in the marketplace. Legitimate Power goes to anyone who has a title, because titles influence people. If you have a title, use it on your business card, nameplate, and letterhead; at the same time, do not feel intimidated by another person's title—some of those titles mean nothing.

Reward Power—the power that makes the buyer feel you can reward him or her, now and in the future. When you perceive someone as being able to reward you, you have ceded power to that person and given him or her the ability to intimidate you. Some buyers may try to use Reward Power on you when they ask for a concession, then just happen to mention they have a big job coming online next week for which you may be in the running. Recognize this power and understand what they are trying to do to you. Then watch their influence diminish as your confidence increases.

Reverent Power—the ability to project a consistent set of values, thereby building trust. When you vacillate on a set of issues, your buyer loses confidence in you. Be certain you do not set up standards only to break them when you cannot live up to them.

Charismatic Power—the power of the personality. Your objective should be to have the buyer like you so much that he is willing to make concessions to you, but not to like the buyer so much that you find yourself making concessions to him.

Expertise Power—the buyer's belief that you know more about the product than he or she does. When you project that you have more expertise than the buyer in a certain area, you gain power. You can also combat this gambit by recognizing it and finding a way to defuse it by referring to another expert or by quickly becoming one yourself.

Information Power—the buyer's vision of you as a storehouse of information. Sharing information forms a bond; withholding information intimidates. Recognize when information is being withheld as a negotiating gambit—you'll shift the power from the buyer to yourself.

business with you, but this deal is just not for us. Let's get together on something else later." A little later, you can ask, "Just between you and me, what do you realistically want to pay for this?" If the buyer tells you, you may yet be able to get back in the running with a better, more informed deal.

Know the Buyer's Personality

Power Sales Negotiators, recognizing when a buyer has taken a firm position, can get the buyer off that position so that they both can focus on their mutual interests. The key to doing this is to become familiar with the personality styles of your buyers and how those styles cause buyers to approach situations differently.

In order to correctly identify the various personalities of your buyers, you should first discern the two dimensions of their personalities: their level of assertiveness (how quickly do they want to make decisions, to get the deal done, or to demand a concession?) and their level of emotion (how creative are they? how caring or warm?). When you combine the assertiveness and emotional dimensions, you come up with four different personality styles:

- **Pragmatic (assertive-unemotional).** Buyers who fall into this category usually negotiate like street fighters whose sole goal in the negotiation is to win. They tend to frighten people, to waver on the edge of hostility, threatening (however implicitly) that things will be very uncomfortable if they do not get their way. While pragmatic buyers' domineering style of negotiating is cause for some discomfort, they also tend to dig into a certain position, unwilling to budge even when it is to their benefit to yield.
  - Don't waste time with small talk when dealing with a pragmatic buyer.
  - Don't overload the buyer with information or give an overenthusiastic presentation; you will come off as phony. Be quick, factual, and expectant of a quick decision.
- **Extrovert (assertive-emotional).** Extroverted buyers are friendly, open, quick decision makers whose prime goal is to influence and inspire other people. They tend not to be sensitive enough in a negotiation to keep up with what's really going on, but they also are not afraid to say no to you.
  - Extroverts respond well to enthusiastic explanations of the situation; if they're excited, they will go out of their way to get others excited also.

○ Talk about their interests and be prepared to receive a quick decision based on their level of excitement about the project.

• **Amiable (unassertive-emotional).** Amiable buyers will set up barriers to keep a safe distance between them and that which makes them uncomfortable, including assertive decisions. They prefer managing in a large corporate situation where they can be protected by the format of the organizations. Their goal is agreement; everything else will fall into place if everyone involved in the decision agrees. Indeed, their guiding philosophy is "If we like each other well enough, we'll all agree." Their soft negotiating style leads them to be too easily swayed, even to the point of accepting losses in the hope that the other side will reciprocate with concessions of its own.

○ When you negotiate with amiable buyers, proceed slowly, gradually building a level of trust. Take care not to offend them, or to use high-pressure tactics with the purpose of goading them into a decision. Give them time to consider all the angles and be comfortable with the decision.

• **Analytical (unassertive-unemotional).** Analytical buyers feel they can manage any situation by providing massive amounts of information. They appreciate and demand accuracy, are flawless time managers, and will likely do anything to make sure there is order in the negotiation. Procedures, in their minds, will produce a solution. They ignore relationships in negotiations, detaching themselves from the

---

WIN-WIN SALES NEGOTIATION

*I*nstead of trying to dominate buyers and trick them into doing things they wouldn't normally do, you should work with them to develop a solution that benefits both of you. Observe the following four rules to create and maintain a win-win negotiating atmosphere:

1. Don't narrow the negotiation down to just one issue.
2. Understand that people are not out for the same thing—that your goals and your buyer's are distinct.
3. Don't be too greedy.
4. Put something back on the table. The little extras you give that the buyer didn't negotiate for mean everything.

personalities involved and preferring to act strictly on facts. They are rigid, sometimes to the point of inflexibility.

Be as accurate as possible when dealing with analytical buyers. Provide facts, figures, charts, and other graphic representations of the information you are providing. Indeed, be prepared to give every little detail about your product and operation and to answer a lot of questions. Try to build rapport by engaging them in a conversation about their interests, which probably include some technical background and/or hobbies.

TIME TRAPS

by Todd Duncan

Benjamin Franklin had many roles during his eighty-four years of life: inventor, statesman, ambassador, signer of both the Declaration of Independence and the Constitution. But salesman? While one can argue whether or not Franklin "sold" the ideas of liberty and democracy to his fellow colonists, there is no doubt he unknowingly contributed a phrase that has come to define the sales profession in a single sentence. In his 1748 piece *Advice to a Young Tradesman*, Franklin wrote, "Remember that time is money." More than two and a half centuries later, author Todd Duncan attempted to help salespeople understand the accuracy of Franklin's simple statement.

The summary of Duncan's book *Time Traps* teaches sales professionals to not accept the common excuse that there aren't enough hours in the day. If anything, American sales professionals should have an advantage in the quantity of their time. This is, after all, the country that has traded the title of "most hours worked annually" back and forth with Japan for the past decade. The causes of wasted time, which Duncan refers to as time traps, are mainly mental in nature. The human predilection for comfort and routine can create some hazardous business practices for salespeople looking to take their results to a higher level. Duncan's mission is to help people climb out of the time stream before they are swept away by its currents.

Duncan's use of a river as a metaphor for a sales career is something with which all salespeople can identify. Depending on the type of industry and size of one's organization, the river might be as long as the Amazon or as treacherous as the Colorado. The depth and speed of each salesperson's river does not matter to Duncan as much as the realization that at no point does the water cease rushing. He acknowledges that most sales professionals assume they can only attempt to navigate the river rather than alter its course. *Time Traps* contradicts this logic by helping salespeople to dam the river and slow its pace to a point where decision making and organization become more manageable.

The management of one's time is improved first by gaining a better understanding of where exactly time disappears. *Time Traps* suggests that poor time management is the result of poor task management. Duncan offers some intriguing suggestions that seem to counter the modern ethic of "instant, constant accessibility." However, sales professionals who take a moment to do some quick calculations may discover that Duncan is right about how much time is wasted due to lack of organization. If a salesperson stops to check his or her e-mail the moment a new message enters the in-box, it actually eats up more time than if he or she designated a ten-minute window every two hours to check messages. While this appears to be a simple notion, sales representatives should try putting it into practice before dismissing it as easy.

A salesperson should be the master of his or her time, not the reverse. Duncan identifies organization, technology, and even sales quotas, among other problems, as thieves that routinely rob the sales professional of time. *Time Traps* attempts to help salespeople get back what is rightfully theirs and, with a bit of ingenuity, exchange it for the currency on which Franklin's portrait appears.

TIME TRAPS
Proven Strategies for Swamped Salespeople
by Todd Duncan

CONTENTS

THE SUMMARY IN BRIEF

Time traps can rob you of your success. As much as 75 percent of the time you spend at work or in your sales career is probably a waste of time. There is a difference between being busy and being productive. At the heart of the many challenges you face—in your sales career, your health, your spirituality, and your most important relationships—is how you spend your time.

In this summary, sales expert Todd Duncan explains all the traps that steal your time and shows why you should abandon the pointless pursuit of time management and, instead, adopt a far more actionable approach: task management. He explains that by focusing your time better you can make more money and have more free time—at the same time.

The summary also asks you to rethink your values as a person while making the case that your work isn't your life: Life is why you work.

In *Time Traps*, Duncan challenges you to invest your time in the areas that will truly deliver dividends: your health, your financial fitness, your relationships, your knowledge, and your purpose.

In addition, you'll learn the following:

- How to extricate yourself from the biggest time traps in order to become more productive.
- The Yes Trap: You lose time by saying yes too much.
- The Control Trap: In order to save time, you must delegate responsibility.
- The Technology Trap: As you may have noticed, e-mail, cell phones, and computers don't always translate into more productivity.
- The Quota Trap: Quotas can create more problems than they solve.
- The Failure Trap: Learn not to be afraid of failure.
- The Party Trap: Don't let success get to your head.
- How to rethink what you think is important. After all, if you gained more free time and wealth, what would you do with it?

THE COMPLETE SUMMARY

Chasing the Wind

The concept of time management is flawed. As a worker, you can't manage or tame or control time any more than you can lasso the wind and tie it to a fence post. You can only manage your thoughts and actions.

We have the know-how and capacity to make time matter. The problem lies in the obstacles that keep us from doing it more often. These obstacles are the time traps, and the lives of salespeople are full of them.

Traps exist to steal your energy and time. Education and avoidance are your best defenses against the time traps.

Since we measure the value of time by how we spend it, task management is the real solution to our overly busy lives. It's the only way to get yourself out of the swamped state in which you find yourself so often.

The Toughest Challenge in Sales

Selling is a profession where time can be a very frustrating thing. Time is the most pervasive and repetitive problem salespeople face. Details vary, but the struggle is constant. Salespeople incorrectly accept this as their lot in life: to never have enough hours in the day to accomplish what they want. But they are wrong. There are immediate and specific actions that you can take in order to shift your business and life into a place where most of your time is well spent—a world of time freedom.

The Identity Trap

When your time is monopolized by your work—and/or recovering from work—the only thing that forms your identity is work. You are known to yourself and to others solely by what you sell, how you sell, and how well you sell. You become lost in your job.

Work has permeated so much of our identity in American culture that we consistently work more hours per year than any other country—leapfrogging the notorious workhorse Japan in 2000 by thirty-seven hours a year.

There are negative consequences to that, including guilt, restlessness, growing frustration, an urge to justify our schedules, and fear or regret. The all-work identity simply doesn't feel right and was never meant to. Author Joe Robinson described it as the "workplace without end." Salespeople, in order to keep this one-dimensional identity viable, trade multilateral satisfaction for unilateral success, trade family fitness for financial potential, and trade childhood dreams for corporate visions. When you think about it, those really aren't good choices.

There's an obvious problem with an identity founded entirely on work. Not only does an identity wrapped up in work sap your identity, it keeps you from realizing your dreams. In essence, it changes who you are now and who you will become in the future.

Rethinking Your Time

Salespeople who are not swamped by their work usually had a breakthrough point where they gained a new perspective on time. They reached common conclusions about time before they were able to make a change in how they used their time. These six conclusions are the foundation for everything else discussed in this piece:

1. Life will never settle down until I choose to settle it down.

2. Working is not living.

3. Time is life first, then money.

4. More work usually means less life; less work, more productivity, and efficiency usually mean more life.

5. How I use my time deeply impacts my self-esteem, my identity, and my fulfillment.

6. I can't control time, but I can control how I use and respond to time.

To reclaim your identity and set the stage for regaining control in your days, you must first understand what is currently defining your identity. Who you are and who you are becoming is foundationally a function of how you are using your waking hours. Most salespeople overlook this in their pursuit of success and become something they never intended to be. What you invest your time in defines who you are.

Time-Trap Swamp

The only thing that will get you out of your time-trap swamp is changing what you spend your time on. In other words, while you cannot manage or tame or recapture time, you can manage, prevent, and change most of the events that fill it up.

In order to capture your true identity you must accomplish two things:

1. Determine how you are wasting your time.

2. Determine how to spend more time on the things that produce the life you desire.

Your true identity will be shaped and your path to freedom will become clear as you accomplish these objectives.

The Organization Trap

The responsibilities a salesperson faces are much like a raging river. There are times when the river flows predictably and you can handle your tasks in an efficient manner. Such days are a rare exception.

On most days your river of responsibilities rages like a flood-high current that threatens to drown you. The more tasks that rain down, the more disorganized and out of control you become. Even if you see obstacles, you rarely have the time or the energy to avoid them. This is a circumstance that most salespeople have to continually work to avoid.

You Have an Excuse, Sort Of

Most salespeople say they are disorganized and lack the time to catch up. As a result, they scramble to get work done every day, but often at the expense of great inefficiencies and gross errors. Once you are in the middle of the river and the current is sweeping you along, stopping to get organized only compounds the problem.

According to one recent study, most salespeople test out in the highly driven or highly relational personality categories. Not surprisingly, these two personality types have the most difficulty when it comes to achieving organization. Both types have traits that make it difficult to multitask or commit to detail and follow through. As a result, salespeople must make special efforts to get their days under control.

Here are two lessons from the world of a professional river guide that can help you construct a mental foundation for cleaning up your days:

1. *Acknowledge the power of the river.* Early on in a sales career, it might seem like a fun challenge to take on everything that comes your way. But the longer you sell, the more you realize that the pace of a sales career doesn't slow down involuntarily. You must first acknowledge the life-sapping power of your river of responsibilities if you are ever to muster the courage to overcome its unforgiving current.

2. *When the river is high and fast, you must scout what's ahead.* If you are sick of working so much, now is an ideal time to pull out of this raging river we call a sales career, if only for a few moments, and survey the scene to determine how you can make it through in one piece.

Damming Your Workload

When you get out of the chaotic current of your career long enough to give it an honest look, you realize there are only two ways to manage your responsibilities: You can either learn to guide yourself through the rapids and attempt to avoid the obstacles as best as you can or you can build a dam. Most salespeople opt for navigation first, but that's very difficult to do when you're in the middle of a raging river. You can only slow the pace of the river by building a dam.

The Blueprint of Your Dam

You have to put boundaries on your business, or you won't have balance in your life. Since you cannot manage your time, the only way to organize your day is by managing your daily tasks. Task management—not time management—is the foundation of organization. The only way to free yourself from the traps that steal your time is to manage the things that occupy your time: *tasks*.

Four phases make up the construction of your dam. Each phase represents different boundaries that you must build in order to slow down the rapid pace of the tasks that fill up your river of responsibilities. The four phases are accumulation, admission, action, and assessment.

- **Accumulation**. In this phase you must learn to stop all unnecessary tasks before they require your attention and sap your time. The primary goal of this phase is to stop all distractions and interruptions from entering your work stream.
- **Admission.** Learn how to admit legitimate tasks into your schedule in the most efficient manner possible. Once you've stopped unnecessary tasks from sapping your time, you must then set up boundaries to help you prioritize and schedule tasks that still require your attention. Decipher the difference between necessary and productive tasks and then set up boundaries that will allow you to maximize your time each day for what is most productive.
- **Action.** Begin to carry out the tasks that are either necessary or productive, based on the boundaries you have set. Learn to increase your overall productivity. Upon completion of the Action Phase, you will have constructed your entire dam.
- **Assessment.** When you get to this phase, you will have a solid system of boundaries—a dam—in place that will provide you at least four hours a day to sell. The Assessment Phase helps you avoid obstacles and teaches you how to remain focused on the tasks that are not only the most productive in your business but also the most productive in your life.

Damming Tasks

The Accumulation Phase and the Admission Phase are the foundation of your dam and represent steps you will take to either eliminate or regulate tasks entering your river of responsibilities. Placing boundaries in these two phases, before you take action, is the key to organization.

There are five things you can do to construct boundaries that regulate or eliminate the most common unnecessary tasks that clutter your days:

1. *Don't give your personal digits to your customers.* Personal digits are your personal cell phone number, home phone number, and personal e-mail address. While you want to serve your customers well, if you don't put limits on when they can contact you, then you will never be able to get out of your personal time swamp. Ask yourself this: Would I rather be known as easily accessible or worth waiting for?

2. *Don't give your work digits to friends.* This may seem radical as well, but it is quite necessary if you intend to gain control of your time. Keep in mind that your friends and family will find a way to reach you during an emergency. The plan here is to avoid all the nonemergency calls and e-mails from friends that make up 99.9 percent of what communication you're getting.

3. *Turn off the e-mail alert and instant message functions on your computer.* You shouldn't need to be told this, but many salespeople have one or both of these functions turned on. Your strategy should be to set a certain time for when you can check and receive your e-mails.

4. *Don't answer the phone unless it is someone you are expecting.* As a salesperson, you very rarely make money on unexpected phone calls. Unless you're in retail or you're expecting the call, the ringer shouldn't even be on. That sounds anti-social, especially if you work in a bigger office, but unless it's a prospect, you shouldn't be on the phone.

5. *Don't check your personal e-mail during work hours.* Although most people ignore company rules that prohibit this, it still adds to your personal river of responsibilities. If you can succeed at either not looking at your e-mail while you work or setting up specific times when you can respond to either e-mails or instant messaging, then you will probably be able to save several hours a week.

Work Without Interruptions

There are scores of endless unnecessary tasks that can saturate our days, including surfing the Web, needless meetings, reading the paper, snacking, checking sports scores, etc. You'll be surprised by how much time is freed up by simply constructing boundaries that keep such tasks from ever entering your river of responsibilities—beginning with the five most prevalent.

The Yes Trap

Most salespeople say yes too often. As a result they end up starting more work than they can finish, and the tasks they do complete are often riddled with errors or inconsistencies.

We are evolving into a nation of yes-people for whom no task is too much to ask and every request is affirmed with "Consider it done." Salespeople are the leaders of this movement.

In sales it is easy to fall into the Yes Trap. If you serve customers, you are granting requests. This translates into taking on many tasks in order to gain rapport and close sales. This kind of mind-set forces you to become an "ideal worker" who becomes a hostage to his or her job. It's the kind of world where parents can't make a living and be effective parents at the same time.

Scaling Back Without Losing Sales

There are only two ways to scale back your heavy workload and free up more time: (1) sacrifice sales, or (2) say no more often.

According to one survey, the average American salesperson sells for only ninety minutes a day. Another study reveals that salespeople spend 80 percent of their time doing tasks that simply don't affect their bottom lines.

More than likely you are spending three-fourths of your time each day on tasks that don't affect your bottom line. A salesperson's inability to spend the majority of his or her time carrying out the most productive, bottom-line tasks is the Yes Trap, and it is rooted in a salesperson's inability to say no.

The Value of Saying No

To best exploit your time, you have to figure out what you're spending most of your time on. There are three categories of tasks that we carry out on any given day: unnecessary tasks, necessary tasks, and productive tasks.

- **Unnecessary tasks.** These are activities that prevent your business from moving forward and therefore waste your time. These kinds of tasks include e-mailing friends, answering random phone calls, chatting with co-workers, instant messaging, making personal phone calls, Web surfing, and playing computer games. These are the tasks you need to stop.
- **Necessary tasks.** These tasks might move your efforts in a positive way but at a less productive pace than other activities. These activities are a good use of your time, but for strategic direction only. They include goal setting and planning, qualifying prospects, dealing with necessary paperwork, observation, and evaluation. These are tasks for which you need to regulate your time investment.
- **Productive tasks.** These activities represent the work that most effectively moves your business in a positive direction and are the best use

of your time. They are often actions that reflect the discoveries you have made completing necessary tasks. The top two activities in this category are strategic prospecting and selling. No other tasks add more to your bottom line.

Necessary Tasks

The goal with necessary tasks is to spend high-quality time on them but not a high quantity of time. The following are the main tasks in this category and the boundaries we must construct for them:

- **Paperwork:** Paperwork can become a major time killer if there are no boundaries in place. Don't spend more than thirty minutes every other hour on paperwork. Delegate your necessary paperwork to an assistant or team member. If you don't have an assistant, a good tactic is to block out at least thirty minutes every other hour for doing paperwork.
- **Planning and Goal Setting.** Spend one or two days planning once a year. If you isolate yourself during your annual planning sessions and are careful to set realistic, value-centered goals, you will not have to spend time amending your plan throughout the year.
- **Surveying Customers.** Don't let this build up. Design a strategic survey that elicits the information you desire from your customers, and then ask for their feedback before you close the sale so that errors are quickly pinpointed and addressed. One restaurant does this between the time you finish your entree and the time dessert and coffee are served. These surveys provide great material for evaluating your progress during your observation and evaluation time.
- **Observing and Evaluating.** Spend one hour on the last workday of every month observing and evaluating your progress against the goals you recorded in your planning session. Record your observations and necessary improvements and file them each month.
- **Communication.** Most voice-mail and e-mail messages can wait. Don't continuously respond to calls and e-mails. Pick two to four specific times a day to answer e-mails or particular phone calls. One salesperson spent twenty-five hours a week listening to and returning calls and e-mails. After she put in some boundaries, her business expanded by nearly 200 percent because she had more time to be productive.

The Control Trap

What begins as an ambitious act of taking ownership often ends up as an unexpected burden that weighs us down, a lid that keeps us from rising higher in our endeavors and realizing our potential. It's a frequent mistake in the sales profession because sales professionals are self-starters. But we can take it too far. And when we do, we end up trapped by the very things we try to control.

Letting Go

There are four basic reasons we maintain control even when it hurts our chances for success. They are:

1. Ego—No one can do it better than me.

2. Insecurity—If someone does it better than me, I will look bad.

3. Naïveté—I'm fine by myself; I don't need anyone else.

4. Temperament—Working with others is too complicated.

Success in any endeavor is a result of focused time. In order for you to realize your true potential, you have to focus on two tasks the most: building trust with the right prospects and adding value to your existing customers. One is too small a number to achieve greatness in sales.

There are three steps you need to take in order to delegate essential tasks and grow your business:

- **Answer the 100 percent question.** Are you devoting 100 percent of your time and effort to achieving your two most important goals? Your goal should be to spend the entire day, every day you work, on your top two productive tasks.
- **Assume a CEO mind-set.** This means looking at your sales job as if you were the owner of a company and then determining what decisions need to be made to grow and to ensure future stability. A CEO invests time in the fertile ground of productive customer relationships and productive business relationships.
- **Delegate in increments.** Salespeople believe they must accept that they have two choices: work more hours or let sales and customer service slide. Yet there is a third option: seek help from other people.

Delegation Steps

Here are four delegation steps you should utilize:

1. *Hire yourself.* You've already done this by blocking out four hours to work on your most productive tasks. This can make a tremendous difference, but it is only a start.

2. *Utilize the help your company provides.* You should get your manager involved. Your company might already have the means in place to help you complete your necessary tasks.

3. *Hire a part-time assistant.* Think of this as an investment that could improve your productivity, perhaps even doubling it or tripling it.

4. *Begin building a team.* A salesman named Harry used to hoard all the responsibilities for himself. After attending a seminar, Harry sat down and decided what jobs he could delegate to his staff. Today, Harry's team runs the company. Harry's income has increased by four times ever since he freed himself to concentrate on what's most productive for the company.

Team Building

When you are ready to build a team, keep in mind that a team needs a purpose to keep everyone excited. Just like professional sports teams, work teams also need an opportunity to gel. A team also needs a coach to empower it. Finally, team members need intimacy, honesty, and accountability to unite them.

You have to take the first step to make these approaches work. Don't quit halfway. Rewards will kick in. If you have a dream and don't have a team, your dream will die. But with a team, your dream will fly.

The Technology Trap

The Technology Trap is made up of many things: the computer, the laptop, the Internet, the PDA, the cell phone, e-mail, etc. The many time-saving devices we laud as efficient may be stealing the very thing they were designed to save.

Technology Traps are everywhere, and we fall into them every day. They not only keep us constantly connected to our jobs, making us slaves to others' schedules, but they also cut deeply into our time. Too often, technology is a hindrance instead of a help.

Regain Control of Technology

Nevertheless, technology can be a good thing—as long as you know how to keep it from impeding your progress. Here are five ways to accomplish this:

1. *Shorten the leash.* If you're a firefighter, a doctor, or police officer, you probably need a cell phone on you at all times. That's not the case for the salesperson. In fact, it's probably detrimental. Phones and beepers simply cause too many interruptions.

2. *Substitute, don't stockpile.* Don't hoard your old technology. If you have to buy a new piece of equipment, get rid of your old one; don't try to use both. Try to use only what saves you time and discard or give away the rest.

3. *Ask directions.* Don't try to figure out every function on your cell phone or PDA on your own. That can waste hours. Ask someone for help so you can figure out what you need right away and get started. We make the assumption that technology can save us time, but the truth is that technology can only save us time if we know how to use it.

4. *Test your tools' efficiency.* Four years ago, the author bought the nicest laptop he could find. Three months later, he discovered he wasn't using half of what the laptop offered and it had turned out to be a ten-pound burden he was forced to carry around. After a while, he bought a smaller laptop and gave away the heavy laptop to a friend who used it as his home office machine.

Evaluate the efficiency of your technological tools. Be honest about what you discover. Don't keep something that just looks good but that gives you all kinds of trouble or has many useless functions. It's wasting your time. Research and test out the tool you feel will give you the biggest boost in time. Don't rule out the old-fashioned way. Technology is not always more efficient than you.

5. *Go backward to go forward.* Sometimes technology isn't better. It's just prettier. If you can accomplish something more efficiently without a tool, don't get a gadget because everyone else has one. If you can use a pencil and paper to do something, do it. It will save you time and money.

The Quota Trap

Most salespeople trade their time far too cheaply. This is primarily the result of one thing: the quota.

Years ago, the traveling salesman was a respected individual. Quotas were used more as goals than as requirements, but they weren't necessary. Steady competition, personal dignity, and family responsibility set the standards that inspired traveling salesmen to trade their time well and succeed.

Nowadays, with competition, greed, and the fear of job loss, quotas can be used like whips on our backs, driving us to produce a certain quantity of sales but fooling us into ignoring the quality of our time. As a result, selling standards have hit the dirt. In fact, the pressure of quotas can force salespeople to act dishonestly. One recent survey revealed that 47 percent of sales managers suspect their salespeople lie during sales transactions. High quotas can actually force salespeople to serve their customers less instead of more.

The Quota Quandary

Since quotas tempt salespeople toward speedy (and even seedy) selling tactics, they often make salespeople counterproductive over the long run. For example:

- Quotas may speed your pace, but they decrease your focus.
- Quotas may increase your action, but they decrease your assessment.
- Quotas may increase your exposure, but they decrease your effectiveness.
- Quotas may increase your short-term turnover, but they decrease your long-term trust.
- Quotas may increase your short-term production, but they decrease your long-term profitability.

Quotas fool you into thinking that quantity of sales is the most important factor in success. Your true value as a salesperson isn't in the number of small sales that you stack up but the investment you receive from your time. Some sales managers hire reps who are less money driven and more relationship oriented.

Your goal as a salesperson, once you've eliminated the time wasters and the extraneous technology, is to use your newfound time as efficiently as you possibly can. Ideally, you should trade your time for only high-value customers. If you work the most with these customers, then you will get the most out of your efforts.

Trading Time for Top Customers

There are four general categories that describe all customers and apply to all industries. To begin trading your time for the highest return, you must understand who the best customers are—because not everyone is worth your time.

1. *High Maintenance/Low Profit.* These are the nightmare customers. You end up spending too much time on them and they usually don't buy very much, or they lower your profit to pennies. It is in your best interest to avoid trading your time with such customers. Don't waste your time: It's more valuable than that.

2. *High Maintenance/High Profit.* Customers fitting this description can produce a lot of business, but they are very difficult to serve. These customers expect more than you can give them, and they don't relent until they get what they want. Avoid this kind of customer. Instead, invest time in the next two types of customers.

3. *Low Maintenance/Low Profit.* These customers probably won't produce great profits, but they are likely to produce greater profits over time as your relationship grows. They are easier to serve because they're more professional. This makes them a wise investment. The goal with these customers is to move them over time into the final category.

4. *Low Maintenance/High Profit.* Invest the majority of your time with these customers. They will trade you the most business for the smallest investment of your time. You will have to groom these customers, but once you have their business, your goal is to hold on to them for life. That's where your time trade-off becomes a highly lucrative deal.

Getting the Full Value for Your Time

Once you understand who is worth your time and then begin to pursue only those types of customers, there are four strategies you need to maintain in order to maximize the value of your prospecting time:

1. *Prequalify prospects before you pursue them.* You need to determine whether the people you call on are fit for an investment of your time before you call on them. To begin a list of qualified prospects, ask the question Whom do I know who knows who I need to know? Remember that current customers and friends are often the best resource for new prospects.

2. *Never call on a prospect unexpectedly.* You're not going to be able to sell to anyone who doesn't expect your call or who isn't excited to talk to you. Try these three approaches to warm up prospects before calling on them: Send a value-added letter that evokes a sense of curiosity and makes you memorable, have a common friend or a colleague introduce you over the phone or in person, or have a common friend or colleague arrange a meeting.

3. *Cut ties with time-consuming customers.* This includes high-maintenance customers. Cut ties professionally and with integrity. You can even write them a business version of a Dear John letter. It is not easy to terminate an unproductive sales relationship, but if you're serious about maximizing your time then you need to free up your time for your best customers. Fewer deep relationships are more valuable and less time-consuming than many shallow ones.

4. *Transition relationships into partnerships.* The most valuable use of your time is not in constantly seeking new business but in deepening your current customer relationships. Do this by figuring out who your best customers are. Then divide your time among your most valuable customers. Set up an annual contact plan for the customers you determine to be the most valuable.

The values of these actions are threefold:

• You will have fewer customers but more income.
• You will be more productive in less time.
• Quotas will never scare you.

The Failure Trap

Those who are brave enough to face their failures understand that to be successful, you have to risk failure. The risk taker pursues dreams, aspires for greater success, is courageous, thinks about succeeding, is a pioneer, is resilient, and is tenacious. The risk maker stifles dreams, aspires to greater security, is cautious, thinks about not failing, is a plodder, is resistant, and is timid.

The risk taker takes risks because he or she understands it is the only way to create greater productivity. The risk maker makes risks by avoiding failure and thus remains unproductive and increases the likelihood of regret.

Three Risks Worth Taking

With the right perspective, you won't ever go back to the unproductive salesperson you were. Here are the top three risks worth taking in your sales career:

1. *Develop an impossible vision.* If you want more time to sell—and live—than you've ever had before, you must stick your neck out. You must dare to have an impossible vision for your business that includes these three parameters: You can't accomplish it alone, it breeds excitement and fear simultaneously, and it requires risk. Take a chance and really dream here.

2. *Become accountable to others.* This is the best way to maximize your potential. Use your personal leverage, associate leverage, and professional leverage to stretch your potential.

3. *Set exceedingly high standards* so that failing to meet them will not have major consequences. It takes guts. You'll need to stick to your guns in some potentially difficult situations. This particular risk isn't just about having high integrity; it's about leaving your office every day when you tell your family you will. It's about paying attention to your health despite the work you need to get done. It's about maintaining one face to every customer. It's about saying no when you must—even when saying yes is more lucrative.

RECLAIMING YOUR HEART AND TIME

"The heart," said Blaise Pascal, "has reasons which reason cannot understand." So don't be surprised if there are moments when what your heart is saying doesn't seem attainable or even practical. The battle between head and heart is lifelong. But you must learn to trust that it's the heart, as Thomas Carlyle said, "that sees before the head can see." It is only your heart, in other words, that holds the answers to the life you truly desire. It is your heart that reveals what makes time matter to you. It is your heart that shows you the way to true time freedom.

The Party Trap

To truly understand failure, we must have a deeper understanding of what constitutes success. Success should appreciate the value of your time; it should give you more time to spend on the things in your life that you value outside your job. However, if you're caught in the Party Trap, like so many professionals, success will actually depreciate the value of your time. Unchanged, this pattern will eventually take back the time it once freed up. Over the long term, the Party Trap will kill you.

Don't use your success just to buy more things. If you decisively invest the time your success creates in the things you value most, sales achievement will truly breed life satisfaction. The five most important investments of your free time should be your health (stop smoking and drink moderately), financial fitness (spend less than you make), relationships (find and be a mentor), knowledge (read and travel more and take up new hobbies), and a higher purpose (discover why you are here).

True Freedom

Remember: You work to live and don't live to work. The point of getting more benefit from your work is to be able to concentrate on the really important parts of your life. Take an honest inventory of your life. Is there a voice deep inside you telling you that there is something more? If there is, then there is still time to do something about it. This is the time to act. This is the time to live. Realize the power you have to change the course of your own history. Your future is not some faraway place. Your future is the result of how you most frequently spend your time. Spend it wisely today and every day hereafter. This alone will lead to freedom.

THE ULTIMATE SALES MACHINE

by Chet Holmes

There are salespeople who are seen as abrupt, direct, and intense, and then there is business growth expert Chet Holmes. He is a believer in the power of the human will to achieve and is willing to take the most direct route to accomplishing a goal. Some of his methods are certain to raise eyebrows. He favors a consumer selling strategy that targets the wealthy over anyone else and champions an interview technique he calls "the Attack," for a start. However, it is hard to argue with the results Holmes has achieved during his career. At one point, Holmes ran nine divisions of a company owned by Berkshire Hathaway vice chairman Charlie Munger, the right-hand man to billionaire investor Warren Buffett. In that time, he grew the business exponentially each year. Upon launching his own company, Holmes worked with nearly one thousand businesses that ranged in size from small operations to the likes of Warner Bros., Pacific Bell, and Wells Fargo.

Sales are at the heart of many of Holmes's principles. He distilled the essence of his road-tested philosophy into twelve skill areas and strategies. Combine his twelve strategies with the intensity Holmes refers to as "pigheaded discipline," and the result is *The Ultimate Sales Machine*. This summary doesn't waste a single word as readers are introduced to Holmes's high-powered lectures on management, marketing, sales, and success. Holmes's words seem to jump off the page, as though they were being shouted in one's ear by a corporate drill instructor.

Sales managers will benefit from the outset from Holmes's time-management secrets. The experience of a sales manager provides a microcosm of the larger adversity that sales professionals face. If a sales manager suffers under constant interruption, what chance do his or her salespeople have of making any inroads with a potential client? *The Ultimate Sales Machine* first tackles the common internal issues that plague many businesses, then demonstrates how to push these improvements out to clientele.

The secret to much of this transformation involves strategy and planning. For each of the twelve key skill areas discussed in *The Ultimate Sales Machine* there are multiple takeaways that readers can immediately apply to their own organizations. Much of what Holmes discusses is backed up by supporting statistics, reassuring the reader that the strategies have been forged in the fires of real situations and are not the product of top-of-mind writing.

The core of selling is the simple pursuit of the word "yes" from one's customers. Whether it's through the "Stadium Pitch" or the "Dream 100" strategy, Holmes is one expert who refuses to take no for an answer. His confidence in his own ideas is evident throughout his book. The adherence to these ideas is what helped Holmes rise to the apex of his industry. The hope is that through an equal amount of determination the reader can achieve the same goal.

THE ULTIMATE SALES MACHINE
Turbocharge Your Business with Relentless Focus on Twelve Key Strategies
by Chet Holmes

CONTENTS

THE SUMMARY IN BRIEF

There are two keys that set the stage for getting powerful results. The first key is to have what I call "pigheaded discipline." This may sound like an insult, but it's one of the best compliments I can pay. This concept is so important I originally titled the book *The Pigheaded Executive Wins Every Time*.

The second key is mastery. How does one become a master? Mastery is about doing twelve specific things four thousand times, not four thousand different things. By focusing specifically on the twelve key strategies—time management, training, meetings, strategy, hiring, getting the best buyers, marketing, using visuals, landing dream clients, selling, following up, and setting goals— you can easily become a master of these skill areas.

This summary is for executives, CEOs, entrepreneurs, and professionals. It is for middle managers, salespeople, and customer-service representatives. It is for everyone who plays a role in operating, marketing, selling, and running a company or department. It offers the kind of information and strategies that are essential for everyone in the trenches doing battle to grow and strengthen their business.

This summary not only offers the tools and pigheaded mind-set for success but also provides you with complete instructions on how to create the Ultimate Sales Machine, as well as how to put yourself and your company on the path to success and stay there.

In addition, you'll learn the following:

- How to master proven strategies for management, marketing, and sales
- How to get more bang from your Web site, advertising, trade shows, and public relations
- How to secure the best buyers for your business
- How to hire top producers every time

THE COMPLETE SUMMARY

Introduction

You can profoundly improve your company or department if you absolutely commit to one hour per week in which you do nothing else but work on making the business much more effective.

It's not going to be hard to apply the twelve strategies or to transform your business into the Ultimate Sales Machine. The key is learning and practicing the pigheaded discipline and determination you need to constantly address and readdress the twelve areas involved.

Time-Management Secrets of Billionaires

Earlier in my career I ran nine divisions of a company owned by billionaire Charlie Munger. I was working seven days a week, ten to twelve hours a day at the office dealing with interruptions, and then I'd bring home work that needed more concentration.

You've heard of "the one-minute manager"—I was the "got-a-minute manager." Anyone could come to me anytime they wanted and interrupt, and a "got-a-minute" meeting would break out.

In contrast, when I had a meeting with Mr. Munger I had to set an appointment, have a tight agenda, know what I was going to say, know the outcome I wanted from the meeting, and be as spot-on as possible. However, every meeting was highly productive and to the point.

Then suddenly it clicked that I needed to take control of my time and my staff. I sent out a memo that said: "Don't come to my door anymore and ask me if I've got a minute. The answer will be no. There are nine primary impact areas reporting to me, so we are going to have nine meetings per week with each of these impact areas. Hold all ideas, unless urgent, until your weekly meeting."

That memo changed my life. The next day, no one came to my door and I was able to get a lot more done at the office. But let me warn you, within a week everyone started slipping back into old habits. It took pigheaded discipline and determination on my part to train the entire organization to respect not just my time but theirs as well.

Instituting Higher Standards and Regular Training

According to an article in *Harvard Business Review*, only 10 percent of the population has what's called "the learning mind-set." These are people who seek out and enjoy learning. The other 90 percent of the population will not look to improve their skills unless they have to as a job requirement. Today, most professions have mandatory continuing education because they have found that without it people wouldn't keep current with the information necessary to be accepted as professionals in their fields.

Deliberate and Constant Training Some companies rely on classroom-style training programs with policies and procedures for all new hires. These programs cover the basics and serve a one-time purpose, but it is the improving and advancing of all the skills and professionalism of every person in your company on an ongoing basis that is going to turn your company into the Ultimate Sales Machine. Training is proactive. It keeps your company healthy and prepared no matter what crisis arises.

Executing Effective Meetings

The best way to build the Ultimate Sales Machine and to keep it running as smoothly as possible is to hold regular, highly productive, workshop-style meetings dedicated to improving every aspect of your company. In each of these meetings you will focus all the relevant people on fixing just one small part of the business. Together, you will brainstorm plans for how to improve this specific area, draft procedures to test, and ultimately create carved-in-stone company policies that everyone will be trained to follow. This constant attention to the "three Ps"—*planning, procedures, and policies*—is essential.

Workshops are an excellent method of focusing your mind and everyone else's on solutions and improvements within your organization. Workshopping means that instead of your talking and your staff listening, all of you get to work together on a problem, developing the ideas and insights to propel the company forward. You never know from where the big ideas are going to come. Large companies should have workshop meetings every week for every department.

Ten Steps to Implement Any New Policy

Here are the ten steps to implement new concepts, change, and growth in your organization:

1. *Get everyone to feel the pain.* To create real change in any organization, you have to help everyone, including yourself, to define, outline, and intensify the pain of not fixing the problem.

2. *Hold a workshop to generate solutions.* Whatever the problem, your staff deals with it every day. They will have many ideas on how to solve it.

3. *Develop a conceptual solution or procedure.* Each solution or procedure is "conceptual" until it is "proven" by you and your staff. More complex solutions will need to be worked on in this phase of your implementation.

4. *Have a leader or top talent personally perform the procedure or task.* Hands-on involvement at every level enables the leader to create the three Ps with certainty.

5. *Set a deadline for testing the conceptual procedure.* Set a deadline so you know that if you aren't seeing results in a certain amount of time, you need to go back to the workshop whiteboard and look at additional options.

6. *Document step-by-step procedure or process.* Spell it out.

7. *Have show-and-tell and use role-playing.* Take your documented steps and work with your staff to test and implement them. Show-and-tell and role-playing are the best methods of gaining experience before you put the process into the field.

8. *Have another workshop on how to improve.* People will have a greater buy-in when you actually take advantage of the ideas they suggest. Make them work at it and perfect it in concept and in practice before you roll it out.

9. *Monitor the procedure directly.* Monitor the procedure closely, observing and correcting behavior.

10. *Measure and reward the outcome.* You must measure your results intently. People respect what you inspect.

The three Ps are magical in your operation because they create the conditions for every aspect of your company to operate with subconscious competence.

CHET HOLMES'S STEP-BY-STEP INSTRUCTIONS FOR AN OUTSTANDING WORKSHOP

*T*he first thing you need to do is schedule your weekly meetings with your staff. Tell everyone to take two minutes and write down three things that they feel need to be improved in the company. You will get better answers if you give everyone time to think. For most companies this will be the first time you have ever gotten the staff together with the proactive goal of improving every aspect of the company. Go around the room getting everyone's take on the company's problems and summarize them on a whiteboard or easel pad.

A meeting like this can give you twenty to thirty things to work on with your staff. Your goal for each meeting is to get at least one incremental improvement. I tell my CEO clients that the only thing you need to bring to a meeting is your judgment. If you have good people, believe me, not only are they going to know the problems, but they will also have plenty of ideas on how to solve them.

Every major area of impact in your company should get one of these weekly meetings. Systematically take each problem and correct it, asking for suggestions from staff. Just remember not to take on too much at a time. A little progress every week can transform your company in a year.

Becoming a Brilliant Strategist

As we've already established, it's harder than ever to get in front of a potential buyer, so when you finally get your company in front of that buyer, you need to maximize what you can accomplish in that moment. You need to think and plan strategically.

To make sure you understand the difference between a tactic and a strategy, here are some simple yet essential definitions. A *tactic* is a method used to achieve a short-term gain, such as ads, direct mail, sales calls, trade shows, your Web site, brochures, and so on.

A *strategy* is a carefully defined and detailed plan to achieve a long-term goal.

In business, a strategy is the overall impact, the ultimate position you would like to achieve in the market. To think like a brilliant strategist, you will design and combine your tactics with the long-term strategy in mind. Constantly ask yourself and your team, "How many strategic objectives can we accomplish with each tactic?"

The Stadium Pitch

Here's an exercise to force you to think like a strategist, called the Stadium Pitch. What if you could be in front of all your prospects in a giant stadium and have the opportunity to present to them all at once? First question: Are you ready right now? Most are not ready.

Here's a practical example. I worked with a billion-dollar newspaper company that had experienced four straight years of declining sales. My job was to help the company increase advertising sales. The tactical sales rep would call a prospective advertiser, for example, and say: "Hi, I'm with the XYZ *Gazette* and we'd love to come and talk to you about advertising." Eight out of ten said they were not interested.

However, with a strategic program, the conversation went more like this:

REP: Hi, I'm with XYZ *Gazette*. We have a new program to teach business owners like you how to be more successful. Have you heard about this?

PROSPECT: No, I haven't.

REP: As the newspaper in this community, we feel it is our moral obligation to help our local business owners be as successful as possible. So we've commissioned some research and found that there are five things that make all businesses fail. Additionally, we've found that there are seven things that make all businesses [name the type of business you are approaching here: restaurant, hair salon, etc.] succeed. So we're meeting with [name a competitor] and showing them this data. Would you like to see it as well?

It would be pretty hard to say no to that appointment, wouldn't it? In fact, the approach, when properly deployed, took the newspaper from getting two appointments out of ten to getting eight out of ten. That's a 400 percent increase in performance.

Back to the stadium for a moment. If that rep had walked out into that stadium and said, "I'm here to tell you why our newspaper is a great place to advertise," probably eight out of ten potential advertisers would've walked out. But if that rep walked out there to tell them the five reasons why businesses fail and the seven why they succeed, who's leaving? No one, if the information is good.

This approach requires you to go the extra mile, but the benefits are significant. A rep who shows a prospect all this terrific data is obviously going to be positioned very differently in the mind of the buyer than a rep who just tries to sell advertising. It shifts the power from the prospect to the sales rep. The one who is teaching has more control than the one who is learning.

This concept is called education-based marketing, and my statement to you is that if you build it, they will come. No matter what business you are in or what product you have, from shaving cream to high-tech sales, you can increase your impact, advertising effectiveness, and ability to take market share by getting deeper and deeper into the concept of education-based marketing.

I'll build on a concept by Jay Abraham. In the dictionary, a customer is someone who buys a product or service from someone else. A client is someone who is under the care, guidance, and protection of an expert in a particular field. So if you have clients, not customers, how deep can you go to care about, guide, and protect them? The deeper you go, the more control you gain over your market.

Hiring Superstars

If you want to build the Ultimate Sales Machine, one of the key pieces of the puzzle is to understand the personality profile of top producers. Breaking it down, you need to learn how to recruit them and keep them and then apply all that you've learned.

The average bad hire costs a company sixty thousand dollars—if you're lucky. Some CEOs estimate that a single bad hire costs them millions.

What Makes a Superstar?

Superstars are those whom you put in a bad situation with poor tools, no training, and bad resources and who still, within a few months, begin to outperform your best people or build your company in ways you never dreamed possible. Hiring someone like this is about understanding the personality characteristics that fit the job for which you are hiring and having the tools to identify the candidates who possess those characteristics.

Three Steps to Interviewing Superstars

Because I've come to understand this at the deepest level, I've perfected an interview method that may seem barbaric to HR executives. I call it the Attack.

Before interviewing anyone, you conduct a five-minute screening call to see if you want to interview a candidate. A screening call might go like this:

YOU: Hi, Bill, we've had a lot of response to our ad; tell me why we would want to interview you.

BILL: Well, let's see. I really like people. I'm a natural bonder, and if I believe in something, I think I can really sell it.

YOU: Ah. I'm not really hearing top producer.

BILL: You're not?

YOU: Nope.

BILL: Well, I guess you would know.

YOU: I do.

BILL: Okay. Well. Thanks for your time. Bye.

This is a person who, if interviewed in a loving and supportive environment, like the environment in which 99 percent of interviews are conducted, might have genuinely impressed you. But when he or she gets in the field and faces rejection, he or she will crumble. Conversely, here's how the conversation might go with a top producer:

YOU: I'm not really hearing top producer.

TOP PRODUCER: Well, what do you think makes a top producer? (Note that the candidate begins to sell. The person can't help it. It's his or her nature.)

YOU: Well, it's a certain type of trait that I'm not hearing in you.

TOP PRODUCER: That's funny, because in my last job I was the new guy and had never sold grommets before, but within a few months I was catching up to salespeople who had been there for eight years.

A person like this will attach his own self-esteem to your product or service, so he becomes more effective when a client tries to reject him.

The final aspect of hiring top talent is to create a performance-based relationship. To get top producers, be clear about how you would reward them. You must reward top producers handsomely. The more you challenge superstars, the more you encourage them to overachieve. But don't forget to compliment them when they meet and exceed your challenge.

The High Art of Getting the Best Buyers

Best buyers buy more, buy faster, and buy more often than others. These are your ideal clients. No matter what else you are doing, you should make an additional effort to capture them. This strategy is called the Dream 100 effort. It is your program for targeting your one hundred (or whatever number is appropriate) dream clients constantly and relentlessly until they buy your product or service.

The fastest way to grow any company is to focus a special and dedicated effort on your dream clients. If you're committed and stay in their faces, you'll be surprised how easy it is.

The Power of Referrals

Referrals are so important you should have a specific strategic objective to gain them. Offer incentives to your current buyers when they refer others to you.

The Dream 100 strategy has doubled the sales of many companies, and it can work for you. You just have to have the pigheaded discipline and determination to build a great Dream 100 program and stick to it.

The Seven Musts of Marketing

Every company that wants to be number one in its industry or profession has to master seven marketing weapons. Here are the ways to turbocharge every aspect of your primary marketing efforts:

1. *Advertising*: There are four rules for creating high-response-generating advertising: It must be distinctive; it must capture attention with a screaming headline; after your headline hooks them, your body copy has to keep them reading; and it must include a call to action.

2. *Direct mail*: If you want massive results from direct mail, pound the best buyers more frequently by far and with more impressive efforts. These buyers are a smaller list and less expensive to target yet yield a far greater reward when they buy.

3. *Corporate literature*: This includes brochures and promotional pieces. Coordinate them so that the look, feel, and content of each weapon is consistent with the others.

4. *Public relations*: You are doing PR work when you throw splashy events such as trade-show parties and benefits for your clients. PR also includes generating press releases, building relationships with the press, getting articles written by or about you, and affiliating with strong forces that can help you, such as trade associations and community groups.

5. *Personal contact*: None of your marketing efforts will have as much impact on your client as personal contact with your salespeople or customer-service reps.

6. *Market education*: Trade shows and other market education efforts must be bold, not boring. The one who gives the most market education will rule the market. There are only three rules to having a great trade show: Get noticed, drive traffic, and capture leads.

7. Internet: A Web site that offers information of value to your prospects can be a community: a place where your prospects go to look at new things, to get information, to interact with you, and to get to know you better.

The Eyes Have It

When you learn how to use visual aids with tremendous effect, you will attract more buyers, influence them more effectively, and close more sales once you are in front of those buyers.

Human beings rewmember 20 percent of what they hear, 30 percent of what they see, but 50 percent of what they both see and hear. Your communication impact nearly triples when you use visual aids. Information that is visually illustrated and communicated has a dramatic and direct impact on the brain.

Since we can take in information three to four times faster than people talk, and since 85 percent of motivation comes from what we see, the great marketer knows to use visual aids everywhere possible. You want to illustrate everything you can visually.

CHET HOLMES ON SECURING THE BEST BUYERS

*I*f you sell to consumers, I recommend a concept I call the Best Neighborhood Strategy or Best Buyer Strategy. If you're a jewelry store, a restaurant, a chiropractor, a dentist, a boat dealer, or high-end retailer, here's a tip: The wealthiest people in your area are your best buyers. For the best neighborhood strategy, I recommend two things:

1. *Keep marketing to them no matter what. You want top-of-mind awareness among those people.*
2. *Make a special offer. They are better buyers, so they are worth making offers you simply would not make to other buyers.*

Rules for Effective Presenting

Here are eight rules for effective presenting:

Rule 1. K.I.S.S. (Keep It Simple, Stupid) Your presentation needs to be easy to follow and understand. Don't clutter the page with text or too many graphics.

Rule 2. K.I.F.P. (*Keep It Fast Paced*) Prospects will get bored if you spend too much time on one page. You should be covering two to three panels a minute. Keep the presentation moving.

Rule 3. *Use "Wow" Facts and Statistics.* You literally want your client to say, "Wow! I didn't know that." Factual information at the beginning of any presentation creates a sense of credibility that carries over even for the "sales" part of your presentation.

Rule 4. *Build In Opportunities for Stories.* Well-told stories increase recall by 26 percent over making a point without a story to illustrate it.

Rule 5. *Make Your Presentation Curiosity Driven.* Unfold the information in a way that keeps your prospects curious. Give them a fact first, and follow it with an explanation.

Rule 6. *Think of Each Headline as Valuable Real Estate.* Every header should work as hard as possible. It should intrigue the prospects and sell the panels.

Rule 7. *Be Confident but Not Obnoxious.* Develop a rapport with your audience, even if it's just one person facing you.

Rule 8. *Focus on Them, Not on You.* Everyone's favorite topic of conversation is him- or herself. The most mature person in a relationship is the one listening the most. He or she is thinking about the other person's needs and how to meet them. If you can be this person when you are presenting to your prospects and remain focused on their needs and how you can help them, you will become a top producer.

The Nitty-Gritty of Getting the Best Buyers

The Dream 100 effort is your plan of attack to reach your best buyers. This is the fastest way to becoming the Ultimate Sales Machine because these dream clients are the people or businesses that will buy your product or service faster, in greater quantities, and more frequently than any other buyers. Landing just a handful of these dream clients can have a seismic impact on your bottom line.

Getting Down to the Nitty-Gritty

Here are six simple steps to help you get your dream clients:

1. *Choose Your Dream 100.* Take a look at your lists of dream clients, neighborhoods, and affiliates. This is your starting point.

2. *Choose the Gifts.* One of the best ways to get noticed by your Dream 100 is to send them small gifts every two weeks. Keep the gifts inexpensive.

3. *Create Your Dream 100 Letters.* A letter should accompany every gift you send. The letter should be short so the prospects will read it. It should tie in to the gift in some clever way. The letter must include a call to action.

4. *Create Your Dream 100 Calendar.* Market to your Dream 100 each and every month without fail. It's even better if you send them something every two weeks. Stay in their faces.

5. *Conduct Dream 100 Follow-up Phone Calls.* After every gift or mailing, you'll need to follow up with each Dream 100 prospect. The goal of a follow-up call is to schedule an appointment to get your core story in front of the prospect.

6. *Present the Executive Briefing.* Use market data, not product data. Set the buying criteria in your favor. Find the "smoking gun," the one thing that undeniably positions you over everyone else.

Remember that getting the best buyers is a process, not a single event. It's a campaign to stay in their faces forever.

Sales Skills

If you have not identified, studied, and mastered every inch of the sales process, you're doing your company a great injustice. The secret to building an excellent sales force (or team of any kind) is repeating core training on basic skills again and again.

The Seven Steps to Every Sale

Work on this extensively, doing workshops on each of these steps.

1. *Rapport.* Do extensive workshops with your sales team on establishing and building rapport. One of the best ways to establish rapport is for your sales staff to be more knowledgeable than any other sales staff they could possibly run into. Ask great questions. Have a sense of humor. Be empathetic and care about them.

2. *Find the need.* Do workshops with your staff to work through every insight you need to serve a particular client. You need to learn everything you can about its existing buying criteria. Reset those buying criteria so your product or service becomes the most logical choice.

3. *Build value.* After you have assessed your customers' buying criteria, you must begin to build value around your product or service. Present your core story/executive briefing. Your Stadium Pitch can do this step really well.

4. *Create desire.* Lead clients through a series of questions in which you intensify their need from their perspective. To create desire, you must motivate your buyers using a combination of problems and solutions.

5. *Overcome objections.* You can't close if there are objections in your way. Remember that *an objection is an opportunity to close.* "Is money the only thing standing between you and the purchase of this product?" If the client says yes, you can now close by being more creative with financing or showing how not buying will cost more in the long run.

6. *Close the sale.* You may need to help prospects make the decision. It's okay to make them feel a little pressure. If you believe that what you have is good for them, close already! Can you add something that motivates them to buy right now?

7. *Follow up.* The process after the sale is crucial.

Follow-up and Client Bonding Skills

It costs six times more to get a new client than to sell something additional to a current client. If you want to build the Ultimate Sales Machine, you need to have highly procedurized follow-up and follow-through.

Enthusiasm is contagious. When you are with a prospect, your enthusiasm rubs off. The second you leave, the prospect begins to cool off. Your job is to keep the prospect hot on two things: you and the sale.

If you made a good impression, you have to keep those cards and letters coming. If you didn't bond very well during the first six steps of the sales process, follow-up is even more important.

Remember, trust and respect are the largest parts of the sale. Every minute that a prospect doesn't hear from you after you leave his office, his respect falls off. Out of sight, out of mind.

All Systems Go

Goal setting and measuring effectiveness are the twelfth core skill area of the Ultimate Sales Machine, and it's designed to soup up all eleven that come before it. Setting goals is not simply about writing them down periodically, although that is a part of it, but about mastering your focus so that you achieve those goals quickly and automatically.

The **reticular activating system (RAS)** is the awesome computer in the brain that most of us never use on purpose. Every day we have thousands of thoughts that seem to leap in and out of our minds. Those thoughts affect every cell in our body. Our cells are completely reactive to the environment in which they dwell, and thought is one of the most powerful sources for creating that environment.

Your RAS screens out everything that won't interest you and then wakes you up to something that will interest you. One example is when you buy a new car. You never noticed that car before, but suddenly you start to see it everywhere. Now that this specific car has become of interest to you, your RAS will pick it out of the thousands of cars you see every day.

Harnessing the Power of RAS

When a company is in trouble, the most powerful thing it can do is get focused on solutions and set goals for improving the situation. The shift in focus shows up in the results the company is getting. With everyone devoting at least an hour a week to focusing their RAS on finding solutions and improving the business, solutions begin to appear and the business begins to improve. One way to harness the power of the RAS is to do proactive workshops to get everyone focused on solving the problems instead of focused on the problems.

Setting goals in every aspect of your life and business puts your RAS to work (on purpose) at attracting great things. This is because the minute you write your goals, you have focused your subconscious on your success and it immediately begins creating that reality. This becomes even more effective when you post your goals and even say them every morning and every night.

Conclusion

Do you want to be the Ultimate Sales Machine and slaughter your competition? Can you see that if you build a machine like this, no company can stand against you? By relentlessly focusing on the twelve key skill areas and strategies we've explored, you can be the Ultimate Sales Machine.

1. Maximize the productivity of yourself and every person in your organization.

2. Train, train, train. The organizations that dominate the future have the best training today.

3. Use the workshop methodology every week in every area of your business to constantly hone and polish every piece of your organization.

4. Become a brilliant strategist. The strategist will slaughter the tactician every day.

5. Hire superstars throughout your organization.

6. Use the Best Buyer Strategy to target the best buyers and pursue them relentlessly with the best marketing and selling in your industry. It's the least expensive, most results-oriented activity you can pursue.

7. Get all seven of your "musts" of marketing working better, smarter, and harder.

8. Build that Stadium Pitch, use visuals everywhere you can, and know how to present better than any of your competitors.

9. Plan every inch of your best buyer attack.

10. Break down those seven steps of every sale and create master-level salespeople.

11. Plan your follow-up steps to the letter.

12. Set goals and measure effectiveness with as much detail as possible.

If you master these twelve strategies, you will never need to know anything else to rule your market, and no competitor will be able to stand against you. But remember that the main ingredient in building this machine is pigheaded discipline and determination.

THE DOLLARIZATION DISCIPLINE

by Jeffrey J. Fox and
Richard C. Gregory

There are numerous sales books that attempt to teach a method of convincing a prospect of a product's or service's value. This approach is intended to combat the single greatest enemy to an otherwise flawless sales pitch: price. The price of a product is an easy target when a prospect wants to dismiss a salesperson without really listening to his or her presentation. When a sales pitch results in a prospect's door slamming shut in front of a seller, it takes the right strategy to reopen it.

Enter marketing strategists Jeffrey J. Fox and Richard C. Gregory. The pair collaborated on *The Dollarization Discipline*, a book based on Fox's years of honing his dollarization concept into a full-fledged sales and marketing principle. Fox, author of the best seller *How to Become a CEO*, created a concept that is simple in theory but complex in execution. The concept is much needed when one considers Fox's statement that most marketers are incapable of completely articulating the full value customers receive from their companies' products.

The secret, the authors point out, is to calculate the exact gain (in dollars) that a customer receives as it relates to the price he or she paid for the product or service. This is an important distinction when one considers that what the salesperson is trying to calculate is generally given the name "value." *The Dollarization Discipline* gives readers a new perspective on a much-used term by asking a simple question. When referring to value, how frequently does one ever hear a number? The fact that most individuals would answer that numbers are rarely, if ever, used demonstrates the disconnection of most sales organizations from an understanding of true value.

The method of dollarization covers a variety of areas in an organization, but it is in sales that the principle is at its most potent. Fox and Gregory demonstrate the power of dollarization and show salespeople how to use it to overcome price objections, sell enhanced or upgraded products, and lower a customer's perception of risk in making the purchase. Dollarization reduces the length of the sales cycle by creating a sense of urgency on the part of the prospect. Fox and Gregory reiterate throughout their book that careful framing of the value of the product should help the customer understand that the purchase of the product will stop the company from losing money rather than cause it to save. With this knowledge, the salesperson has turned the customer into a hero within his or her own organization, a preferable position for the customer.

Fox's success with the dollarization principle led him to found Fox & Company, a successful management consulting firm. Gregory, as the firm's senior consultant, specializes in consulting on the dollarization concept and training organizations of all sizes in its application. The fact that *The Dollarization Discipline* continues to be considered a key sales technique shows the success of Fox's years of work. It's all part of growing the understanding between sales professional and client. As the authors note, to make money from a customer, a salesperson should first look to help the customer make more money.

THE DOLLARIZATION DISCIPLINE
How Smart Companies Create Customer Value and Profit from It
by Jeffrey J. Fox and Richard C. Gregory

CONTENTS
1. Getting Started with Dollarization
2. Why Dollarize?
3. Dollarization and Selling
4. Dollarization and Marketing
5. Dollarization Techniques
6. The Dollarization Doctrine

THE SUMMARY IN BRIEF

At the heart of The Dollarization Discipline lies the concept of understanding the financial impacts a product or service has on its buyer. Although this involves the idea of "total cost of ownership," it focuses on more than just cost reduction and cost avoidance. In The Dollarization Discipline, marketing guru Jeffrey J. Fox, best-selling author of How to Become a Rainmaker and other books, and management consultant Richard C. Gregory describe how organizations can also measure the financial impact of noncost benefits, including increased market share, increased sales volume, and increased pricing power. The authors explain that dollarization should be a discipline that businesses apply across a broad set of sales, marketing, and management activities, forcing organizations to be customer focused and customer driven.

Helping companies to stay focused on the financial performance that is the ultimate arbiter of their customers' success is a primary ingredient of dollarization, and throughout *The Dollarization Discipline* the authors describe how the difficult task of dollarization can be put into practice.

In addition, you'll learn the following:

- How to effectively communicate the economic value created by your products and services
- How to use a step-by-step strategy to calculate the monetary gain a customer receives in exchange for the price paid
- How to handle price objections, shorten sales cycles, protect business from competition, and get appointments
- How to apply the techniques of dollarization to new-product pricing, advertising, and communications
- Ways to discover how customers make money and align resources to help those customers make more money

THE COMPLETE SUMMARY

Getting Started with Dollarization

You are shopping for paint and find many choices at the local paint store. Product X costs twelve dollars a gallon; product Y costs twenty dollars a gallon. Which paint should you buy?

The salesperson says, "I strongly recommend product Y. Its price may be higher, but it will last eight years, while the other paint will last four at best. That means that over eight years, you'd have to buy product X twice, for a total of twenty-four dollars a gallon, versus just twenty dollars a gallon for product Y. In reality, product Y costs less!"

You reply, "That's very interesting, but I'm preparing to sell my home, so I don't care about how long this paint will last. I think I'll go with product X for twelve dollars."

The salesperson listens and responds, "I understand, but I think product Y is still your best choice. You see, product Y contains 50 percent more pigment, which results in better coverage than product X. This means you will need to apply only one coat to your house. Product X will require at least two coats. This will also cut your labor costs in half. Plus, you are guaranteed that your house will look freshly painted, which will improve your success in selling your home. Wouldn't you agree that an extra eight dollars per gallon is a great investment to sell your house at the price you want?"

Finally, you decide. The twenty-dollar paint is actually less expensive than the twelve-dollar paint.

Financial Consequences of Choosing

When businesses make purchases, too often they are myopic and overemphasize the importance of price. They overlook the many other financial consequences of choosing one offering over another. This is a failure on the buyer's part, because it may very well result in financial harm to the organization. But more important, it is a failure on the seller's part because the seller has missed the chance to demonstrate the true financial impact that could be provided to the customer.

The meaningful way to compare the cost of two offerings is by evaluating the *total cost* of using each. In order to help customers to understand the true net cost of your product, you must *dollarize* the product's *true value*.

Dollarization is figuring out what your offering is really worth—in dollars and cents—to your customer. It is the management discipline that is missing in many sales and marketing organizations, and its impact can be great, and its applications are many.

Dollarization can help your company better understand, articulate, and profit from the value you create for your customers and clients. Dollarization should become a standing discipline that guides your thinking about pricing, selling, positioning, new-product development, and nearly every other area of your sales and marketing.

Value Is a Number

In sales and marketing, value takes the form of value added, value chain, value proposition, or value engineering. When sales and marketing people talk value, they use words—words that lack precision—and rarely use numbers.

The solution is an approach to sales and marketing that goes beyond articulating features and benefits but in fact calculates the full economic value a customer receives from a product or service; the seller is then able to price the product or service as a true reflection of that value. This approach is called dollarization.

Businesses do not buy; they invest. Every time a company makes a purchase decision, it is committing company capital. In theory, that capital is constantly being allocated and reallocated to achieve the best available return. Too few companies exercise this discipline for all purchases. And far fewer companies market and sell in a way that permits customers to understand the economic value provided in return for the investment. Whatever you do, you must map exactly how your offering translates to value for your customer's business.

Why Dollarize?

Keep your fair share of the value created. Companies receive value from suppliers, and they compensate those suppliers by returning a portion of the value created. In turn, they create value for their customers and are able to extract some value in return, which allows them to generate positive net value for their owners. Too many companies allow their customers to keep more than a fair share of the value created. Those customers are often unaware of and therefore underappreciate the actual value created by their purchase of the supplier's product. Dollarization is the bridge that enables a company to link and leverage the value it creates and the value it extracts.

Find new ways to grow your top line. Once cost cutting reaches diminishing returns, companies must look for ways to grow the top line, through expanded sales, higher prices, or both. The traditional growth levers available to marketers include:

- earning a greater share of volume or "share of wallet" from existing customers;
- adding new customers in current markets;
- introducing new products or services to existing or new customers;
- entering new geographies;
- selling new applications or uses for existing products/services;
- entering new market segments;
- raising prices;
- reducing controllable customer attrition.

In the following pages, you will learn how dollarization can improve the effectiveness of each of these marketing endeavors.

Help your organization at all levels protect price. An important motivator for many companies that utilize dollarization is protection of a price premium or defense against price erosion (or both). While companies may recognize these as strategically important, it is important for all frontline sales and marketing staff to appreciate just how much profit leverage can be gained by protecting price.

For example, if a salesperson is considering a 3 percent price cut and the current gross margin is 40 percent, the salesperson would have to gain 8.1 percent in incremental unit volume at the new reduced price in order to generate the same number of gross margin dollars he or she was producing before the price cut.

Strategic Value of Dollarization

Understand your customer better. In addition to winning new sales and improving pricing, dollarization also enables the marketer to gain a deeper understanding of the customer. This understanding keeps the marketer focused on what is truly important to the customer and helps the marketer make strategic marketing decisions—about product direction, sales approaches, pricing strategies, channel development—that are fundamentally more sound than traditional approaches.

Companies that use dollarization disciplines find that inside-out decision making gives way to a customer-focused mentality. Every decision that impacts the customer can be tested through the dollarization filter: How does this impact the value we create for our customers?

Value of Competing for Inches

The power of dollarization typically lives in the leverage of a few incremental gains. The economic benefit of effective dollarization is far in excess of the cost of implementation. When an organization develops the discipline to dollarize, it wins on multiple fronts. The company begins to win more of the close competitive fights that were once lost. It also grows business with existing customers through a new recognition of the economic contributions made. Overall profit margins inch upward due to smarter pricing and an increased sense of organizational confidence.

Dollarization and Selling

Dollarization is used most often as a competitive tool in personal, face-to-face selling. Within this realm, there are many specific situations that demand dollarization, including handling a customer price objection, dealing with a customer request for a price reduction, and escaping treatment as a commodity.

The price objection can come in many forms, and somewhere in the course of every sale at least one of these forms is likely to present itself. In order to buy something, customers must give up money, of which they have a limited supply. This creates tension driven by the implicit economic reluctance to part with cash. In the absence of other financial information, the customer focuses on the price, which represents the imminent sacrifice of dollars.

If the seller truly believes that his or her product is worth the price, then the burden is on the salesperson to demonstrate the price/value relationship to the customer. It is the rare customer who will accurately assess this relationship without help from the seller.

BUYING MOTIVATION

*T*here are two fundamental reasons that drive all purchase decisions: People buy either to feel good or to solve a problem. But because our personal lives are not strictly profit-driven enterprises, not every personal problem we solve can be dollarized.

On the other hand, the primary driver behind nearly all business expenditures is the need to solve some type of problem. Further, in business, the solution to a problem represents either the avoidance of loss or the chance for gain. Both of these can be measured in dollars and cents ... or dollarized.

Examples of Avoidance of Loss

- *Reduce cost of materials.*
- *Reduce downtime.*
- *Reduce labor costs.*
- *Reduce regulatory penalties.*
- *Reduce product-liability costs.*
- *Eliminate manufacturing waste.*

Examples of Chance for Gain

- *Increase sales.*
- *Increase prices.*
- *Expand market share.*
- *Enter new markets.*
- *Earn new customers.*
- *Enable ne w products.*

Dealing with the Price Objection

To first overcome the psychological difficulties of dealing with the price objection, the seller needs to keep two simple facts in mind:

1. In most cases, the simple question *"What is your price?"* has no subversive intent. Usually, the customer simply wants to know the price.

2. Often, the customer is fully aware of the seller's price, the customer's own budget, and the competitive price situation before agreeing to meet with or talk to the seller. Despite knowing all this, the customer is still willing to discuss a potential purchase. Certainly, the customer will want to negotiate to ensure he or she pays the best price possible. And certainly, some customers use the price objection solely as a tool to drive down the seller's price. But most customers simply want or need the seller to help them understand why they should invest in the seller's offering over other options or why they should move budget money around to enable an investment in the seller's offering. Often this is motivated by the customer's need to make the same case internally to his or her colleagues. The customer *needs the seller to demonstrate the dollarized value of investing in the seller's solution.*

It is also important to understand as sellers that the price-only customer is fickle and probably not a healthy addition to the selling company's customer portfolio. Price-only customers do not merit much investment of selling resources. Guard against price-only customers!

A true dollarization-discipline salesperson handles the price objection by bringing it up long before the customer voices it. Early in the sales process, this salesperson says, "You need to be aware of something right from the start. When it comes time to propose a price for this program, I can guarantee we will not be the lowest. In fact, our price will likely be at the high end. However, as I work with you, I intend to show you how that does not matter. I will help you evaluate how my product will reduce your costs in areas other than price, so that your total cost picture will be much more attractive, even with my higher price. If that's okay with you, let's get started, okay?"

By establishing this understanding at the outset, before price is even on the table, this salesperson changes the rules of the game in favor of a total-dollarized-value approach. If the customer disagrees, the salesperson knows to invest his or her selling time elsewhere.

Selling Something New

One of the more difficult challenges in selling is persuading customers to purchase a new product or service when they are currently satisfied using an established, entrenched technology or methodology. Dollarization can help move even the most reluctant customer to action.

The challenge when selling a new concept is to demonstrate to the prospective customer that, despite the apparent risks of leaving behind the tried and true, the new product will produce a financial return so attractive that the customer would be committing management malpractice by not—at a minimum—testing the new product.

The financial argument plays out as follows: The customer considers the "net value" delivered by a product or service, which can be expressed as follows:

$$\text{Net Value} = (\text{Dollarized Value} - \text{Cost of Risk}) - \text{Price}$$

In other words, to understand the true net value of a product offering, the customer must assess the dollarized value the offering is expected to create, adjust that for any perceived risk, and then subtract the purchase price.

When comparing two established products, the customer analysis is simplified, because the cost of risk associated with the two established products, due to experience, is comparable and perhaps even negligible. However, when a customer is considering a new, unproven product or service, the net value for the new offering can be greatly impacted by the customer's perceived cost of risk for the new product.

In order to move the customer to buy, the new product seller must demonstrate that the net value of the new product is greater than the net value of the old product.

$$^{Net\ Value}\text{New Product} > {}^{Net\ Value}\text{Old Product}$$

To accomplish this, the seller's missions are (1) to articulate the dollarized value of the new offering, (2) to develop and execute a strategy for minimizing the customer's perceived cost of risk, and (3) to present a price that makes financial sense given the other variables involved.

Mitigating the Customer's Perceived Cost of Risk

There are two key challenges in dealing with the customer's perceived cost of risk. First, the customer is frequently comfortable with and complacent about the current product or service. Second, because newness brings with it a vacuum of experience and reviewable data, buying companies tend to overestimate the risk of switching to something new.

One selling strategy that has been successful in these situations involves three steps:

1. *The seller works with the customer to generate a preliminary understanding of the new product's benefits and applicability to the customer's situation.*

2. *The seller works with the customer to conduct a pro forma dollarization analysis.* This analysis is typically based largely on the seller's own background data.

3. *The seller asks the customer for a conditional buying commitment.* For example: "As we agreed, this widget could save your company more than fifty thousand dollars per year. If it performs as promised when tested, is there any other reason that would prohibit you from going forward with it?"

This approach works on several levels. First, it acknowledges the customer's need to test and validate the promise of the new, unproven product. Second, it puts the burden on the seller to prove the preliminary claims made about the product's performance. This creates a feeling of comfort for the customer. Third, it firmly puts the decision in financial terms: In order to save fifty thousand dollars per month, the customer must test the product. This makes the testing more likely to proceed in a timely manner. Fourth, the "Is there anything else?" question prompts the customer to verbalize any other hidden objections or roadblocks. And finally, once these are cleared up, the decision criteria are clearly established: If the product does indeed test as promised, the customer has committed to move ahead.

Unless there is a legitimate misunderstanding between the buyer and seller about the compatibility or applicability (or both) of the new product, this approach significantly increases the odds that the product will be tested and will perform acceptably for the customer. Testing the product greatly diminishes the perceived cost of risk, allowing the dollarized value to stand on its own.

REDUCTION TO THE ABSURD

When you have exhausted all available strategies and the buyer's focus on price continues to go beyond what is rational and reasonable, it can be useful to employ reductio ad absurdum, or reduction to the absurd. This technique can be useful, but be warned: It must be used carefully! It is often saved as a last resort and should be delivered with good humor (and low expectations). Consider this conversation:

> BUYER: As far as we're concerned, we will buy from whatever gear company offers the lowest price. I don't care about your supposed "advantages."
> SELLER: So, if you could spend nothing on this gear, you'd be happy.
> BUYER: Exactly. Very happy.
> SELLER: Well, there is a way you can do that and save all the money you would spend on gears: Don't buy any gears.
> BUYER: Excuse me?
> SELLER: That's right. Don't buy any. That would save your entire budget.
> BUYER: Yes, it would. But our machines wouldn't run without gears.
> SELLER: Oh, the operation of your machines is a factor in your decision?

The conversation has now returned to the underlying reason why the customer needs to buy the seller's product. By bringing it to an absurd level, the seller has made the point that product performance and price must be considered in concert.

Shortening the Sales Cycle

Dollarization *does* shorten the salets cycle. There are three requirements to get a business to accelerate its decision-making process on a purchase:

1. *Dollarize.* The seller must present a compelling dollarized financial story. This changes the way the customer views the decision. Rather than another buying decision, the customer sees an opportunity to make money, to save money, or to stop losing money. The presentation of a dollarized economic reason for moving ahead with a purchase decision can distinguish an offering and place it in a unique light. The dollarized story alerts the customer to the financial impact of making, or not making, a decision to move forward.

2. *Make someone a hero.* An important step in using dollarization in any customer situation is to earn the trust of one or more of the players on the customer side. You must help them understand that your dollarization approach is intended to be used not as a selling ploy but as a tool to make sure the customer is making a valid business decision.

3. *Create a sense of urgency.* Whether or not you are able to develop a partner on the customer side, the words used in presenting the dollarized case must be chosen very carefully. Telling a customer he or she "can stop losing X dollars" is more compelling than telling him or her that he or she "could save X dollars by investing in product Y."

Dollarization and Marketing

While the application of dollarization in advertising and marketing communications can take many forms, it is typically best executed using the following devices:

- **Testimonials.** A customer or other expert provides a third-party reporting of the dollarized story.
- **Case histories.** The marketer relates the experiences of prior customers in describing the dollarized outcomes.
- **Head-to-head comparisons.** The marketer states the dollarized advantages of its product versus a prominent competitive offering.
- **Test-driven data.** The marketer reports test data (third-party or its own) that demonstrates a dollarized advantage for its product versus the competition.

Sandvik Coromant

Dollarization can lead to clear positioning, messaging, and communication, as seen in the following example.

Sandvik Coromant is the world's leading maker of highly engineered carbide metal cutting tools. These tools are used heavily in the automotive and aerospace industries and in nearly every industrial segment for shaping steel and other metals, drilling holes, threading bolts, and many other applications.

Sandvik is a prolific new-product marketer. Every year, it introduces thousands of new products. These products are built on technological improvements—sometimes incremental, sometimes revolutionary. The improvements tend to focus on a few key performance areas: extending tool life, making cutting faster, and improving quality of cutting.

An implicit side effect of these improvements is that the consumption of tools by customers can decrease over time. For example, if a tool that currently cuts one hundred pieces before breaking is replaced by a new tool that lasts for two hundred cuts, the number of tools required by a customer is theoretically cut in half. Over time, this creates a governor for unit growth, so Sandvik must try to price its products to reflect the performance improvements to the customer in order to avoid long-term revenue erosion.

Every new product that Sandvik launches is backed by detailed comparative test data developed by the product marketing teams. This data illustrates performance claims that can later be tested by individual customers. Every Sandvik salesperson is equipped with analytical tools to estimate the financial payback of converting to new Sandvik tooling. Dollarized thinking pervades the entire Sandvik approach to marketing, including its print advertising, which has distinguished itself from industry competitors for years.

Pricing New Products

Although new-product pricing is an inherently imperfect combination of marketing art and science, there are ways to add more science to the mix. New-product pricing should not be strictly formulaic, as in target margin pricing, nor should it be a game of blindman's buff. Understanding the dollarized value of an offering to the target customer group is a critical ingredient to seeing new-product pricing options more clearly.

The following sequence can be adapted for different product types and different markets, but the essential discipline remains the same:

1. *Estimate the product's dollarized value.* First you must understand the economic value your new offering delivers to your target customer. The value created by every unit of your offering establishes the dollarized price ceiling for your offering.

2. *Compare the dollarized value to the price floor.* The total dollarized value provides an initial snapshot of your potential pricing window. You must next compare that value to the minimum price you would accept for the new product offering.

This price floor is constructed by evaluating the direct cost of producing and delivering each unit, plus the minimum markup that would generate an acceptable contribution to your business. If the total dollarized value per unit is less than the price floor, the marketer must conclude that the product is economically viable. If instead the total value per unit does indeed exceed the marketer's acceptable price floor, the next task is to determine how far above that floor the marketer can manage to price the offering.

3. *Consider the target customer's investment criteria.* In order to be enticed to buy, the customer will demand to keep some of the incremental value created by the new product. The amount kept must satisfy the customer's investment criteria for making the outlay of the price of the product. Whatever the customer's method for evaluating the attractiveness of an investment, you must understand it and account for it in your pricing strategy.

4. *Account for other marketplace dynamics.* Dozens of factors come into play here, but some of the common considerations are the following: How defensible is your competitive advantage? What is the conventional market price? How homogeneous is the market?

5. *Consider unconventional pricing structures.* If you anticipate emotional customer resistance, look for ways to unbundle your pricing. This could involve charging for use instead of a one-time price, or charging one stripped-down price for the core product and then charging extra fees for other components of the offering. Some companies charge special handling fees, odd-lot fees, engineering surcharges, environmental fees, etc.

Dollarization Techniques

When a company decides to put dollarization to work in sales and marketing, there are three major disciplines that must be addressed. Each requires a different set of skills and each can be accomplished through a variety of approaches. However, a dollarization strategy that underinvests in any one of these activities will underperform.

Dollarization Process Steps

The three process steps are:

1. *Dollarization discovery.* Determine how your offering results in financial value to your customers. The outcome of this step is the arithmetic formulas required to calculate your dollarized value. The actual data needed to populate those formulas must be developed separately.

2. *Data development.* Develop the data required to calculate the dollarized value you deliver to customers. This step enables you to complete the equations developed in the discovery phase with real numbers.

3. *Strategy integration.* Determine how to use your dollarized story to shape your marketing and sales approaches. This is where dollarization is put to work to improve your business.

THREE STEPS IN ONE MEETING

*I*n some cases—especially when the marketer's offering is engineered or tailored for each customer—the "needs analysis" phase of face-to-face consultative selling might encompass all three steps.

For example, a salesperson might enter a conversation with an existing or prospective customer with a dollarization mind-set and proceed to probe for customer problems for which the seller's offering provides potential cures. In the course of that probing, the seller might discover the economic consequences of those problems (discovery) and, if prepared and alert, might also discover the building-block data required to calculate the actual dollarized values (data development). Additionally, during the same visit, the salesperson might learn about the decision-making process at the target customer and thereby gain insight as to how to use his or her dollarized story to shape his or her selling strategy (strategy integration).

Discovery and Data Development

The strategy-integration opportunities offered by dollarization were covered in the previous pages of this summary. The remainder of the summary looks more closely at how to implement the discovery and development phases of the dollarization process.

Whenever you start identifying and quantifying the value you create for a single customer or an entire population of customers, it is important that you methodically review all the potential impacts. Leave no stone unturned. Whatever sources you use to develop your understanding of the value created, the following steps will guide you:

1. *Determine who is your competition.* You must know what you are selling against before you can begin to dollarize. Often, you will need to dollarize against multiple enemies.

2. *Articulate your differentiating features.* When compared to the competition you are facing, what are the specific differentiating elements of your offering? Consider every element of your total offering, from the product itself to the service package that comes with it to your overall company picture. You must be precise and comprehensive in this assessment.

3. *State your benefits.* Next, you must identify all the ways your differentiating features benefit your customer. It is helpful to ask yourself the following questions and to try to answer them from the customer's perspective: How does this feature help the customer? Why should the customer care about this feature? What customer problems does this solve? What are the consequences if the customer does not get this feature?

4. *Quantify your benefit.* The next step is to determine how to quantify each benefit delivered by your product or service. This is where you convert benefit words into numbers. For example, "improved productivity" becomes "eight more units per hour," and "better performance" becomes "a 3 percent gain in market share for the customer."

5. *Dollarize.* Finally, you must determine how the quantified benefit results in dollars-and-cents savings for the customer.

CUSTOMER BUY-IN IS A MUST

*D*ollarization without customer buy-in will not succeed. If a customer views your analysis as a self-serving tool to coax the customer into paying for your solution, that customer will likely be reluctant to share information, will discount your claimed outcomes, and will undermine your efforts with other colleagues. An important early selling step is to help the customer understand that, as a consultative seller, you are sincerely interested in helping improve the customer's business situation. Dollarization is your tool to make sure the economic returns to the customer are acceptable.

After you have worked through this five-step process, you will have drawn the connection between your offering and the value it creates for your customer. Also, you must always probe beyond the obvious benefit of your solution. This requires knowing your customer's business, knowing contacts throughout the organization, and asking excellent needs-analysis questions. Identify the real value and you will be rewarded for it.

Developing Dollarization Data Once the marketer has developed an understanding of the mechanisms by which his or her offering creates value for customers, the marketer is faced with the challenge of actually quantifying and dollarizing that value.

The two key areas of information requiring development are

1. data that *quantifies* the performance advantage;

2. data that *dollarizes* the quantified performance advantage.

Often, both of these discovery steps can be accomplished in the course of routine interactions with the customer, or the marketer will find that the required data can be developed quite fully through internal means, with just a few bits of data needed from external sources. But in many cases the data are elusive, so the marketer must develop creative means to collect the necessary information.

Direct Interviews with the Customer
When a company is selling products that are custom engineered, services that are specifically tailored, or other offerings that are unique to each buying customer, the only feasible approach for developing applicable dollarization data is to pursue a direct, preferably collaborative approach with the target customer. Because much of this work is done face-to-face (or by phone) with the customer, it requires careful training, practice, and diligent planning.

Indirect Customer Research
When a product or service offering is expected to impact the way your customer's customers benefit from enhancements to your customer's offering, it is useful to seek the perspective of the end market when assessing your value. People in your customer's sales and marketing organization can be a good source of intelligence here. You might ask them, for example, how a specific enhancement to their product would be received in their marketplace. You also might ask them how certain aspects of your product or service offering might help them to raise prices, attract more customers, or both.

The Dollarization Doctrine

Here are ten rules to successful dollarization:

1. *Always remember that "price" and "cost" are not the same thing.* Price is one of many costs. When convenient, buyers will discuss price as if it were the only cost. They will use the words interchangeably. Don't succumb!

2. *Ask, "So what?"* Don't let your sales and marketing people talk about features and benefits without answering, "So what?" How do those features and benefits translate to money in your customer's pocket? What are the consequences if they do not buy from you?

3. *Let dollarization guide you.* A key criterion in your new product-development process should be the value a product can deliver to customers. If your current offering lacks meaningful value, look for enhancements that will fill the void.

4. *Use numbers.* Resist the temptation to use words when numbers can do the job so much better. The phrase "25 percent faster" is more compelling than "much faster."

5. *Sell the concept first.* A great dollarization story will fall on deaf ears if the customer does not first understand that the analysis is meant to help the customer and his or her organization. Worse yet, it will be viewed as a selling ploy and discounted accordingly.

6. *Show your calculations.* Show every step in the math to make your dollarization work. Otherwise, a customer might be unable to recreate the math in your absence, preventing him or her from sharing it with peers, which is a critical step in the commitment process.

7. *Do your homework.* Before sitting down with a customer to work through your dollarization math, you will need two things: a set of calculations that will dollarize the value points you have identified (with the numbers left blank) and a set of pro forma numbers based on your homework. These numbers will be your fallback if your customer is unable to provide a piece of data.

8. *Use customer numbers.* Whenever possible, ask your customer for the pieces of information required to build your dollarization analysis. In selling, customer participation begets persuasion. Any number you provide will be discounted. The customer's own numbers are indisputable.

9. *Competition will always be a downward force on your prices.* This downward force of competition will never go away, so you need opposing forces on your side.

The dollarized value you create and document will counter the negative pull of competition.

10. *Don't forget to dollarize defensively.* If you have a customer you can't afford to lose, be sure to periodically report the dollarized value you deliver as part of your day-to-day relationship. Don't let an information vacuum allow your customer to be tempted by the lure of a low-priced competitor.

MAKING THE NUMBER

by Greg Alexander, Aaron Bartels, and Mike Drapeau

I t's the term that haunts some salespeople (and nearly all sales managers) in their sleep. It's a word that can strike fear into more and more hearts the closer a company gets to the end of a fiscal quarter. That word is "number." Sales advisers Greg Alexander, Aaron Bartels, and Mike Drapeau take on the challenge of discussing the number, whether in dollars or closed sales, that sales departments are expected to attain. The trio are leaders of Sales Benchmark Index, an Atlanta-based strategic advisory firm that pushes a unique perspective on what it takes to succeed in selling.

The prevailing attitude toward achieving higher sales has largely rested on theory rather than hard science. Companies rely on contests, motivational messages, and the occasional managerial "ride along" for purposes of spurring an increase in the bottom line. Alexander, Bartels, and Drapeau feel that this is the equivalent of rowing a boat on dry land. Pull as hard as you wish, but the boat won't budge. Their alternative is *sales benchmarking*, a profound new method to improve sales via the use of, as they put it, "data-driven decision making."

Making the Number: How to Use Sales Benchmarking to Drive Performance is the product of their breakthrough and is one of the most valuable yet underappreciated recent sales-based books. The authors push away from the emotional and take sales into the realm of statistical measurement, where, truth be told, it probably should have been the entire time. Other areas of business have relied on benchmarking for decades. Marketing, accounting, and even core management structures are built around a systematic monitoring of statistics. *Making the Number* is the first book to apply this principle strictly to the sales realm.

What differentiates the Sales Benchmarking process from merely scanning numbers on a spreadsheet is the five-step process the authors describe. Of the five steps, the first one, metric identification, may prove the most challenging for readers. This is where the strength of Alexander, Bartels, and Drapeau becomes apparent. They understand the need to bring simplicity to abstract concepts, something that benefits anyone without prior benchmarking experience. The authors give careful explanation of each of their five sales metrics and guide a sales executive through the process of collecting the data, the step they refer to as the most labor intensive. Upon analysis, the organization's new benchmark will not only give it a glimpse of internal operations but will also provide a mark by which to measure the business against competitors of equal or superior stature.

Making the Number continues to impress veterans of the selling field as well as other creators of new business methodology. Bradford D. Smart, author of the revolutionary human-resources guide *Topgrading: How Leading Companies Win by Hiring, Coaching, and Keeping the Best People*, is one such innovator who sees the value in the Sales Benchmarking method. In his foreword, he refers to the book as "a tour de force, a masterful guide that connects all the important dots, showing exactly how almost every sales organization can improve dramatically." While the effort involved in compiling and analyzing the various metric numbers may appear daunting to some, it is "the Number," the all-important bottom line, and its sharp increase that will make the effort worthwhile.

MAKING THE NUMBER
How to Use Sales Benchmarking to Drive Performance
by Greg Alexander, Aaron Bartels, and Mike Drapeau

CONTENTS
1. Sales Benchmarking: The Time Has Come
2. Sales Benchmarking: What's in It for the Executives?
3. Diving Deeper Into Sales Benchmarking
4. Five Steps to Effective Sales Benchmarking
5. Call to Action
6. Case Studies

THE SUMMARY IN BRIEF

In *Making the Number*, the authors make a convincing case for improving the sales function of an organization through benchmarking. Sales benchmarking, they explain, takes the guesswork out of sales and turns the sales function into a highly predictable, dependable engine that ultimately increases shareholder value.

Greg Alexander, Aaron Bartels, and Mike Drapeau first explain why sales benchmarking is valuable for the sales force, for executives, and for sales professionals. Then they break down benchmarking, delving into process, strategies, best practices, and world-class status.

Next, the authors identify and expound on the five steps to effective sales benchmarking: metric identification, data collection, comparing and contrasting, focused action, and sustained improvement.

Understanding that there will be resistance inside organizations to sales benchmarking, they list the most common objections and provide responses for sales leaders who wish to implement sales benchmarking. Finally, they let benchmarking speak for itself through case studies of companies that have successfully employed sales benchmarking.

In addition, you will learn the following:

• Why sales benchmarking should replace the concept of sales as an art
• How sales benchmarking can increase company profits
• How to increase a salesperson's annual sales
• The five steps to effective sales benchmarking
• How to overcome objections to sales benchmarking within your organization
• How to overcome implementation obstacles to sales benchmarking
• How other companies have succeeded with sales benchmarking

THE COMPLETE SUMMARY

Sales Benchmarking: The Time Has Come

In order to appreciate why sales benchmarking is critical for executives, managers, and frontline salespeople, it is necessary to take several steps backward. In doing this, consider some macro trends that are shaking up corporate America and how they are impacting the sales profession.

There has been an ongoing debate on the significance of globalization, even as its reality is now too well established to deny. To understand how your organization might form a coherent and compelling response to the threat of global competition, let us examine the sources of competitive advantage.

Sources of Competitive Advantage

Michael Porter has published two seminal works on this topic—*Competitive Advantage* and *Competitive Strategy*. Porter outlines three basic approaches organizations can use to establish and maintain competitive advantage in their respective marketplaces:

Overall cost leadership describes how companies can achieve and defend a low-cost-provider position yet retain enough return to sustain the business model achieved through technology, labor-force selectivity, or even process innovation.

Focus is built around the ability to orient a product or service toward a specific market segment, buying group, or geographic market. It succeeds when you can convince the customer that the higher price is worth the value you deliver. This can be an approach that is profitable in the long-term but is limited by the size of the chosen target market; the larger the market, the more likely it is that the twin strategic forces of cost and differentiation will make the focus strategy more difficult to defend.

Differentiation is about establishing and leveraging the uniqueness of a product or service such that customers demand it from the supplier and substitute offerings are insufficient. Customer service is the most sustainable differentiation strategy available to twenty-first-century companies.

Customer Experience

The Internet has armed the consumer against ineffective, legacy corporate messaging efforts. The sales profession must understand that marketing departments have already been disintermediated by citizen marketers. Sales is next.

Consider these statistics:

- The average shelf life of a sales manager is fifteen months.
- Nearly four out of ten salespeople will lose their jobs this year.
- An average of 27 percent of salespeople do not produce enough even to cover their loaded employment costs.

Armed with these numbers, CEOs will increasingly demand quantitative evidence that supports whatever the sales leaders are trying to sell to senior management about their ability to hit the number. No other function within a company is allowed to underperform this way.

The Sales Force

The bottom line is that salespeople who miss their numbers cost the company.

Many organizations are prevented from achieving their revenue goals or improving market penetration because they embrace the mind-set that there is an intangible "golden secret" to the sales profession—something that simply can't be quantified. Many CEOs have been cautious in demanding accountability of the sales leader in the same way that they have of the other functional heads. The "hall pass" that sales executives have received from their CEOs is coming to an end.

Sales benchmarking can dramatically increase revenue growth and decrease the cost of sales.

What's in It for the Executives?

The importance of benchmarking lies in its ability to increase profits and positively impact each business function within the organization. There is nothing different when it comes to sales.

The application of benchmarking to the sales function can be so transformative that it should be a matter of interest from the individual sales reps all the way up to the corporate boardroom.

No matter who you are in a public firm—salesperson, sales leader, CEO, CFO, or board member—shareholder value affects you. Shareholders control the firm and are focused on maximizing the value of their shares. A board of directors focused on sales performance should embrace sales benchmarking because it improves shareholder value.

Conflicts between management and shareholders arise when corporations pursue managerial goals at the expense of shareholder goals. Sales benchmarking helps realign the two again.

The Power of Sales Benchmarking

Let's look at the fictional company Consolidated Inc. to see the power of sales benchmarking. Assume that Consolidated will generate $1.1 billion in revenue during the next fiscal year and will have earnings of $55 million, an EPS (earnings per share) of $1.10, and a P/E (price/earnings) multiple of 20. This will translate into a share price of $22 and a market cap of $1.1 billion. Consolidated expects to enjoy a return on investment 0.4 percentage points behind the average—if it hits its numbers. This is where the sales-benchmarking discipline can be used to improve Consolidated's situation.

Consider what happens if, in the first year, Consolidated cuts back on those expense items that are least likely to negatively impact the top line. Using this low-risk, cherry-picking approach, Consolidated is able to reduce its cost of sales by $22 million, resulting in an earnings growth of nearly 7 percent rather than 5 percent. This approach would generate $77 million in earnings, compared with the previous estimate of $55 million. EPS will now be $1.54 (up from $1.10). With a P/E ratio of 20, the stock will now be valued at $30.80 per share, driving market cap up to $1.54 billion. The result of this seemingly low-impact sales expense reduction effort is more than $440 million in increased shareholder wealth.

Following is a list of some of the sales metrics against which companies can benchmark themselves to achieve top-line revenue improvements:

- Sales productivity per sales rep
- Ramp time to full sales productivity

- Annual sales rep turnover rate
- Sales rep time allocation
- Sales deal size
- Sales cycle length
- Close rate

By analyzing and improving performance in these dimensions, companies can determine the extent of shareholder wealth that can be created.

Business Benchmarking

Benchmarking is one of the most universally effective management disciplines available in business today. But it will not correct a flawed business model, nor will it force an organization to make the necessary changes—that is the job of the leader. It does, however, serve up a wealth of positive possibilities.

Sales benchmarking helps organizations understand how to use data to uncover the root cause of individual sales problems.

WHY SHOULD A CEO EMPLOY SALES BENCHMARKING?

Most CEOs did not rise through the sales function. As a result, they don't really understand sales. With sales benchmarking, CEOs can accelerate their knowledge of the sales department's capabilities.

Much like CEOs, other key members of the leadership team also often have no experience in sales. This prevents many members from contributing to the overall effort of growing revenue. Sales benchmarking provides the CEO with a tool to educate other leaders in the organization in a language that everyone can understand—numbers.

When a CEO is armed with an objective analysis of the sales department, he can better direct other parts of the company about exactly how to enable the sales force to grow new sources of revenue. Sales benchmarking allows CEOs to explain to a sales force its specific role in bringing the corporate vision to life. It gives the CEO the chance to convince the sales force why the vision is viable and calculates the payoff for the sales department if it is able to successfully execute it.

Sales benchmarking transforms the sales department's capabilities from tribal knowledge to a bastion of intellectual property embedded in company systems. This reservoir of data forms the basis for a new sales culture and more predictable sales behavior patterns.

Diving Deeper into Sales Benchmarking

The four key assets that must be present to ensure an effective sales-benchmarking initiative are a sales-benchmarking taxonomy, a sales-benchmarking repository, automation technology, and subject-matter experts. A taxonomy should cover, at a minimum, the definitions for all data inputs, metric formulas rendered from these inputs, and sales processes into which these metrics are grouped.

A sales-benchmarking repository is a robust, extensive, layered, archival, verifiable, and integrated data resource that possesses a series of attributes, including industry segments, geographical areas, sales channels, sales force/ organization, company type, and history.

Sales-benchmarking automation technology enables a series of steps from data collection to analysis to display long-term integration.

Sales-benchmarking subject-matter experts perform a variety of assessment and analytical tasks.

Process Sales Benchmarking and Strategic Sales Benchmarking

The majority of sales professionals find themselves working for organizations that have poorly designed processes, rather than no process at all. Poor process design manifests itself in inaccurate workflows, bad governance, inadequately defined roles, and insufficient standard operating procedures.

Process is the road map by which sales gets things done. Sales managers who say, "Too many deals fail to progress from upside to forecast" or "Why does it seem that it takes so long for new hires to become productive?" are giving voice to the fact that the process is insufficiently defined or poorly controlled.

The purpose of process sales benchmarking, according to John Davis, who wrote the book *Magic Numbers for Sales Management: Key Measures to Evaluate Sales Success*, is to identify the "most effective operating practices from many companies [in a peer group] that perform similar work functions." When an organization is able to elevate an entire sales process so that it attains world-class status, it can achieve breakthrough performance improvements.

Strategic benchmarking examines how companies compete. It involves considering high-level aspects such as core competencies, development of new products and services, and improved capacity for dealing with changes in the external environment.

Strategic benchmarking helps identify winning approaches that have enabled world-class companies to succeed in their respective marketplaces.

At its most basic level, strategic sales benchmarking usually reveals some sort of indication of which process areas are deficient and by how much.

Best Practices and the Importance of Being World Class

Best-practices benchmarking is about understanding and improving the processes within the business, not about comparing sets of numbers. It is what comes after you have diagnosed the problem areas and quantified the magnitude of the opportunity for financial gain. Best-practices benchmarking is the "how" of closing the gap between current performance and an improved one.

Best-practices benchmarking encompasses the effort necessary to

- identify those companies that are known for excellence in a certain discipline or process;
- gain agreement from them to study their unique set of policies, operating environment, and techniques;
- determine if and how this discipline should be modified so that it can be imported into your organization's unique culture and systems;
- make those modifications;
- implement the new discipline/process and enter into a cycle of continuous improvement.

Every organization has the potential to field a world-class sales force. To get there it takes a firm commitment to deploy benchmarking as a habit. There are many different techniques to measure world-class status—a bottom-up approach through individual metrics, one that focuses on the sales process, and one that takes an overall view. All are potentially valid. Once your sales organization has been benchmarked against your peers and world-class performance, you can then develop a plan to consistently outsell the competition.

The Self-aware Sales Force

Sales benchmarking is not a one-size-fits-all proposition. Organizations and their sales forces have distinguishing characteristics that influence whether and how they should be compared to each other. The results of sales benchmarking—metrics, scores, gaps, comparisons—all need to be evaluated when they are finally produced.

Sales forces can best be characterized by their dominant trait, which typically falls into one of the following six categories:

- **Delivery.** Example: courier services
- **Order taking.** Fulfills demand; example: Internet orders
- **Missionary.** Educates the marketplace to build brand awareness
- **Technician.** Employs sales reps who cannot complete a sale without the direct assistance of a presales engineer
- **Demand creator.** Is a classic transaction-based, business-to-business sales force
- **Solutions provider.** Focuses on solving customer problems

With the sales category determined, the next step is to perform a snapshot analysis of your sales force maturity. The five levels of sales management maturity are, from least mature to most mature:

- Level 1: Chaos. Processes, if they exist, are ill defined and unmanaged.
- Level 2: Defined. Most sales processes have been developed and documented.
- Level 3: Reportable. Sales processes have been adopted by the sales force.
- Level 4: Managed. The sales management team relies primarily on quantitative internal data.
- Level 5: Predictable. The sales management team is able to sufficiently predict sales performance.

WHAT SALES BENCHMARKING IS AND WHAT IT IS NOT

Sales Benchmarking Requires:	Sales Benchmarking Is NOT:
A detailed taxonomy	Valid without accepted definitions
Empirical and validated input data	A series of opinion-based answers from only those who decided to respond to a survey
Comparison of your performance against a relevant peer group	A simple comparison of your current performance against past performance
A statistically valid sample set cut by significant dimensions	A summary of survey results
Coverage of all major sales processes and subfunctions	Limited to one subfunction (such as compensation planning)
Strategic and tactical sales metrics	A list of qualitative questions
Tools to automate the series of steps from data collection to analysis to display	Accomplished manually without Herculean effort
A living repository with sufficient data and OLAP-like (online analytical processing) functionality to enable multidimensional and trend analysis	A collection of disparate data sources, surveys, and spreadsheets that lack integration, consistency, and analytic functionality
Subject-matter experts with specific expertise in comparative data analytics	Possible with ex-salespeople trying to perform data analytics without applicable training

SALES FORCE MANAGEMENT MATURITY MODEL SCALE (SM3)

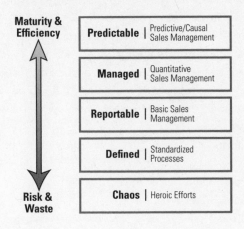

Five Steps to Effective Sales Benchmarking

Now that benchmarking has been defined and its applicability to the sales function understood, how do you get started? Benchmarking is a data-intensive exercise and derives its value from comparing information at different points in time. The first step in executing a sales-benchmarking effort is to identify which key sales-related metrics to measure.

Metrics Identification (Step 1)

It is unreasonable to think that any organization could measure (or would want to measure) every possible sales metric. Therefore, the first step is to pare down the possibilities to a strategic list of twenty to forty that are judged the best indicators of future performance and have the greatest likelihood of positively impacting the organization.

By using the customized approach, organizations gain control over the metrics and their input definitions, but they may find themselves without meaningful external data sets for comparison. Identifying the strategic metrics you want to measure will teach you a lot about your organization. Most companies have never thought of their sales performance in terms of a prism like the formula for sales success or ever considered measuring their sales force according to the many metrics from which to choose.

Data Collection (Step 2)

The Data Collection step is the most labor intensive of the benchmarking process, but it is necessary in order for the organization to determine how it stacks up, both internally against past performance and externally against peers and world-class entities.

Sales benchmarking is concerned with both qualitative and quantitative data. It uses descriptive statistics to depict raw data patterns and inferential statistics to leverage the power of leading indicators.

Sales benchmarking uses sampling to draw conclusions about a sales population (all sales receipts in the month of November, for example). If performed in the proper, nonbiased manner, sampling can support statistical results with sufficiently high precision.

The goal of data collection is to have a statistically valid sample that can be used to identify where an organization is underperforming or overperforming in relation to its peers and other world-class organizations.

Compare and Contrast (Step 3)

Compare and Contrast describes the actions necessary after having collected the internal data and assembled the relevant peer group data to compare them to each other. This comparison effort requires the use and understanding of a series of statistical techniques that help benchmarkers better interpret the data. In this way, organizations can determine how they stack up against peers and world-class organizations and, more important, they can determine the magnitude of any return they are likely to receive by closing these gaps. Usually these findings are summarized in some sort of report that goes to the board for review.

Some sales benchmarkers prefer to highlight areas of weakness and strength with graphical flourishes. They draw big red circles around the sales metric results that contribute disproportionately to failure and big green circles around those metrics where performance is well above the peer group and occasionally above world-class. This latter indication identifies centers of competency, which is every bit as important as determining where improvement must be made to exposed areas of weakness.

Whatever format this report takes, it should clearly indicate the gaps by sales metric and summarize the financial opportunity for improvement.

Focused Action (Step 4)

Focused Action is an antidote for use by the typical sales leader who is urged to implement a major improvement program across the board as soon as possible without first having ensured success through a well-designed pilot effort.

Focused Action is based on the concept of hypothesis testing. Hypothesis testing provides managers with a structured, analytical method for making decisions in such a way that the probability of error can be controlled or at least measured.

Sales Benchmark Index recommends a seven-step methodology to help organizations identify, test, and select the most effective solutions to the business problems exposed by sales benchmarking.

- 1. *Frame the problem.* Define the problem being addressed in specific terms.
- 2. *Develop hypotheses.* List potential causes for the problem and key drivers that impact or influence each potential cause.
- 3. *Gather data.* Gather relevant data, information, and background on the key drivers that will allow each potential cause to be proved or disproved.
- 4. *Test hyphotheses.* Analyze each potential cause to determine if the data supports the hypothesis as the most likely cause of the problem.
- 5. *Create solutions.* For those hypotheses that prove to be valid, identify possible solutions and examine each solution's feasibility for successful implementation.
- 6. *Develop plans.* For those solutions determined to be viable, estimate all necessary tasks, investments, milestones, resources, metrics, and returns.
- 7. *Select solutions.* Determine which solutions should be implemented using some form of program-approval criteria (e.g., hurdle rates for internal rate of return, or IRR).

Sustained Improvement (Step 5)

Completing step 5, Sustained Improvement, will ensure sustainability for the benchmarking program.

Is sustainability possible? Much research has been done on the tendency of corporate performance to revert to the mean. Although the details are somewhat arcane, the conclusions lend powerful support to the notion that benchmarking, as a form of modeling, can improve an organization's chances of staying continuously above the norm in performance.

Sustained competitive advantage is the goal, and it will be obtained only if the program transitions from being a one-time event to being one that is thoroughly embedded in the company's operating procedures.

Sales benchmarking can become standard operating procedure without replicating the heavy lifting of steps 1 through 4. The benchmarking process can be administered by a small number of staff members. When an organization is ready to move the benchmarking process into the mainstream of its sales operations system, it should implement a form of quality improvement.

Control charts monitor variations in data, highlighting trends that allow for correction before a process gets out of control. Control charts show when variation is due to a special cause and help highlight problems that need to be corrected.

Implementing the techniques of statistical process control and applying them to the sales force will enable sales benchmarking to become a best practice inside a company.

WHAT ARE THE FOCUS AREAS OF STRATEGIC BENCHMARKING?

*T*ypical focus areas for strategic benchmarking include

- acquisition strategy;
- business partnerships and strategic alliances;
- competitive dynamics;
- core competencies;
- foreign markets;
- marketplace segmentation;
- outsourcing, offshoring, and insourcing opportunities;
- process capabilities;
- product offerings and product development;
- service portfolio;
- strategic intent;
- technology enablement.

Call to Action

Sales leaders have very strong personalities. They sometimes suffer from the "not invented here" syndrome, particularly with regard to any attempt to change sales processes, tactics, or strategies that did not originate within their organizations.

Overcoming Objections to Sales Benchmarking

There are several common objections that sales leaders tend to present when faced with the question of whether to adopt sales benchmarking. Each one can be overcome. One objection is that "sales benchmarking is a fad." This objection has some teeth in that innovative concepts can boast of longevity only if they yield continual value for those who adopt them. From a logical perspective, sales force leaders should adopt sales benchmarking as a means of driving improvements in their businesses. However, when assessing the advisability of such "risky" ventures, emotions can affect our decisions. And fear, the most powerful of all negative emotions, can distort otherwise rational views and prevent sales benchmarking from gaining a foothold.

Another objection is "Sales benchmarking won't really work." The counterargument is that sales benchmarking delivers large, company-changing results. It is a "skewed bet" that presents a large payoff when allowed to succeed. The key question to ask when comparing sales benchmarking to other sales ideas is not how likely it is that it will work but how much will be gained when it does work. It is the magnitude of the outcome that counts.

One additional example of an objection is "Things are going well—we don't need it." The response is that sales benchmarking allows a company and a sales leader to compare themselves against a large sample size. This raises the bar to what is possible. It is a common occurrence for a sales leader to mine internal data and present it in a way that makes senior leadership feel good about the results. But when the first quarterly target is missed, the sales executive is greeted with looks of astonishment. Objectivity and external measurement are musts.

Overcoming Implementation Obstacles

You may be tempted to think that obstacles pose too stiff a challenge. Maybe you are beginning to believe that deployment of sales benchmarking would be too difficult and time-consuming. Overcoming these challenges appears daunting and putting forth the effort seems perilous, but for those who leave their comfort zone to adopt benchmarking, the results will be dynamic—competitors will be eclipsed and business transformed. Despite the obstacles, sales benchmarking can be deployed with success.

For those few CEOs still resistant to the idea that the sales leader should be a key participant in strategy creation, a mountain of literature argues to the contrary. The key to this discussion is making sure that the CEO understands that the sales organization is crucial to strategic plan execution. This justifies a sales seat at the table.

Sales leaders must master the discipline of change management and ensure that their own sales forces do not derail an otherwise well-constructed benchmarking improvement program. Developing staff behaviors conducive to change management will be the best approach to achieving sustainable success with sales benchmarking.

Do you have the organizational fortitude to introduce sales benchmarking? It is true that embracing sales benchmarking can be risky, and there are few sales leaders currently doing so. Many will doubt the worth of sales benchmarking, and you will face some dogged resistance. But persevere and address the obstacles, and the results will be dramatic.

Case Studies

Two real-world examples of sales benchmarking follow.

Discover Financial Services

Credit, Debit, Stored-Value Cards In an effort to increase acceptance of Discover Network–issued cards and grow its transaction volume, Vice President of Sales Gerry Wagner and his team have conducted extensive analysis, identifying areas for improvement. They have studied their accounts to determine levels of transaction volume. These metrics, along with several submetrics, are the key drivers of their success.

When Gerry and his team identify a gap in acceptance, they gather external data from sources such as the Nielsen Report to identify partners that can perform the activities necessary to close the gap.

Discover brings innovative offerings to market in an effort to convert more of the available market to Discover transactions. Each product's effectiveness is measured in conversion rates. Each new program has a volume goal, which is then projected on a percentage basis to a group of merchants.

Gerry gathers real-time data comparing actual results to goal results and determines the variance. Armed with this level of granularity, Gerry can speak to his team members responsible for the program and the merchant and make midcourse corrections in order to drive volume.

Nine years ago, Gerry had approximately seven hundred people in his sales and service force. Today he has around 150. The key difference between then and now is that Gerry now outsources the acquisition of small-business owners to an independent network of sales professionals who work on a commission basis. This has dramatically lowered his acquisition costs while significantly and rapidly expanding acceptance points for Discover.

Discover invested in the proper infrastructure to sustain its level of performance. It streamlined its processes, allowing for few people to produce high levels of productivity. The resources deployed are focused, and the organization's priorities are clear to all.

Covad Communications Group

Broadband Innovation Covad's leads are generated primarily from three sources: marketing, customer referrals, and old-fashioned cold calling. In the past year, David McMorrow, executive vice president of worldwide sales, and his team performed a lead-generation benchmark where closed sales were tracked back to the originating activity, with effectiveness measured in terms of closed business per dollar spent generating the lead.

For the first time, Covad could clearly rank lead-generating activities in terms of the returns they produced. These findings revealed that the traditional investments the company was making in radio and print were largely ineffective. After deploying a pilot, Covad rolled out a new program focused on search-engine optimization. The result was a 30 percent improvement in yield in the first year, measured as a dollar earned compared to a dollar spent.

Covad measures several metrics, including customer churn, deal size, revenue per sales rep, channel yield, rate of up-sell/renewal, and postsale cancellation. Covad learned that the primary events leading to customer "fallout" were typically a rough implementation, an outage, or renewal time. It has cut its churn in half, but it is still almost a percentage point above the industry benchmark. Customer churn and fallout, the two items that have the largest impact on companywide profitability, will continue to be an area of focus.

THE GIANTS OF SALES

by Tom Sant

I f one were to undertake carving a Mount Rushmore of the sales industry, who would be the four faces that would be chiseled from the stone? This question would spur endless hours of debate among sales professionals, managers, and consultants. Many of the names featured in this collection of summaries would certainly be in contention. Some could be cited for their methods of motivation, while others deserve recognition for contributing new techniques to the profession of selling. The field of sales is fortunate to continue to forge professionals who find new ways to innovate and update the simple act of getting a prospect to exchange money for goods and services.

While Washington, Jefferson, Lincoln, and Theodore Roosevelt were representative of the presidential greats of the country's first 150 years, author Tom Sant's quest for the titans of the sales industry is limited to the twentieth century. After exhaustive research, he arrived at four names: John Henry Patterson, Dale Carnegie, Elmer Wheeler, and Joe Girard. This quartet forms the focus of Sant's book *The Giants of Sales*, a thought-provoking look at sales success through the words and actions of four masters of the craft.

It's not idle praise to be named a giant by Sant. He is considered an expert in persuasive communications, something to which *Selling Power* magazine attested when it named him among the top ten sales trainers in the world. His attention to detail makes him an insightful chronicler of the evolution of the industry, and he doesn't fall prey to myth making when discussing the exploits of these celebrated salesmen.

Innovation is the key to the four men profiled in *The Giants of Sales*. Each one contributed a new idea that added vibrant color to the sales palette. In the case of Patterson, he started a process-oriented sales method. Carnegie became synonymous with relationship-oriented sales. Wheeler was a master linguist whose endless pursuit of the perfect sales pitch led him into previously uncharted territory. Girard was a brilliant tactician whose early forays in car sales laid the groundwork for the technique we now know as relationship marketing. In each case, the contributions of the respective sales giant continue to have far-reaching impact in the industry. It's no coincidence that Carnegie's book *How to*

Win Friends and Influence People continues to be a best seller, despite its being first published during the Great Depression.

The stories contained in *The Giants of Sales* are intended to provide a broad-based look at the fundamental ideas that underscore sales success. More than just providing historical information, Sant intends the innovations of his four giants to continue to help sales professionals achieve and exceed their goals. He integrates the lessons provided by each sales legend into four fully formed sales methods. By borrowing the essentials from Patterson, Carnegie, Wheeler, and Girard, Sant simplifies the ways in which sales are made and gives sales professionals one of four paths to follow. *The Giants of Sales* is as much about self-evaluation as it is about technique. The professional who is able to successfully recognize and implement the points delivered by Sant is sure to strengthen his or her numbers. The next step, the one of innovation, may land him or her on Sant's list for the twenty-first century.

THE GIANTS OF SALES
What Dale Carnegie, John Patterson, Elmer Wheeler, and Joe Girard Can Teach You About Real Sales Success
by Tom Sant

CONTENTS

THE SUMMARY IN BRIEF

John Henry Patterson faced financial ruin from his investment in the first cash register, but he turned National Cash Register into one of the most important companies of its day. He also introduced a highly organized sales process that focuses on understanding customers' needs and selling a solution that meets those needs.

Dale Carnegie began his life as the son of a pig farmer in Missouri, but his book *How to Win Friends and Influence People* has been a best seller for nearly seventy years. In that book, Carnegie made famous many lasting principles, such as tapping into the power of enthusiasm, that would lead to the relationship-oriented approach to selling.

Elmer Wheeler tested thousands of sentences on millions of consumers in his Wheeler Word Laboratories, searching for combinations of words that produced the best results. In the process, he developed an influential selling program and wrote more than twenty hit books. His classic selling points include "Don't sell the steak, sell the sizzle!"

Joe Girard was born into deep poverty in Detroit. He took his first job at the age of eight, shining shoes in a hardscrabble saloon. After drifting from one bad job to another, he turned to car sales. Soon, he was single-handedly selling more cars than 95 percent of all the dealerships in North America. His system for generating leads and gaining referrals still forms the basis of today's permission marketing and closed-loop marketing.

The stories of these four sales gurus and their key sales innovations offer readers a broad and deep understanding of the entire selling field.

In addition, this summary will show you:

- how to tap into the power of the selling methods developed by these sales pioneers;
- the difference between linguistic approaches and tactical methods;
- how process-oriented sales methods can improve sales;
- how to make some of the most powerful ideas in the history of selling work for you.

THE COMPLETE SUMMARY

Selling in the Twenty-first Century

Professional selling is the most important American invention of the twentieth century. Without professional sales methods, the development of our society and our economy would have been delayed. Professional selling is the engine that has powered our economy for the past hundred years.

Our predecessors figured out how to sell effectively by figuring out what works.

John Henry Patterson, for example, developed a process for selling that kept his company growing even in the midst of recessions, and that became the foundation for the methods used today by the most successful sales organizations in the world.

Dale Carnegie discovered truths about human relationships that have been used by such powerhouse business leaders as Lee Iacocca, Mary Kay Ash, and Tom Monaghan to build businesses.

Elmer Wheeler developed and tested ways of delivering sales messages, boiled down to brief statements, to figure out which ways worked the best.

"The World's Greatest Salesman"

And Joe Girard, born into abject poverty in the slums of Detroit, discovered a technique for generating qualified leads that put him in the *Guinness Book of World Records* as "the world's greatest salesman."

A particular method of selling may work wonderfully in one environment and rather poorly in another. Matching the method to the situation is one of the challenges the salesperson, the sales manager, and the company all face. By going back and looking at what the early masters of modern selling taught us, we can avoid wasting our time on fads and foolishness. More important, we can avoid damaging our customer relationships by adopting lousy advice. Most important of all, we can sell more effectively.

Four Ways to Sell

Generally speaking, sales methods fall into four broad categories. Each of the four basic ways to approach selling has some real strengths and can improve results. But each also has some significant limitations. The goal is to understand the basic approaches and to recognize when and why each of them works. Then we can match the method to the particular selling environment in which we are working. Here are the four categories of sales methods:

1. *Process-Oriented Sales Methods.* This type of approach treats sales as a process, a series of identifiable steps. The assumption is that when salespeople follow the steps correctly, they will be successful—provided they have a reasonably competitive product or service to offer. These process-oriented approaches have dominated the sales-training market for the past generation. Their success stems from a number of factors:

They are relatively easy to teach.

They address the needs of sales management.

They tend to be effective in complex sales.

They have been adopted by highly influential corporations.

2. *Relationship-Driven Sales Methods.* In the view of the trainers and authors who recommend this kind of selling strategy, what matters the most in winning a sale is how strong a bond you forge with the decision maker. That bond, that individual relationship, which is based on trust and mutual respect, is the basis on which one vendor will be chosen over another. For a long time, these methods dominated sales training, but about twenty years ago they began to fall out of favor. However, they have a number of unique strengths that make them effective in the right situation:

People prefer to buy from people they trust.

Relationship-driven approaches tend to result in more repeat business.

The salesperson's value is maximized.

These methods work well in selling intangibles, such as intellectual capital or services, and in selling commodities, where there is little differentiation between products.

3. *Linguistic Approaches.* For some reason, people believe that certain words or phrases can exert tremendous power over a customer's mind. As a result, salespeople eagerly seek insights into both verbal and body language. Although fewer in number, the sales experts who advocate these methods have tremendously loyal followings. Why? There are two reasons:

Scientific research backs them up. Linguistic approaches are often tied to empirical research in cognition.

They are testable. A salesperson can quickly determine whether or not the method is working simply by trying it in the course of a sales call.

4. *Tactical Methods.* This type of sales training focuses on tricks and techniques. Often this kind of training tends toward the manipulative, but there are sound techniques in selling that can make a person's job easier. The reasons why salespeople support these methods include:

They believe that their success is limited only by a particular skill deficiency. Specific, tactical training can be exactly what the salesperson needs.

Techniques are often trainable in short, focused sessions.

John Henry Patterson: The Process of Selling

In 1884, when John Henry Patterson was forty years old, he and his brother sold their coal business and made a fateful decision: They decided to invest in high technology.

The cash register had been invented and patented in 1879 by James Ritty, a saloon keeper in Dayton, Ohio. Ritty founded the National Manufacturing Company in Dayton to manufacture and sell cash registers. The company was barely staying afloat when Patterson bought it. He knew about Ritty's machine because he was one of the few people who had bought one. Once the register had proved its value in one of his retail outlets, he ordered two more. Patterson concluded that every retailer should have a cash register and that every intelligent retailer would quickly buy one. And so, for $6,500, he bought the rights to Ritty's patent and operation.

Patterson took over the business, which he renamed the National Cash Register Company. Patterson faced the classic dilemma faced by many contemporary entrepreneurs: He was producing a product so innovative that there was no market for it, a product in which the world had no interest, a product so complex that its largest group of potential users couldn't understand it. He had to find a way to sell his complicated, innovative product to skeptical consumers.

The answers he found have had repercussions throughout American business for more than one hundred years. Some of the most powerful and influential leaders in American industry worked for Patterson and took his methods to their next positions as leaders at IBM, General Motors Corporation, Packard Motor Car Company, Burroughs Adding Machine Company, and other top companies.

The First Sales Convention

In 1886, Patterson organized the first sales convention. He had all five of his sales agents come to Dayton, where they received training on some new features of the cash registers and how these features increased value for the customer. He also had his top-producing sales reps share their selling tips with the others. In this sales conference, Patterson had come up with two of many innovations in modern selling: holding a regular sales meeting and having sales reps trained not just in product features but in sales techniques as well.

Patterson's brother-in-law, Joseph Crane, also attended the sales conference as an observer and offered his advice. Once Crane had joined NCR as a sales agent, he developed a process in which he would uncover the customer's biggest worry, problem, or fear; show which feature addressed that issue; and then demonstrate the value of buying the machine to the merchant in a systematic way so that the prospective purchaser fully understood it. By quickly focusing on the particular set of problems that the given customer worried about, Crane was able to position the cash register as a solution, not merely a piece of equipment. He was selling value, not technology. And he was saying the same basic words in the same order, time after time.

Systematizing the Sales Force

Patterson realized what he had in Crane's method: a way of systematizing the sales force to maximize its results. He had Crane give his presentation while a secretary transcribed it. Patterson sent the script out to the other salesmen with a note: "Crane sells more machines than any of you fellows, and he sells them this way. I suggest you all learn this."

Patterson soon revised the text, making it a bit more flexible, and issued it again, this time as the NCR Primer. He presented it at the sales conference in 1887 and told the men they had to learn it.

A Primer on Process

After Patterson insisted that every sales agent in the field use the sales method that Crane had developed, the company's sales began to soar. Crane's approach was so powerful because it focused entirely on the customer's needs rather than on the company's product. Although Patterson didn't use the term, what he was developing was the first sales force to use a consultative approach.

The four steps of Crane's process are:

- **First, the approach—identify the customer's problems.** Where are customers losing money? What goals are they failing to achieve? What gaps in their current capabilities are keeping them from being successful?

- **Second, the proposition—develop a specific value proposition.** Identify the specific areas where losses are occurring and quantify them. Summarize the losses and show the potential for increased profitability in concrete dollars and cents.

- **Third, the demonstration—show how the solution fits.** Summarize the customer's problems and the potential for increasing profits. Then show how the solution works, not in terms of its technical functions but in terms of its business impact.

- **Fourth, the close—ask for the order.** Assume that an intelligent businessperson will want to buy. If a customer has objections, answer them and close again.

For the first time in history, a selling argument was consistently developed from the customer's point of view rather than from the company's desire to make a sale. It was also the first time that selling was seen as a process, something that could be repeated over and over, rather than as a transactional event. This was Patterson's most important contribution to modern selling. Defining sales as a process—a sequence of specific steps that can be identified, tracked, and measured—means that sales can be taught, measured, and improved.

Making It Work for You

Take an objective look at your sales process. If it's not explicitly defined, go ahead and identify the typical steps that must occur for you to close business. Once you have a firm grasp of the steps in the process, whether there are three or seven or nine or some other number, identify what you must accomplish in each step in order to move to the next one. How do you know when this step has been completed? Identify training or resources that can help you improve your execution in those steps.

For some people, thinking about sales as a project to be managed or a process to be executed is not a natural way to view the job. That was true for many of Patterson's sales reps, and it's no different today. But if you have that feeling of resistance, it's worth overcoming. Knowing your process and following it will make your job as a sales professional easier and will enable you to work more efficiently and effectively. You'll close more deals faster if you know what it takes to get to a close.

Learn your process, use it, and respect it. In return, the process will make you more successful than you could ever be without it.

THE FIRST SALES TRAINING SCHOOL

*N*ational Cash Register sponsored a display at the Chicago World's Fair in 1893. A group of young men was hired specifically to staff the display, but Patterson found to his horror that they knew almost nothing about cash registers. He pulled them all into a hotel room, where he created a short, focused presentation based on the Primer. He also listed the most common questions that the crowd was likely to ask, along with the best answers. Patterson then drilled the young men in small groups until they were all perfect.

Patterson decided that he could do the same thing with his sales reps. The first sales training school was held on April 4, 1894. It was attended by thirty-seven men. The company paid all expenses. Crane was in charge of the instruction, and the men were drilled on the Primer and the newly developed Book of Arguments, a handy guide to overcoming objections.

As usual, Patterson kept records of everything. By tracking performance, he was soon able to see that sales veterans who went through the training doubled their sales afterward.

Dale Carnegie: The Apostle of Influence

Dale Carnegie was born in 1888 in a small farmhouse in Missouri and was raised on hog farms in rural parts of the state. After a streak of bad luck, his family moved to a farm near Warrensburg, Missouri, so that he could attend the state teachers' college nearby. Dressed in shabby, ill-fitting clothes, beset by insecurities and worries, he sought recognition by becoming a champion debater. Carnegie saw that the winners "were regarded as the intellectual leaders in college," he said. The public-speaking contests and debate competitions drew crowds from the town as well as the college community. This, Carnegie thought, was his opportunity.

His first year at Missouri State Teachers College, Carnegie entered a dozen competitions. He lost every time. Yet he was stubborn enough to try again. So he practiced every night, reciting passages from Abraham Lincoln and Richard Harding Davis, a popular journalist who became the managing editor of *Harper's Weekly*. A year later, he won the schoolwide public-speaking contest by delivering Davis's "The Boy Orator of Zapata" and Lincoln's Gettysburg Address. He also won the debating contest.

Other students sought him out to coach them in public speaking. During his last year in school he won the debating contest again, a boy he had tutored won the public-speaking contest, and a girl he had trained won the declamatory contest.

With his recognized skill for talking, he decided to become a salesman. After a short stint selling courses for the International Correspondence Schools, he was hired as a sales rep by Armour and Company in Omaha, Nebraska. Carnegie thrived in his new job and eventually became the top salesman in his territory. When his managers approached him about a promotion, he declined.

From Selling to Acting to Selling

Taking the money he had made selling for Armour, he quit his job, headed to New York, and enrolled in the American Academy of Dramatic Arts to become an actor. After graduation, he was hired for the road company of a goofy musical about life in a circus. After the tour ended, Carnegie couldn't find work as an actor anywhere, so he went back to selling. He wanted to stay in New York, so he took a job as a car salesman for the Packard automobile company. He found that he hated it.

The 125th Street YMCA in Harlem offered a few courses in an evening school that it ran to help working-class men and women get ahead. Carnegie wanted to become a night-school instructor there so he could free up his days to write the Great American Novel. Since the YMCA director wasn't sure that anybody would sign up for Carnegie's class in public speaking, he refused to pay him the standard salary of two dollars a class.

"So I said," Carnegie later remembered, " 'I will work on a profit-sharing basis.' "

The director agreed. Some three years later, Carnegie was making thirty dollars a night in commissions. His class had become a huge success.

The Twenty-five-Year Overnight Success

Carnegie never planned to write his most famous book, How to Win Friends and Influence People. He was sailing along running his popular public-speaking workshops, which were making him a lot of money even in the middle of the Great Depression. For nearly twenty-five years he had delivered the same basic course. After a representative of the publisher Simon & Schuster attended one of Carnegie's public-speaking courses, he approached Carnegie about writing a book about getting along with people. Although Carnegie initially refused, he eventually agreed. Two years later, in 1936, the first edition of How to Win Friends and Influence People appeared in bookstores. Within weeks, more than five thousand copies had been sold. Sales continued to build quickly until the book was selling almost five thousand copies a week. The book went through seventeen printings in five months. In the first year, Carnegie made $150,000 in royalties, based on twenty-five cents a copy.

Overnight, Dale Carnegie was famous, wealthy, and eagerly sought after by business leaders, politicians, and celebrities.

Why Does It Work?

At the heart of Carnegie's philosophy is a simple idea: Influence is linked to trust. Gaining influence means building trust, and trust is fundamentally a relationship. Carnegie correctly surmised that unless you get the other person to like you, you're not going to get very far in your efforts to persuade him or her. It's the emotional connection between people that will get you started on the road to trust. The second most important element is displaying interest in the other person—in other words, minimizing the appearance of self-interest. Research studies into buyer/seller relationships have indicated that these are exactly the variables that are most likely to produce a successful relationship.

How to Establish Rapport

Here are some tips for establishing rapport and building conscious relationships with your prospects:

1. *Be your professional self.* Don't try to act like somebody other than who you are. If you do, it'll come across as insincere or fake.

2. *Dress simply and professionally.* Minimize jewelry and wear a good watch and polished shoes. Keep the focus on the customer and away from your wardrobe.

3. *Be forthright.* Extend your hand, look the other person in the eye, and tell him or her how good it is to meet with him or her.

4. *Take a second to scan his or her office.* Do you see signs of a similar interest? Are there pictures of the family or a hobby? Are there awards? Make a connection. If you truly don't have the same personal interests, look for a professional connection.

5. *Always set a time frame at the beginning of the meeting, whether it is on the telephone or in person.*

6. *At the start of a meeting, resist the temptation to show off all you have learned about the customer's business and industry from reading the company's 10-K and annual report.* You'll make a bigger impression if you wait to display your knowledge by asking incisive questions later, after you've established rapport.

7. *When the customer talks, listen.* Look directly at him or her. Nod. Don't interrupt. If you like to take extensive notes, ask permission to do so. When the other person has made his or her point, wait for three counts before you say anything back to him or her. Linger on what was said. Give the person a chance to take a breath. Show that you are listening by stopping to absorb what was just said.

8. *After listening, always feed back what you heard.* This is the highest compliment you can pay someone. It is the most important sign of a truly conscious relationship. You listened, and you want to get it right.

9. *Stay on the topic, but don't try to control the conversation too tightly.* As need statements emerge, be sure to write them down so that you can later match a solution or benefit to each need.

10. *Treat your customers or prospects as your equals, as partners in having a successful meeting.* Let them explain their problems and how their business and their decision process work, and then carefully explain to them how your sales cycle usually progresses.

11. *Never argue with the customer.* Instead, if you disagree, take a few minutes to make sure you understand his or her position. Make sure you truly see the customer's point of view. One of the best ways to resolve conflict is to ask, "Why?"

12. *When leaving, extend your hand and offer a firm handshake and a smile, look the customer in the eyes, and thank him or her for his or her hospitality.* Remind the customer of your next agreed-upon step.

The Carnegie Approach

The Dale Carnegie approach is fundamentally about improving our relationships with other people, not about selling them more stuff. It's about getting what you want by helping someone else get what he or she wants. It's about establishing a trusting relationship built on sincere acceptance of the other person's point of view, on honest communication, and on sharing an open agenda.

You want to do your homework before you meet with a client, so that you can come to the meeting prepared with insights and information relevant to the client's business. But the most important thing you can do is to listen closely and attentively. Nothing builds trust and rapport faster than listening.

Elmer Wheeler: The Magic of Words

Elmer Wheeler did some of the twentieth century's most innovative thinking about how to sell and came up with phrases that have shaped American culture. For example, he coined the phrase "Don't sell the steak, sell the sizzle," as a way of making the point that bland, factual details don't work. You have to show the customer what the benefits are.

Wheeler came by his interest in language naturally—early in his career he sold display advertising for newspapers. Wheeler was pretty successful working for the Los Angeles Herald, the Rochester Journal, the Albany Times-Union, and the Baltimore News-Post, but he became frustrated because he wasn't able to establish a causal link between the ads a merchant placed in a paper and an increase in that merchant's business.

"Wheelerpoints"

In 1937, after some research and experimentation, Wheeler published Tested Sentences That Sell, his first major book. In it, he presented five "Wheelerpoints," gave his readers examples of how they worked, and even speculated about why they worked. Here they are:

- **Wheelerpoint 1: Don't sell the steak, sell the sizzle!** People want to know, What's in it for me?
- **Wheelerpoint 2: Don't write—telegraph.** In Wheeler's words, you need to get the customer's "IMMEDIATE and FAVORABLE attention in the fewest possible words."
- **Wheelerpoint 3: Say it with flowers.** You must prove your claims. Wheeler said, "Give a quick customer benefit—but then prove it the next second."
- **Wheelerpoint 4: Don't ask if—ask which!** He explained, "You should always frame your words (especially at the close) so that you give the prospect a choice between something and SOMETHING, never between something and NOTHING."
- **Wheelerpoint 5: Watch your bark!** It's not just using the right words; it's saying them in the right way that delivers results.

Over the next twenty years, *Tested Sentences That Sell* outsold all other books on selling ever written. Wheeler became one of the best-known speakers in the country, delivering thousands of speeches to businesses, associations, and conferences. He established training programs that were taught at 125 business schools and colleges around the world. He also wrote more than twenty books on retail sales, direct sales, overcoming shyness, losing weight, setting goals, and quitting cigarettes!

The psychological insights that were the foundation of Wheeler's points were based on his own common sense and his observations—his "testing" of the various approaches embodied in specific words, phrases, and sentences. Today we would use different words to make the points and different examples to illustrate them, but that doesn't mean they don't still work.

Wheeler's genius was in recognizing that the way you say something can make a huge difference in whether or not you convince the customer. He tried wording sales messages in different ways and testing them to find the wording that produced the best results. In both respects—focusing on the power of language to influence a customer and using empirical methods to find out what really works—he was way ahead of his time.

Language, used effectively, is an enabling mechanism that allows people to connect. There are no magic words. There is only word magic: the skillful and insightful use of words to communicate a message clearly and persuasively.

Elmer's Wheelerpoints work in sales calls and writing. Here are some additional tips for communicating effectively with your prospects.

Oral Communications

1. *Questions are more effective than statements in engaging a customer, particularly during the early stages of a sales process.* Think about the questions you need to ask in order to guide the customer's thinking and to obtain the right information.

2. *Create a printed agenda and share it with the customer.* Even informal, one-on-one meetings will benefit from having an agenda.

3. *Stay flexible and responsive to your audience's interests.* If your meeting goes off on a tangent but you build rapport or gain insight into your client's concerns and values, it's still a successful meeting.

4. *If you have a written proposal, a price quote, or other printed material, don't hand it out until the end of your presentation.* Otherwise, your audience will be distracted, reading the text while listening to your presentation and getting little from either source.

5. *Welcome interruptions, objections, and questions from your audience.* They indicate interest and involvement.

6. *Share responsibility for the outcome of your presentation with the audience.* That means giving up some of the control, being flexible, and articulating common objectives.

7. *Use visual aids in formal presentations and don't skimp on them.* It's better to have many charts and move through them quickly than to have only a few and spend a lot of time on each.

8. *Practice important presentations using videotape to identify distracting mannerisms or habits.*

9. *Learn to control your nervousness.* Develop a routine for calming yourself. Visualize success and breathe!

10. *Use the following pattern during initial meetings with the client to begin the probing and fact-finding process:* Establish your purpose, probe for needs and goals, gain concurrence, and close the call.

Written Communications

1. *Check whether your sales proposals are client centered or self-centered.*

2. *Put the important stuff first.*

3. *Send out the best work you're capable of producing.* Have someone you trust proofread and edit documents that you are sending to a client before you send them.

4. *Always use your spelling and grammar checker.*

5. *Kill the marketing fluff.* Be ruthless about removing it from anything you send to a client.

6. *Eliminate weasel words and booster words while you're at it.* Booster words are words thrown into a sentence when we suspect we're not making a point very well, such as "very," "really," "certainly," "obviouswly," "somewhat," and "significant." Weasel words try to imply that we're saying one thing when we mean something slightly different. For example, the words "can be" in "can be of value . . ." don't necessarily mean it will be.

7. *Keep your documents as short as possible.* Short documents are easier to understand and make a stronger impression.

8. *Highlight your documents.* Use headlines, subheadings, boldface type, lists, and other devices to make sure that the reader who skims sees key points.

9. *Use familiar, everyday language.* When in doubt, leave it out. Instead of "implement," "optimum," and "utilize," write "do," "best," and "use."

Joe Girard: Priming the Pump

Joe Girard was born at the start of the Great Depression. His father was a physically abusive Sicilian immigrant with no trade and no skills and seldom worked more than a few days at a time. Mainly his family survived on relief checks and handouts. The six of them lived in a tiny apartment in one of the worst neighborhoods in Detroit, Michigan.

Girard started working in saloons when he was eight years old, shining shoes late into the night for a few nickels. Later he took another job delivering the *Detroit Free Press* before heading off to school. When the paper had a contest for signing up new subscribers, he sold enough new subscriptions to win the prize—a case of Pepsi, which he turned around and sold one bottle at a time for still more nickels.

After getting expelled from high school for fighting, he drifted from one lousy job to another. After he was turned down for a car salesman position, one sales manager hired him on straight commission. Not long afterward, he went to a funeral home to pay his respects to the deceased mother of one of his friends. At the Catholic funeral, he wondered how the funeral director knew how many Mass cards to print. After some research, he discovered that the average number of people who come to a funeral was about 250.

When Girard and his wife were attending a wedding, he asked the caterer what the average number of guests was at a wedding. "About 250 from the bride's side, and another 250 from the groom's," he was told. Girard discovered that there was a principle at work here, one that he could use to build business.

Joe Girard's Law of 250

The principle is this: Most people have about 250 other people in their lives who are important enough to invite to a wedding or to a funeral. In other words, each person with whom I do business represents 250 other people. If I do a great job, 250 more people are likely to get a recommendation to buy from me. If I do a lousy job, I have just made 250 enemies. Consistently doing a good job—building strong relationships, treating people fairly, and giving them what they want—will make selling much easier in the long run. What Girard had realized was that it made more sense to "prime the pump" by generating awareness and interest among prospects well before they ever needed a car.

Using the Law of 250, Girard became the greatest car salesman in the world, and the only one ever honored with admission to the Automobile Hall of Fame. From 1963 to 1977, Girard sold more than thirteen thousand cars, all at retail, one customer at a time. He sold more retail automobiles from his small office at Merollis Chevrolet in Eastpointe, Michigan, than anyone else anywhere in the world.

Girard learned that one satisfied customer can lead to referrals that can dramatically shorten the sales cycle and help fill the pipeline. Each customer has a circle of influence that potentially includes many people who might also become customers.

The system of generating leads and maintaining awareness among prospects that Girard developed has been revived in recent years under several new names: permission marketing, nurture marketing, relationship marketing, and closed-loop marketing. Even today, the idea of priming the pump with creative presale activities that generate leads and keep prospects aware of you has tremendous potential for improving sales force efficiency.

The first step is to create a profile of your best customers. Next, you have to figure out how to approach the prospect. You have to earn the right to communicate with these people who have never heard of you. Write a series of brief and focused messages that will be of interest to your target customers. Then start sending them. This is the kind of activity you need to do every day.

It's all about marketing yourself. And it's about recognizing that for every impression you make on somebody, you potentially are making an impression on 250 other people as well.

HOW TO NURTURE RELATIONSHIPS

To turn happy customers into willing recommenders, Girard realized that he had to take action. He had to nurture the relationship and keep it alive. One way he did this was by sending out a greeting card every month to every one of the nine thousand people in his prospect file. By the time he had been selling for a decade, nearly two-thirds of his sales were to repeat customers.

Looking Back to Look Ahead

Which sales methodology is the best? The answer depends on you, on your typical customers, on what you are selling, and on the competitive environment in which you are working. There are six characteristics for which you should look in your current methods. If you find that your sales methodology is lacking in one, take steps to correct the deficiency.

1. The sales method matches the customer's preferred mode of buying.

2. The sales method is flexible enough to be self-correcting, incorporating lessons learned.

3. The sales process itself creates value, usually in the form of intellectual capital, for both the customer and the vendor.

4. The methodology increases the efficiency of the sales process, making the sales cycle shorter or enabling the salesperson to handle a larger volume of accounts successfully.

5. The methodology is transferable across all skill levels.

6. The methodology is based on objectively measured events or tasks.

ZIGLAR ON SELLING

by Zig Ziglar

To call Zig Ziglar a sales icon is something of a misnomer. Hilary "Zig" Ziglar's presence as a speaker and educator in the areas of personal and professional development transcends the sales arena. He is the author of twenty-seven books, nine of which have reached best-seller status. Today, he is perhaps as well known for his works on his Christian faith as he is for motivating corporate executives. Now in his eighties, Ziglar still participates in speaking engagements around the globe and is widely considered a pioneer in the area of executive coaching.

In the sales realm, Ziglar's body of work stretches into the stratosphere. "Selling," he notes in *Ziglar on Selling*, "is more than a profession; it is a way of life." This way of life, according to Ziglar, hinges on the need for the sales professional to continue to approach the profession as an ongoing opportunity to learn. Ziglar never relents in his belief that salespeople, like athletes, scholars, and artists, need constant reinforcement of the basics. From these essential building blocks, Ziglar expands on his ideas and helps the sales professional become a more open, prepared, and battle-ready individual.

With more than a half dozen sales books to his credit, why focus on *Ziglar on Selling*? As its subtitle notes, the book promises to be "The Ultimate Handbook for the Complete Sales Professional." This is not a charge Ziglar takes lightly. What makes *Ziglar on Selling* a defining moment for Ziglar is that it may be the best combination of classic selling techniques and forward-looking strategies. Critics who point out that some of Ziglar's advice is a relic of the era of door-to-door salesmen (note, sales*men*) miss a fundamental aspect of selling. The door to which today's sales professionals travel may be in a Fortune 500 company, at the other end of a phone line, or in someone's e-mail in-box, but it is a door nonetheless. The act of presenting oneself and one's products or services is still person to person, even in the digital age.

Ziglar on Selling offers the advice that beginning salespeople need to learn and experienced professionals need to remember. Ziglar provides essential reminders that the customer is looking not for a product but for the solution the product provides. He champions the "win-win" method and instructs sales professionals to be advocates for the customer. He makes clear that selling is not something to be left to chance. Preparation and execution are two skills that *Ziglar on Selling* emphasizes, and through easily applicable examples, it teaches sales professionals the right way to find and approach prospects.

Readers will quickly benefit from Ziglar's approach to selling. He is a substantial believer in the power of positivity. *Ziglar on Selling* is one of the few sales books to recognize the true grind that is a life of "making your numbers," but that doesn't stop Ziglar from giving sales professionals the perspective to help turn the grind into an opportunity for greatness. The advice provided in *Ziglar on Selling* is universal, and it may lead sales professionals to, as Ziglar suggests, return to this volume again and again, finding something new in each reading.

ZIGLAR ON SELLING
The Ultimate Handbook for the Complete Sales Professional
by Zig Ziglar

CONTENTS
1. You Made the Right Choice
2. Finding Someone Willing to Buy
3. Questions Are the Answer
4. Making the Lights Go On
5. Closing More Sales More Often
6. The Successful Sales Support System
7. Organization and Discipline

THE SUMMARY IN BRIEF

How do you succeed in the profession of selling—while also maintaining your sanity, avoiding ulcers and heart attacks, continuing in a good relationship with your spouse and children, meeting your financial obligations, and preparing for those "golden years"—and still have a moment you can call your own?

Zig Ziglar shows you how, sharing information, direction, inspiration, laughter, and tears that will help you make the necessary choices for a balanced life.

Selling is more than a profession; it is a way of life. And the sales professional of today is concerned about being fundamentally sound. In addition to fundamentals, any resource tool claiming to be "The Ultimate Handbook for the Complete Sales Professional" must be prepared to address those areas outside the actual time spent in face-to-face selling. This book is designed to do just that.

Zig Ziglar has included not only selling techniques and procedures that will add to your income, but also ideas and principles that will add to your "intangible" income (quality of life). Selling is a magnificently rewarding and exciting profession. It is, however, more than a career. It is a way of life—constantly changing and always demanding your best. In *Ziglar on Selling*, you'll discover that the kind of person you *are* is the most essential facet in building a successful professional sales career. You've got to *be* before you can *do*.

In this summary, you'll also learn the following:

- The sales professional of today clearly understands that you can finish school but you never finish your education. Education is a lifelong experience.
- Today's successful persuader must have a specific plan of action.
- When we provide solutions, we do not sell products. People do not buy products. They buy products of the products—known as benefits.
- If you are the "right" kind of person selling the "right" kind of product at a fair price with the "right" intentions, you are in a win-win situation.
- One extra hour per day in high-payoff activity will allow you to outdistance most of the field and surprise yourself in terms of people helped and dollars earned.

THE COMPLETE SUMMARY

You Made the Right Choice

Selling can and should be fun, so let's make it clear from the beginning that a sense of humor combined with self-esteem that allows you to laugh at yourself will play a significant part in your success in your chosen profession.

The Benefits Are for You

As you enter professional sales (whether this is your first experience or you are rededicating yourself to a new level of professionalism), you must stop to realize that choosing to be a sales professional is a daily task. As a matter of fact, make this first entry on your "to do" list: "Today I will be a successful sales professional, and I will learn something today that will make me even more professional tomorrow." If you will begin each day with this commitment to this great profession, there are many benefits that await you, the successful sales professional!

- One of the many great things about the profession is that you are truly your own boss.
- Opportunity is born of independence handled in a responsible manner, and in the sales profession, your opportunities are unparalleled.
- With the possible exceptions of medicine and the ministry, no one is in as good a position to solve problems as you, the professional persuader.
- The family benefits are also enormous. They want to *feel* and *be* a part of your trials and triumphs. Having your spouse and children hear from the boss about what a great job you are doing has significant benefits for the entire family.
- Salespeople consistently move into the executive suites.

Selling in the Modern Market

Today's sales professional is not the plaid-coated, white-belted, snake oil–selling carnival barker or the outdated stereotype of the fast-talking, back-slapping, joke-telling used car salesman. Today's sales professional has the appearance of the Harvard MBA, even if he or she didn't complete high school. Today's sales professional is educated in what is necessary to be successful in the modern world—from computer literacy to market knowledge.

The sales professional of today clearly understands that you can finish school but you never finish your education. You might have finished school with ease, but continuing your education is seldom easy. Education is a lifelong experience. Many men and women who have not earned a degree are brilliantly educated because they never really left school.

Formal Education

Acquire as much formal education as possible and understand that if you do not have that degree, you can still make it big in the world of selling . . . if you take advantage of the learning opportunities all around you.

- One trademark of an "educated" person is the commitment to grow and keep pace with the rapidly changing technology of the time.
- The words we hear most in today's selling world are "change" and "technology."

• The salesperson who refuses to adapt to the changes and capitalize on the technology of today is going to be left at the starting gate and will have a limited career that will not be nearly as productive as it otherwise could be.

Finding Someone Willing to Buy

An ongoing debate at every sales get-together (meaning when two salespeople start talking) is this: "What is the most important part of the selling process?" A disproportionate number believe that "closing sales" more effectively would solve all their selling problems; some say that the only way to sales success is to sell the proper product; others say that handling objections is the key to success; one group claims that making a powerful presentation is the most important area; and still another group believes determining the specific wants and needs of the prospect is most important to sales success. The reality is, if you can't handle all phases of the sales process, you will not sell enough to stay in the profession.

Prospecting

Regardless of how good your closing skills, your product, your ability to handle objections, your presentation, or your skills at determining wants and needs, you are out of business if you don't have a prospect. Here are three vital points:

1. A prospect is an individual or group capable of making the decision on the product or service the salesperson is selling.

2. Prospecting is not an eight-to-five job. Prospecting, when done graciously, can be done in virtually any environment—in social situations, on an airplane, in an airport, at a luncheon or a club meeting, or wherever people are present.

3. The best way to begin prospecting is to display a genuine interest in the other person, which brings us back to an oft-made point. When you're the right kind of person, your chances of becoming an effective salesperson are much, much better.

Selling in the Real World

Few who join the proud profession of selling avoid the anxious and excited feelings that accompany the sales call. In fact, according to a study done on "fears in performance" by George W. Dudley and Shannon L. Goodson, authors of *Earning What You're Worth? The Psychology of Sales Call Reluctance*, salespeople who struggle with call reluctance earn an average of 80 percent less in commissions per year than those who overcome the problem—even if they are equal in talent, ability, motivation, intelligence, preparation, and experience.

To Overcome Call Reluctance, Remember the Following:

1. Take personal responsibility for building self-confidence and self-esteem.

2. Selling is a transference of feeling.

3. You can have everything you want in life if you will just help enough other people get what they want.

4. Tame the telephone. Make it work for you instead of against you.

5. To be the winner you were born to be, you must plan to win, prepare to win, and expect to win.

6. Use the "Experimental Syndrome" to overcome feelings of rejection by making each call a positive "experiment" instead of a negative "experience."

7. Get on a regular schedule and make an appointment with yourself to be face-to-face with a prospect at the same time every day!

THE SALES WORLD IS A STAGE

*P*rofessional persuaders, such as stage and screen actors, professional speakers, managers, teachers, doctors, and sales professionals, have many things in common, not the least of which is anxiety at "the moment of truth." Whether that moment comes in front of an audience, a camera, a crowd of people, the office staff, students, patients, or prospects, anxiety is real. The good news is that you can join the group of achievers who have overcome reluctance by getting the feeling of anxiety to work for you instead of against you.

Sell by Design, Not by Chance

Today's successful persuader must have a specific plan of action. Since there is a direct correlation between money earned and time spent with a prospect, you can eliminate unnecessary planning by applying a formula with transferable value. In the world of selling, we need a plan of action that will transcend product line and situational differences. Our planned selling process consists of a four-step formula:

1. Need Analysis
2. Need Awareness
3. Need Solution
4. Need Satisfaction

Pavlovian Selling

In 1904, Russian physiologist Ivan Petrovich Pavlov won the Nobel Prize in Medicine for his research. Pavlov did research on digestion and the nervous system. He conducted experiments with dogs in which he rang a bell just before feeding time. In subsequent experiments, he would ring the bell and the dogs would salivate—whether the food was present or not.

Too many salespeople are ringing a bell and hoping the prospects will salivate when, in fact, just the opposite happens. If your actions come across as what some perceive as stereotypically "salesy," the prospects are turned off. Successful sales professionals use a process or design—a blueprint.

Questions Are the Answer

If you were to ask someone a series of questions in a professional manner that showed a sincere interest in him and his company, what would he think of you? If you handle this portion of the sales presentation in the proper manner, he would learn that you are not just another salesperson out to separate him from his money. Instead, he would discover that you are truly interested in helping him!

Questions demonstrate that the purpose of the call is to find the prospect's needs and interests while gathering information, so that together you can learn how your goods or services meet the prospect's need (solve the problem). You communicate this message: "Let's work together to discover the need (problem) before you offer a solution." The sales professional of the twenty-first century must clearly understand that the sales prospect of the twenty-first century is better informed and more cynical than any consumer in history.

The Proper Questioning Process

Three basic types of questions allow us to discover the needs and wants of our clients and potential customers. And all questions—emotional or logical—fall into one of these three categories:

Open-Door Questions. These questions allow the persons being questioned to go wherever they like with their responses.

Closed-Door Questions. If an open-door question is designed to allow prospects to move freely wherever their thoughts take them, then the closed-door question is designed to keep them in a certain area for clarification or embellishment.

Yes or No Questions. This third type of question demands a direct response.

MOTIVATION OR MANIPULATION

Thomas Carlyle said, "A great man shows his greatness by the way he treats the little man." The value you place on people determines whether you are a motivator or a manipulator of men. Motivation is moving together for a mutual advantage. Manipulation is moving together for your own advantage. That is a substantial difference. With motivation, everybody wins. With manipulation, only the manipulator wins.

The Conversational "Interrogation"

Even some very successful sales professionals have difficulty firing off a series of questions to a prospect they are meeting for the first time. Still others struggle with asking for information without giving some first. The **POGO** formula will allow you to get involved in a conversational interview process that will be comfortable for you and the prospect.

- **P** stands for "**person**." Anything that expresses a sincere interest in the prospect will be valuable to you.
- **O** stands for "**organization**." As the conversation about the person draws to a close, move to the organization.
- **G** stands for "**goals**." This is the time for gathering information about personal and professional goals, for example, "What do you plan to accomplish in the next six months?" and "What goals do you have in place for the next year?" (both open-door questions).
- **O** stands for "**obstacles**" to reaching the goals just discussed.

Get to the Point

Some prospects are incredibly impatient, and even as early as Need Analysis they show their impatience. They are driven and impetuous and want "just the facts" without any "window dressing" along the way. When the prospect demands to know "what it will do for me and how much it will cost," you need to move immediately into benefit selling.

There is no need for you to get off track or panic or begin closing immediately. The prospect has sent you a definite signal: Get to the point. So get to the point in the manner that is best for the prospect. Each step is important or you would not have planned it, so stay with your plan but do an abbreviated version of each step. Just "move along."

Making the Lights Go On

Even when you are sure you have discovered the client's need, you must continue to probe for two basic reasons: (1) to be sure you have identified the true need and not a symptom of the need; and (2) to be sure the prospect understands that there really is a need.

Since companies, especially small ones that do not have an active, competent board of directors, are often run or dominated by one person, they often deny problems even when they are told and shown the specifics. However, when a skilled sales professional probes with the right questions, the same person who was denying the problem is permitted to "discover" the problem. Since he has discovered it, he will be far more open to discovering solutions—your goods or services (which he has also discovered).

Training for Need Awareness

If you are going to help the prospect become aware of specific needs, four areas of knowledge will benefit you:

1. *Product Knowledge.* You can never know too much about your product. Get information on its history, how it is made or manufactured, and how it does what it does and why.

2. *Industry Knowledge.* The more you know about your industry in general, the more you are able to understand the all-important "why." The more you understand about the industry you have chosen to invest your career life in, the more effective you may become.

3. *Pricing Knowledge.* Why does your product or service require the investment that you are asking from a prospect? Focus on showing prospects how and why the price of your product is fair to them. Never forget that price involves a great deal more than money!

4. *Application Knowledge.* The use or application of your product will help you enormously in showing the prospect the need for your product. If you understand how your product, goods, or services can be used and you can help others understand the process, you will help more people and make more sales.

All the Lights Are On

Once the light has gone on for you (you know the prospect's need and know you have the solution) and has gone on for the prospect (the person knows that there is a need and that you have a solution), you must move to the Need Solution segment of the sales process.

Selling Solutions to People's Problems When we provide solutions, we do not sell products. People do not buy products. They buy products of the products—known as benefits.

Personalize the benefits for the prospect.

Paint the person into the picture driving that luxury car, receiving compliments on the beautiful dress or suit, looking at the sunset on the lake where the new home has been constructed, or sitting in the comfortable retirement environment provided by the investment being made.

Paint the picture so your prospect sees personal benefits.

Feature—Function—Benefit

In the great profession of selling, there is much talk about features, functions, and benefits, but what are these wonderful things? In order to "lead with need," we must have an understanding of the basic definitions of these three key words:

1. By definition, a *feature* is a part of the product or service—or what the product or service is.

2. By definition, a *function* is the act that a particular part of the product or service performs—or what that particular part of the product or service does.

3. By definition, a *benefit* is the advantage in using the feature and function—or what the feature and function do for the prospect/client.

To avoid confusion and make the proper use of feature, function, and benefit, we need to add the bridge. The bridge is a phrase preparing the prospect to hear the benefit. Sample bridges might include:

"The advantage to you, Mr. Prospect, is . . ."

"You will enjoy this because. . . ."

"The benefit to you, Ms. Prospect, is . . ."

The ABCs of Closing Sales

Closing sales doesn't have to be painful for you or the prospect. On the contrary, if you are the "right" kind of person selling the "right" kind of product at a fair price with the "right" intentions, you are in a win-win situation. And a win-win situation means that closing the sale is a positive and pleasant experience for both you and the prospect.

People Want to Say Yes Remember, as a persuader, whether you are a doctor, dentist, or computer salesperson, in most cases the prospect really does want to say yes, particularly if you are pleasant, professional, and at least reasonably friendly. The prospect might not be able to verbalize the feeling, but it is there, so the odds are in the professional salesperson's favor. So ask for the order. Do it pleasantly and professionally, but ask!

Asking and Receiving Although there are literally hundreds of ways to ask for the order, you should focus on only three.

If you use one or all of these three ways of asking for the order for ninety days, you will close more sales more often, and you will be prepared to develop three closes of your own based on your experience. The key is not to reinvent the wheel. Let these three methods be the foundation upon which you build your successful sales career.

1. The *three-question close* helps ask for the order:

"Can you see where my product or service would _____?"

"Are you interested in _____?"

"If you were ever going to start _____, when do you think would be the best time to start?"

2. The *probability close* helps the prospect understand how close he is to making the purchase:

"On a scale of 1 to 10, with 10 meaning you are ready to place your order, where would you stand right now?"

"What would it take to move you to a 10?"

3. The *summary close* may seem basic, but don't be fooled. Summarize all the reasons the prospect has given you for buying and ask for the order! Relight the fire through summarization.

Closing More Sales More Often

Let's look at a concept that will allow you to handle real objections in an efficient and effective way so you can close more sales more often. When objections occur, the professional salesperson will get "QUIET." Each letter in the formula stands for a word that will allow you to help your prospects gather enough information to overcome their objections. When you get an objection, you pause and think QUIET.

- **Question.** Begin with a question.
- **Understand.** You must ask questions so that you can understand the objection.

- **Identify.** Once you understand the objection, you must identify the objection.
- **Empathize.** To identify the proper objection (and not be fooled by a false objection), you must empathize with the prospect.
- **Test.** If you empathize instead of sympathize with the prospect, you are ready to test the objection. When you test the objection and prove it real, you can eliminate the prospect's concerns and dramatically improve your chance of making the sale.

This Is Why You Are in Business—to Make Sales

The professional salesperson will bring out all the objections as early as possible so each objection can be dealt with effectively. As a matter of fact, sales professionals often take the objection and use it as the major reason the prospect should buy.

Remember, your goal is not to prove how many objections you can answer but to prove how much your goods and services can benefit the prospect.

Beyond "Customer Service" to "Customer Satisfaction"

The days of "customer service" as the standard of excellence are long gone! Today, everybody talks about the importance of "customer satisfaction." In this competitive market the only way to get ahead (and sometimes, the only way to survive) is to go beyond customer service to customer satisfaction.

Can We "Afford" Unhappy Customers? Research indicates that roughly 90 percent of our unhappy customers simply stop doing business with us without saying anything at all about it to us. Unfortunately, they do tell friends, relatives, neighbors, and complete strangers. Question: Can we afford unhappy customers?

All of us can be kind, gentle, courteous, friendly, enthusiastic, and optimistic to the people who give us the order, treat us in a friendly manner, and are easy to deal with.

Your value to your company comes basically from the skills you develop in dealing with everybody, including disgruntled customers and prospects, in an effective and professional manner.

The Glamour of the Road

Since the earliest days of recorded time, there has been confusion and misconception about what happens when the "provider" leaves home for an extended period. The person left behind often feels left out of all the fun and excitement.

Today's selling professional realizes that the glamour of travel wears off (if not out) after a very few trips, and what remains is plain old-fashioned hard work! With the proper perspective, one can take this potentially negative situation and turn it into a positive winner!

- **Variety.** No two days are the same.
- **Competitive Edge.** The sales professional who learns to travel success-fully on a regular basis, represent the company properly, and keep family life well balanced has a competitive edge in the job market.
- **Education Opportunities.** Travel time in the car or plane can allow you great quantities of listening or reading time that you just cannot get in an office setting.
- **Cultural Enrichment.** When company travel takes you to areas of cultural interest, you can broaden your cultural base and enrich your personal and family life.
- **Social Skills.** Travel invariably forces you into daily use of social skills that might lie dormant in the office environment.
- **Physical Fitness.** Too many of our friends in selling use the road as an excuse for poor physical fitness instead of a reason for success in this important area of life.
- **Creative Time.** Thinking time or creative time is different from solitude. In your quiet time, there will most often be no agenda; in creative time, you will focus on a specific client, customer, situation, scenario, or concern.

Withdrawal One of the most difficult parts of traveling is the actual leaving. If you have ever been involved in a tearful "Daddy, please don't go" or "Mommy, can't you please stay home with me today?" scene, you know the agony of withdrawal. From time to time all of us have suffered from the pains associated with "withdrawal" or leaving home for the road.

As in so many areas of our lives, the key to success in departing for the road is preparation. Leave a complete itinerary, including addresses and phone numbers, with each family member. Predetermine how emergencies are to be handled. Let the children know the essentials: when, where, for how long, with whom, and why.

Decompression There are times when coming home can be more difficult than leaving. The road has a rhythm and pace of its own, and rarely is it similar to the flow of activity in the home. Ask yourself these questions:

1. Do you begin by inquiring about how the week of the nontraveler has gone or by sharing information about the trip?

2. Do you initiate conversation or respond to conversation?

All of this is to say that when you return home, you should have an agreement with your mate that you will first talk about and deal with the positive and pleasant aspects of what happened to you and the family during your absence.

Once the pleasant reentry has been established and things have regained some sense of normalcy (no sooner than after dinner), the challenges of the time away need to be quietly and calmly addressed.

The Successful Sales Support System

To build a career in the world of sales, you will need the support and cooperation of many people. Let's begin with the members of the company team: the accounting department, the billing department, the shipping department, and perhaps the public relations department.

Have you ever stopped to realize that you have two sets of customers? The clients and prospects to whom you make presentations are your external customers, those outside your organization. The second group includes the internal clients and prospects who work for your organization. Obviously, you are not selling the same products and services to both groups, but you are selling!

When you fail to treat co-workers with the same courtesy and respect shown to customers, you will pay the price all unsuccessful salespeople pay for forgetting who their customers really are.

The Family

Since the entire family is involved in the salesperson's career, the wise salesperson not only confers with the family but also shares the results of efforts. For example, there are frequently contests involving trips and prizes. These might necessitate a heavier workload and more absence from the home. The salesperson should call a sales meeting, share with the family the details of the contest, solicit their help, get their involvement, listen to their input, and then let them share in the rewards.

Work to Eliminate Financial Pressures

Your co-workers and family have financial concerns. All of us can be more effective in dealing with financial pressures by following a few simple guidelines:

1. Begin financial planning today.

2. Plan with your spouse.

3. Use a record-keeping system.

4. Establish spending priorities.

5. Break away from financial myths.

Organization and Discipline

Because salespeople have so much freedom and independence in the world of selling, they do not always exercise good judgment or sound integrity as they go about the business of selling.

Discipline yourself to do the things you need to do when you need to do them, and the day will come when you will be able to do the things you want to do when you want to do them.

Recipe for Sales Success

Generally speaking, the high-producing sales professional does work harder than the average producer. The reality is, simply outworking your competition will put you in the upper echelons of selling. You do not have to work eighty-hour and ninety-hour weeks. One extra hour per day in high-payoff activity will allow you to outdistance most of the field and surprise yourself in terms of people helped and dollars earned.

Add integrity, discipline, and organization to the recipe, and you catapult very quickly into the top 10 percent of all salespeople. Throw in a constant quest for knowledge and learning about how to become "even better" as a professional salesperson while becoming adept at the new procedures and the latest industry trends, and you will move into the upper 5 percent.

Getting the Person Right

In the world of selling, when we get the "person" right, it's much easier to get the "salesperson" right. Realistically, until you get right, your sales world won't be right. The secret to getting you right is getting your attitude right.

An Attitude "Vaccination"? How can you inoculate yourself against the wrong attitude? Truthfully, there is no way you can completely build an armored shell to totally protect against feelings of frustration, disappointment, and fear. If you could, you would not be a very successful salesperson. The reason is simple: You are an emotional person and feel a full range of emotions. If we didn't feel disappointment when a prospect refuses to take action on the "greatest product on the face of the earth," we couldn't feel enthusiastic about what we are selling. To be successful in selling, we must have the capacity to feel both "up" and "down."

Since we are not immune to those "down" feelings, the question is, What can we do to limit their frequency, length, and severity? Taking control is important because our attitude determines how many calls we make, when we start, how we finish, and what results we obtain each day.

You cannot control the circumstances in your life, but there are many things you can do to control your mental attitude as you deal with those circumstances.

Finding the Right Mental Attitude Here are some specific action steps for you to take in developing the right attitude:

1. Accept the fact that you *can* control your attitude.

2. Make the commitment to do whatever is necessary to take control of your attitude.

3. Evaluate each book, television program, movie, and video before you actually start reading or viewing it with a question: "Is this going to help me in my personal, family, or business life, or is there a better use I could make of this time to advance my personal, family, or business life?"

4. Learn one new word each day.

5. Read something of value to you personally and professionally for at least twenty minutes every day—something that is informative, inspiring, and educational.

6. Turn your car into the University of Automobile.

7. Choose your associates carefully.

How Do You Maintain the Right Attitude? Each of us can be number one. You are number one when you can honestly look in the mirror at the end of the day and say, "I used my ability today. I gave it my best shot." In short, you realize that true success is not necessarily beating someone else; real success, enjoyment, and happiness come from using your own ability.

HOW TO MASTER THE ART OF SELLING

by Tom Hopkins

The commission-based pay structure of most sales jobs creates a unique setup in which to work. Success, whether financial or otherwise, is limited only by the salesperson's own abilities and drive. Unlike an office job, where extra work rarely creates a dividend in one's paycheck, more sales will always translate to more money for salespeople. The job comes with a built-in motivational method, and it's part of the reason why sales draws some of the most determined individuals to its ranks.

Tom Hopkins is one individual who saw sales as his opportunity for a better life. He went from carrying building materials on construction sites into the field of real estate sales. His success was anything but instant. In fact, Hopkins's first few months on the job nearly left him bankrupt. It was a chance trip to a sales training seminar by master trainer J. Douglas Edwards that turned Hopkins from also-ran to superstar. According to his bio, at Hopkins's peak, he sold the equivalent of one house per day for an entire year.

As more and more people clamored for the secrets of his meteoric rise, Hopkins overcame his fears of public speaking to address the questions coming his way. Where less than a decade earlier he had been an audience member, Hopkins was now the expert giving the advice to up-and-comers. He decided to put the essential elements of his years as a sales trainer into a single volume. The result, *How to Master the Art of Selling*, is one of the classic books for salespeople at any level. Hopkins's goal is as straightforward as his writing style: to turn average performers into champions.

Readers may wonder if Hopkins's days laboring on construction sites gave him the work ethic that's infused into the heart of his message. He is praised for acknowledging that the sales profession is one that requires constant hard work. Like great athletes or musicians, salespeople operate in a finite number of situations with a basic set of skills. As Hopkins discusses in the text, it is the repetitive drilling and refinement of these skills that pushes the best sales professionals to new heights. His insights on the questioning process and the need to study objections will motivate salespeople to examine their own processes.

So much of a salesperson's success is tied to the ability to prospect, and Hopkins delivers excellent advice in this area. His discussions of referral and non-referral prospecting will help newer sales professionals discover the varied ways to meet and connect with potential buyers. Hopkins's instructions for prospecting are coupled nicely with his thoughts on dynamic presentations. All of these ideas ride atop the undercurrent of effort. Hopkins is as much a drill instructor as he is a workhorse salesman. He frequently points out that there is no secret formula that will turn an average performer into a great one. The champions of the sales world are those who are relentless in their pursuit of the mastery of the basics. This book gives salespeople the knowledge, but the effort must come from within.

HOW TO MASTER THE ART OF SELLING
by Tom Hopkins

CONTENTS
1. The Sources of Sensational Selling Success
2. The Basics of Questioning
3. Creating the Selling Climate
4. Finding the People to Sell
5. Nonreferral Prospecting Methods
6. Finessing the First Meeting
7. Closing Is Sweet Success
8. Fortune Building Starts with Time Planning

THE SUMMARY IN BRIEF

Selling is the highest-paid hard work—and the lowest-paid easy work—that you can find. And another exciting thing about selling is that the choice is yours, all yours. What you achieve in your selling career is entirely up to you, and what anyone else wants won't make much difference.

What so few of us are willing to accept is this fundamental truth: Great salespeople, like great athletes, simply do the basics very well. Some of us would like to believe that there's a shortcut around the basics, that there's a secret formula out there somewhere for just sitting back and letting the money roll in. The sooner you can get rid of that illusion, the sooner you can get on with reaching the heights you want to reach through effective use of the basics.

So stop excusing yourself from the hard work of learning how to be competent in your sales career. Whether you think you're a wonder or a nonwonder, top sales trainer Tom Hopkins can lead you on a journey to help you succeed in the profession of selling.

Hopkins writes with a very simple premise: The skills, knowledge, and drive within you are what will make you great, and these qualities can be expanded and intensified—if you're willing to invest time, effort, and money in yourself.

In this summary, you will also learn the following:

- How to create the perfect selling climate
- How to prospect effectively
- How to finesse the first meeting
- How to handle objections
- What to do when you hear the word "no"
- Why it is important to master different closes

THE COMPLETE SUMMARY

The Sources of Sensational Selling Success

Those new to selling or veterans wanting to boost their incomes are smart to ask about qualities they can develop within themselves in order to succeed. Here is a list of twelve that seem fairly common to those who achieve champion status in selling:

1. Champions project the unmistakable stamp of competence with their attire and grooming. Just by looking at them, you know that you're in the presence of a powerful force—people who have a purpose and are ready to carry it out to the fullest.

2. Champions take tremendous pride in the profession of selling and in themselves as human beings.

3. Champions radiate confidence.

4. Champions close warmly. They never close people they know shouldn't be closed. Champions don't push people with warmth. They are sincere in their desire to help clients.

5. Most Champions look to only one person for their self-assurance, and that one person is themselves.

6. Champions want to get rich.

7. Champions have a burning desire to achieve. They don't quit no matter how much pain and how many challenges they encounter, because those things are nothing compared with their desire.

8. Champions learn what their fears are, and often that's not easy, since we're all so good at concealing them from ourselves. But Champions persevere in this. They learn what they fear. Then they attack what they fear and overcome it.

9. Champions know that no matter how good they get, they're still going to fail some of the time between their successes. It's all a part of the game we call selling. So they don't have to hide their true feelings while they're failing because they're still filled with enthusiasm.

10. Champions get emotionally involved with the folks they serve. Champions really care about their clients, and this true feeling comes through loud and clear.

11. Champions don't take rejection personally. Do you take rejection personally? You can't prevent situations of this kind from happening, but you can train yourself to take them in stride. These prospects haven't rejected you as a person. They've rejected your product.

12. Champions believe in continuing education. They study technique. They learn new skills. The place to start improving your environment is inside your own skull.

The Difference Between the Have and the Have Not

Champions collect sales objections. They like to hear them from other strong salespeople, read them in books, and think them up themselves. They enjoy finding new objections anytime—except when they're with customers. And you can be sure that as fast as Champions find new objections, they develop their best responses to them. But they don't stop there. They practice, drill, and rehearse their best responses. Before they ever hear the new objection in a sales situation, they're ready to instantly fire their best answer at it because they've practiced, drilled, and rehearsed the answers to all the objections they have already heard. That's professionalism. That's the type of thinking and action that brings in the big money.

The theory is simple, but its application is demanding, specialized for every product or service, and in a constant state of evolution. You don't just learn a few objections, memorize the answers, and then turn your mind off the subject of objection response forever. Constant alertness for new objections and better responses to old objections marks the Champion.

Question Right and Sink Your Teeth into Sales Success

Most salespeople have a tendency to talk too fast too much and to try to control every conversation. That's probably where the stereotypical image of a salesperson as pushy originated. Champion sales professionals are just the opposite. They understand that to be successful in selling, you need to learn to listen twice as much as you talk.

Twelve Pointers on Question Technique

1. Ask questions to gain and maintain control rather than letting a potential client take control of the conversation and provide important details in a random fashion. You gain and maintain control of the selling situation by asking questions that help you determine the best solution to the client's needs.

2. Ask questions to indicate the broad areas the client is interested in where you might be of service.

3. Ask questions to get the minor "yeses" that will start the stream of minor agreements that will swell into the major river of acceptance of your proposition.

4. Ask questions to arouse and direct the client's emotions toward the purchase.

5. Ask questions to isolate objections.

6. Ask questions to answer objections.

7. Ask questions to determine the benefits that the prospect wants to own.

8. Ask questions to acknowledge a fact. If you say it, the client can doubt you; if the client says it, he or she must believe it to be true.

9. Ask questions to confirm that (a) the client is going ahead and (b) you should now go on to the next step in your selling sequence.

10. Ask questions that involve the client in ownership decisions about your offering.

11. Ask questions to help the client rationalize decisions that he or she wants to make. You do this because you want the client to make those decisions, too.

12. Ask questions that close the client on the purchase.

Don't make the mistake of concentrating solely on what you're going to tell clients. Don't overlook the vital importance of asking the right questions and varying your methods to fit their answers.

The Basics of Questioning

Before you ask anyone a question, be sure it's a question they'll know the answer to. If they don't know the answer, they may feel threatened by it and you.

For example, if you help people make buying decisions on computers, don't assume they know every bit and byte of information about computers. Begin by asking them questions that will be easy for them to answer.

For instance, "Jim, most people who are looking for a laptop do so because they move around a lot. Do you travel mostly in town where it will be with you in your car, or will you be primarily taking it on airplanes?" He'll know that answer. If you had asked, "What weight of machine were you looking for?" or "What type of carrying case will you need?" Jim might not have known because he doesn't even know what the choices are.

Open questions are those that require thought on the part of the person you're asking. They have to think about their responses. Remember in school the who, what, when, where, why, and how questions? When you ask a question beginning with one of those words, prospects can't give you a quick or reflexive answer. They have to think and give you some bit of information that will be helpful to you in your sales presentation.

Closed questions are aimed at getting a specific answer. Normally, the answers to closed questions are fairly short. They could even be simple yes-or-no questions, the answers to which allow you to move the sales process forward.

Making These Strategies Yours

One of the great challenges in training salespeople is to provide an effective framework of techniques, theories, methods, and knowledge without stifling the creativity of those who learn.

Professional salespeople never give prospects the impression that they're pushing—for the simple reason that they never push. But they do lead. By not talking all the time, by listening most of the time, by asking artful questions, Champions lead their prospects from the initial contact to happy involvement in owning the product or service. In all this alert and pointed questioning, true professionals maintain a friendly attitude of interest and understanding that encourages prospects to open up and give the desired information freely.

It all starts with your intimate and detailed knowledge of what you're selling. You can't prospect with strength unless you know your offering; you can't demonstrate or present with strength unless you know your offering; and you can't close with strength unless you know your offering—which is the product or service that you're selling.

That knowledge will include an adequate understanding of the competition and a superior knowledge of what qualifications your buyers must have. Without such knowledge, how can you intelligently decide, for both yourself and the other person, whether any given prospect can—or should—become your client? It's impossible. From product knowledge springs the expertise to work with clients in the effective and professional manner that earns high income.

Creating the Selling Climate

Champions sell only the benefits and features that the prospect they're working with wants to buy. It's critical to success: Don't sell what you want; sell what they want. Champions don't sell benefits before finding out what benefits the prospect wants.

People want more than they can get. They want it all but you know they can't have it all, so you have to decide, among your many products and services and their many desires, what specific item will work best for them.

Catch the Change on the Move

What is the emotional process that leads to a purchase? It begins with a new development in the buyer's self-image. That is, the buyer sees him- or herself in a new way. If the projected purchase is small, that change need only be small, but if the purchase is a large one in relation to the buyer's income, the change in self-image that makes the purchase possible will be large. Such a change can come about very quickly. Champions are adept at spotting these changes in self-image as they occur during sales interviews.

- First, be genuinely interested in doing your best for clients and show this interest by asking questions that will tell you what they're seeking to accomplish. Rise above the limitations of your own taste and preferences.
- Second, use your expertise to guide clients to the best solution for them that your inventory provides.
- Third, wait for positive stimulus from clients. When you get it, if you believe they've found something that helps them achieve whatever effect they want, reinforce their image about that purchase.

Emotion. That's where it's at. Unless you're arousing positive emotions, you're raising negative emotions—and you've lost the sale. Positive emotions trigger sales; negative emotions destroy sales.

Why Don't I Do What I Know I Should Do?

The reason why you don't do what you know you should do is that you're in conflict with yourself. This conflict comes about because the forward push of your wants and needs can't overcome the backward push of your fears and anxieties. Resolving these fears and anxieties is surprisingly easy when you know how to do it. The first requirement is to admit that you're like everyone else—you have them. The next one is to decide that you're not going to let those beatable fears and anxieties stand between you and what you want in life.

If you're depressed now about your sales performance, ever have been in the past, or think it's possible that you could be in the future, you need to review the sources of motivation.

The Motivators

- **Money.** Money is good so long as what you earn is in direct proportion to the service you give. Money is a scoreboard reflection of the service you give.
- **Security.** Maslow's Hierarchy of Needs teaches that the average human being strives daily to supply physical needs—that is, to obtain security. Money is a tremendous motivator, both as a direct measure of success and as a provider of a sense of security.
- **Achievement.** Almost everyone wants to achieve, but almost no one wants to do what's necessary to achieve. Look at this from another perspective as well. Everyone you know also wants to achieve. If what you offer through your products and services helps them achieve what they're after, they'll help you with what you wish to achieve.
- **Recognition.** We all crave and require recognition. That's why this motivator has such awesome power when it's used at full throttle.
- **Acceptance.** Surround yourself with people most like the person you want to become. Don't hang around with people whose financial and emotional thinking is on a lower level than yours. They won't help you expand your horizons, and they can't inspire you.
- **Self-acceptance.** Self-acceptance marks the day when the opinions of other people don't control you anymore. Why do so many of us fail to attain self-acceptance? Because we don't limit the number of people we must have approval from. Because we demand more approval from the world than the world is willing to give—and weaken our action in a vain attempt to get it.

Learn to Love "No"

What's the only thing that stands between you and everything you want from your selling career?

The word "no."

The challenge afflicting most of us here is fundamental: We have the wrong attitude toward that most basic word. This attitude, held since early childhood, has long outlived its usefulness in our lives—especially since we're now in the profession of selling, where the word "no" keeps us from serving others and achieving our goals.

Confronted by a prospect who has suddenly turned hostile, average salespeople get anxious. Champions see the situation in an entirely different light. They know at once that their prospect is in pain—that countering the prospect's hostility with more hostility is nonproductive, and that their own dignity is beside the point. As human beings, they want to help relieve the prospect's pain; as businesspeople, they want to move that pain aside so they can get on with business.

Here's how Champions win by casting themselves as the good guy: They keep calm, listen carefully, and speak to the heart of the matter at the first opportunity.

How to Reject the Negative Effects of Rejection No one in sales will dispute that being able to overcome the ill effects of rejection is vital to success in our chosen field. What's needed is a system that will allow us to do that all the time—the Champion Formula for Rejecting Rejection.

The first step in this formula requires you to determine the cash value of each rejection that you received. Step two is to determine how many people you have to contact in order to close one sale. You are not paid by the sale; you are paid by the contact. This isn't a weird, twisted, nonsensical way of looking at sales activity—it's reality. No contacts mean no sales, which mean no earnings. Earnings are not started by sales; they are started by contacts.

Finding the People to Sell

It's sad, but the average salesperson doesn't really believe that getting to know people is the key to every door in selling.

Selling is finding people to sell and selling the people you find. In the beginning, you'll try nearly anything. As you grow in your skills, you'll see what works and what doesn't work. You'll constantly tweak what you say, how you present yourself, the material you send people, the number of times and ways you keep in touch. The only way to know what's working best is to keep track of the results. That's where ratios come into play.

Ratios that will help you manage your selling business are serious stuff. Here are some that you should be keeping track of—and striving to improve:

- Prospecting calls/hours spent
- Prospecting calls/appointments made
- Appointments/sales

- Hours worked/money earned
- Prospecting calls made last month/income this month

A Champion always makes one successful call after a rejection. Why? If you stop on rejection, what do you carry with you the rest of the day? Rejection. Champions are determined to keep their winning attitude. If they hang up on a negative note, their winning attitude is damaged for the rest of the day.

Four Ways to Hover Until You're Ready to Fly

If you're in a situation where no business at all is coming at you, you're dead. You have to either change your attitude or change your job, because you're not going to make a dime at what you're doing.

But you may be in a situation or territory where there's a flow of business that comes at you without any prospecting on your part: company-supplied leads, repeat business from established customers, things of that sort. The following methods will allow you to hold that business, and even build it up, while you're also building confidence and learning your product or service:

1. *Handle problems fast.* If someone has a challenge with your product or service, take care of it right now.

2. *Call people back immediately.* One of the biggest challenges most salespeople have is that they don't want to pick up messages and call people back. Return calls now. It's the only way you can build up a happy clientele.

3. *Keep every promise made.* To make the sale, some salespeople will promise everything. And then they don't do one thing they promised to do if they can avoid it. You'll never get a referral that way.

4. *Keep in touch.* Call or see your clients regularly. Letters and mailing pieces can't carry the full load because there's no feedback from the disgruntled or from those being wooed by a competitor. Phone them. Listen for their itch cycles.

Nonreferral Prospecting Methods

These are the leads you generate where there's no referral involved. Keep this in mind: They're not prequalified, so you'll only be closing 10 percent of them. Therefore, you need to learn not only how to find new leads but also how to prequalify them. A lead is prequalified when you know that the emotional and logical requirements for benefitting from your product or service are all present.

The sale depends on emotion backed by logic. The emotion comes first and the logic follows. It does not happen the other way around. You prequalify people by finding out whether the emotion that's necessary to carry the sale to completion exists or can be created.

Each general type of product or service has its own set of vital qualification factors. You probably know those that are important in selecting the people most likely to buy what you're selling. If you don't have a clear idea of who buys what you sell, one of your top priorities should be to research this question. A careful study of your company's files of completed sales should quickly tell you all you need to know. Here are a few ideas:

- **The itch cycle.** A Champion keeps in touch with all his or her past buyers. These buyers are an important group among the select few who have favored him or her with their trust. So he or she makes certain to be there to scratch when the itch strikes.
- **The orphan adoption.** Every company has turnover in its sales force. When salespeople leave an organization, what do they leave behind? Their clientele. Their abandoned clientele can become your gold mine.
- **Your local newspapers.** Newspapers carry lots of little items about people who have been promoted, because that's one of the ways newspapers build their own clientele. You can count on a steady flow of these notices. Skim these articles and send those who were promoted a note of congratulations.
- **Claim staking.** Make yourself known, learn the ropes, and get acquainted with carefully selected organizations where you feel comfortable and are meeting people who are prequalified—by income and interests—for owning your offering.
- **Servicing your service department.** Check with the service department and find out who's calling in to get their existing equipment worked on. Service calls give you the perfect opportunity to go over and get these people happily involved in the new model that'll do a better job for them with no downtime.
- **Community involvement.** Consider getting involved in local community events. This will allow you the opportunity to meet others while doing good.

Referral Prospecting

The referral lead is the easiest to close. In fact, you'll spend half the time selling the referred, prequalified lead than you will selling the company-generated, nonqualified lead. Even more exciting is the fact that Champions will close 40 percent to 60 percent of their qualified referrals. Compare this with the results they get working with their nonreferred and unqualified leads. The success rate with referrals is 400 percent to 600 percent of what it is with nonreferrals.

The process of getting referrals—or "quality introductions"—begins the moment you meet people. When you first meet potential clients, you work on building their trust. People won't buy from you if they don't trust you. During your initial rapport-building chat, you must be like a detective and look for clues as to the small groups of people this person knows.

A Spectator Sport Buying Is Not

Operating their mouths at high speed, some salespeople put on amazing demonstrations. They flip levers, punch buttons, zip stuff around in a high-tech presentation. And out of the product they're demonstrating, be it a stamping machine, software application, or copier, comes a flood of perfect parts, data, or copies, respectively. But they don't sell much with these superb performances.

Why? Because apathy rushes in where involvement fails to tread. Buying is action. It can't take place unless there are decisions, and decisions require a switched-on mind. Watching instead of doing is a switch-off. The longer your prospects are switched off, the harder it'll be to switch them back on again when you want the paperwork approved at the end of your demonstration.

The truth is that you're the star twice when you master the client-participation demonstration: first when you have your prospects happily involved in your demonstration and product and second when you walk out with the endorsed file copies of an order.

Put Champion Selling Power in Your Presentations and Demonstrations

Now we're getting into the area you probably enjoy most: working face-to-face with buyers. Likely you're good at this—and you spend too much of your time doing it. Research indicates that most salespeople put in 80 percent to 90 percent of their time presenting and demonstrating, leaving only 10 percent to 20 percent for other things.

Champions, on the other hand, spend only 40 percent of their time presenting or demonstrating and no more than 10 percent prospecting (some Champions spend no time at all prospecting because referrals keep them busy); about 50 percent of their time goes into the vital areas of qualifying and planning. These percentages apply to net selling time—that is, to the total amount of working time remaining after the trade shows and company meetings are attended, the routine paperwork is done, and the old accounts are serviced.

Repetition is the mother of learning, yet average salespeople don't like repetition. For one thing, they've used their material so many times that it's stale to them. In many cases, they've begun to think that anyone who doesn't get what they're saying the first time they say it is a lost cause. All too often, non-Champions have gone worse than stale on their presentation and feel it would be better off buried.

Champions, on the other hand, never tire of phrases that work, strategies that sell, and ideas that make sense to their buyers and money for them. Champions discard things in their presentations when they stop working, and not before. And Champions never forget that they're working with people who don't know their specialty as well as they do: They're always courteous and deferential about their superior knowledge in the narrow area of their expertise. Champions work happily with lines they've said ten thousand times.

Finessing the First Meeting

The first impression you make with potential clients will make or break your chances of serving them today and for many years down the road. The first principle of approaching potential new clients is to come on softly so that you relax them enough to allow their desire for your product to overcome their fear of being sold or talked into something.

The steps involved in meeting a potential client correctly are smiling, looking into his or her eyes, offering a proper greeting, and, if you're greeting a nonreferred prospect, not expecting to shake hands (if it's a recontact or referred lead, let the prospect decide).

Qualification Is the Key to Quota Busting

Many salespeople never qualify before presenting or demonstrating. They simply never do it. As soon as they get near warm bodies, they put their heads down and plow right into excitedly telling them all about the product or service, whether they need it or not. Some of them do it because they don't know how to qualify, and others aren't organized well enough to tone down their excitement by learning more about whom they're talking with and whether or not it would be wise to proceed.

Whatever explanation there may be for failing to qualify prospects before giving a full presentation, the salespeople who don't do it are often depressed because they aren't making enough sales. The problem is that they try to close the wrong people too often and too hard.

An evaluation of the selling skills of more than two hundred thousand salespeople revealed that the biggest difference between those making high incomes and others who were just getting by was their strength in the area of qualifying. Since it can be learned and done simply and professionally, why don't more salespeople build their skill in this area? Because they don't realize how much it's costing them.

The word "needs" is really what you're after when qualifying. You must determine their "NEADS" before knowing how to proceed with potential clients:

Now. Ask your prospect, "What product are you currently using?"

Enjoy. Follow up the first question by asking, "What is it about that product that you like best?"

Altered. Ask your prospect, "What would you like to see altered or improved in your new [name of product or service]?"

Decision. Then ask, "Who, in addition to yourself, will make the final decision?" Be certain you're talking with the real decision maker.

Solution. "If we were fortunate enough today to find the right solution for your needs, would you be in a position to proceed?"

Give Them a Triplicate of Choice

Complete knowledge of your product line is the first essential. Let's say that your line includes eight different copy machines. Instead of trying to go from eight possibilities to the one machine that given prospects will buy, frame them in the most likely three first, and then in a second step isolate the one that's best for their particular needs.

Next, focus them on triplicate of choice for money. This is a beautiful strategy for overcoming what, in many cases, is the trickiest question of all. Average salespeople baldly state the price, in effect daring the client to come up with the cash. That's not the way to close.

Stick as close to the exact wording as you can when adapting this technique to your offering—all the elements are important. Here's how it goes:

"Most people interested in acquiring this machine with all its features are prepared to invest twelve thousand dollars. A fortunate few can invest between fifteen and twenty thousand dollars. And then there are those on a limited or fixed budget who—with the high cost of everything today—can't go higher than ten thousand. May I ask, which of these categories does your company fit into most comfortably?"

In actual fact, clients possibly don't have an exact amount in mind. They don't want to be in the bottom category, though, so they opt for the middle figure. Structure this technique so that you come up a winner no matter what figure they pick.

The Objection Connection

Here is a short lesson that will take you far in sales. If the people you're talking with don't object to anything during your time together, they're either not listening or not qualified. In other words, they won't buy.

Objections (concerns) are nothing more than ways for your potential client to slow things down—to keep themselves from making a rash decision, from feeling as if they're being "sold." Objections are a common aspect of every sale you'll attempt to make. Accept this fact and you'll open your mind to the ways to handle, address, and overcome objections.

Until you learn how to handle objections, you're not going to approach your potential in sales. Champions have affection for even the peskiest objection because it's something concrete. They know they've reached the Klondike and are digging for gold when they start hearing objections.

Closing Is Sweet Success

Some people get sold fast. If you keep talking instead of closing them, you'll unsell them just as fast. After all, they can only buy it once today, so don't risk having to sell them twice. Some salespeople get so excited that they can't stop talking when buyers give a sign that they're ready. Curb your urge to tell all. Don't be one of those who keep on plowing when it's time to harvest. I've watched salespeople literally grit their teeth as though to say, "You haven't heard it all yet, and you're gonna hear it all before I'll take your order."

More talk just triggers more opportunities to raise concerns. When the clients are ready to run with it, shut up and start filling out the form. The most dangerous time in the closing sequence is when you're busy doing any

---

OBJECTION VERSUS CONDITION

An objection is a statement by a potential client that he or she wants to know more. Of course, an objection doesn't usually come out sounding like a polite request for additional information.

A condition is a valid reason for not going ahead. It's not an objection to overcome; it's a total block to the sale that you must accept and walk away from.

Some of us have a severe challenge here. If we spend time with people and get into our selling sequence with them, we get emotionally involved to the point where we lose our ability to see the difference between an objection that can be overcome and a condition that can't.

kind of calculating or writing and the silence brings on the buyer's anxieties. This is why Champions know their forms so well that they can flash through them while talking casually to a client and keeping him or her interested. You must have your paperwork down to a reflex action that won't soak up all your attention.

Fortune Building Starts with Time Planning

"I must do the most productive thing possible at every given moment." If you live by this saying, you'll not only become a Champion and enjoy a high income but also become a finer, happier person. The most productive thing is not always something aimed directly at making money. Planning your time with productive activities is a vital key to success in selling.

BE A SALES SUPERSTAR

by Brian Tracy

There are salespeople in every organization who seem to find ways to outpace the competition. Quarter after quarter these individuals can be counted on to convert a tough prospect or generate revenue via a clever combination of add-on items. Instead of lurking in this person's shadow, harboring some form of professional jealousy, the salesperson currently hitting for average should seek to find a way to join the record breaker at the top. Enter Brian Tracy, one of the icons of the professional development industry. Tracy has spent thirty years training nearly one million sales professionals. In that time, his keen powers of observation granted him the ability to spot subtle, nuanced differences in the upper echelon of sales professionals. Granted, it helps that Tracy himself was a high-flying seller at one point in his career.

Subsequent to his sales career, he served as chief operating officer of a $265 million development company. His experience stretches from marketing to real estate to importation and distribution. Years of high-stakes performance in a variety of industries helped him launch one of the most notable and high-profile management consulting careers in recent memory. However, the sales profession is at the root of what propelled Tracy to greatness. In some respects, it's fortunate he found sales when he did.

Never content to remain stationary, Tracy set a blistering pace as he moved through life. He was born of modest means and never graduated from high school, and he admits that his exit from education came via expulsion on three separate occasions. After no less than seven manual-labor jobs in a variety of industries, Tracy describes his entry into the sales world as the result of drifting rather than a sudden desire for direction. During his initial foray into selling, he was plagued by the question of what separated the superstars of selling from their also-ran counterparts, of which, at the time, he was one. With a focus finally arriving for his restless energy, Tracy hammered away at the disparity in sales until he was able to lead the pack. This achievement afforded him the knowledge to start advising others about selling. He continues to write and produce sales training materials to this day, and some of his works on selling and performance enhancement are classics in the field.

One of these gems is *Be a Sales Superstar*, a collection of twenty-one essential performance tips to push sales professionals into the elite realm of the top 10 percent of sellers. In selling lore, this exclusive circle is rumored to earn more than 80 percent of the money brought in by sellers. This book is intended to be the key that unlocks the door. Tracy is quick to acknowledge that an untrained eye may lose his book among the sea of sales titles that populate the professional-improvement landscape. What distinguishes his book, he notes, is the brevity and forthrightness of his observations. Tracy bases this on a simple principle he learned at the outset of his own sales career: *Small differences in ability in key areas can lead to enormous differences in results*. The skills in question are familiar to every salesperson, but every one of them must be mastered if the reader hopes to join the ranks that Tracy himself eventually conquered.

BE A SALES SUPERSTAR
Twenty-one Great Ways to Sell More, Faster, Easier in Tough Markets
by Brian Tracy

CONTENTS
1. Commit to Excellence
2. Learn Continuously
3. Accept Responsibility and Become Brilliant
4. Use Educational Selling and Build Credibility
5. Keys to Building Megacredibility
6. Close the Sale and Make Every Minute Count
7. Set Clear Goals and Manage Your Territory

THE SUMMARY IN BRIEF

In *Be a Sales Superstar*, Brian Tracy creates a blueprint for salespeople who want to reach the top of their profession. Tracy breaks down the sales process into an easy-to-understand guide that teaches the art of selling from prospecting to closing the sale.

He begins with the mental process of preparing to sell and then walks the reader through everything from proper preparation for sales calls to handling objections effectively.

Tracy's prose is concise and to the point, and every tip in the book is aimed at helping the salesperson increase his or her income. His action plan is presented logically and simply, and Tracy provides concrete steps that, if followed, should result in sales success.

He opens his book with a pep talk about the power of optimism and the importance of getting into the game and staying there. Then he launches into an explanation of the mind-set necessary to be a top salesperson and follows that with usable, understandable directions for becoming a sales superstar.

In this summary, you will also learn the following:

- How to prepare for successful selling
- How to get prospects to listen to you
- The four stages of building sales relationships
- How to become a financial-improvement specialist
- How to calculate a company's internal rate of return
- How to help your customer determine time to payback
- How to do educational selling
- How to establish megacredibility

THE COMPLETE SUMMARY

Commit to Excellence

Optimists, people with high expectations of eventual success, are ambitious. The more optimistic they are, the more ambitious and determined they become. Ambition is, therefore, the single most important expression of optimism, and it is the key quality for the achievement of great success in sales or in any other field.

Ambitious people have one remarkable characteristic in sales. They dream big dreams. They see themselves as capable of being the best in their fields.

Get in Line

Everyone who is in the top 10 percent today started in the bottom 10 percent. Everyone who is doing well today was once doing poorly. Everybody who is at the front of the buffet line of life started at the end of the line.

How do you get to the front of the buffet line of life? The answer is simple. It consists of two key steps: First, get in line. Second, stay in line.

The way that you get in line is by making a decision that you are going to be excellent in your field and then by taking action to learn and apply whatever knowledge and skills you need to get ahead.

Turning Point

Here is the turning point in your life. Make a decision. The dividing line between success and failure is contained in your ability to make a clear, unequivocal decision that you are going to be the best and then to back your decision with persistence and determination until you reach your goal.

The world is full of people who are wishing, hoping, and praying for their lives to be better, but they never make the kind of do-or-die decision that leads to great success.

Act as if It Was Impossible to Fail

The two major fears that stand as the greatest obstacles on your road to success are the fear of failure or loss and the fear of criticism or rejection. These are the major enemies to overcome.

You can neutralize the fear of failure by repeating, "I can! I can!" over and over. Even more effective is to say to yourself, "I can do it!" I can do it!" over and over until you actually believe it. You create within yourself the mind-set of a high-performance salesperson.

Put Your Whole Heart into Selling

Top salespeople believe in their companies. Above all, they believe in themselves and their ability to succeed. Your level of belief in the value of a product or service is directly related to your ability to convince other people that it is good for them. The more enthusiastic and convinced you are about what you are selling, the more contagious this enthusiasm will be and the more your customers will sense it and act on it.

The more you love your work, the more caring you will be. The more committed you are to your company, products, and services, the more you will naturally and honestly care about your customers. The more you honestly care about your company and your customers, the more concerned you will be about helping customers make good buying decisions.

Since you become what you think about most of the time, you should repeat the words "I love my work!" over and over. The more you enjoy your work, the better you will do it. Selling will become easier and easier.

Position Yourself

Top salespeople see themselves as consultants rather than as salespeople. They see themselves as advisers, helpers, counselors, and friends to their clients and customers. Perhaps the single most important determinant of whether or not someone buys from you is how that person thinks and feels about you. In marketing, this is called positioning.

Once a customer views you as a consultant and friend, he or she will never buy from anyone else, no matter what the small difference might be in price or product/service features.

Become a Consultant

From now on, think of yourself as a consultant. Walk, talk, and behave like a consultant. Dress, groom, and prepare for every sales meeting as if you were a highly paid and competent consultant and adviser in your field. When people ask you what you do, tell them, "I'm a consultant."

The best positioning you can have among your prospects and customers is that of an expert, an authority in your area of expertise. Your customers look to you to give them valuable advice they can use to improve their work or life in a cost-effective way.

Prepare Thoroughly

Preparation is the mark of the professional. The highest-paid salespeople review every detail of an account before every sales call. They study their notes from previous calls. They read the literature and information they have gathered on the prospect. And their prospects can sense it almost immediately.

Your goal is to be among the top 10 percent of salespeople in your field. To reach that goal, you must do what the top people do, over and over, until it is as natural to you as breathing. And the top people prepare thoroughly every single time.

Preparation for great success in selling consists of three parts: precall research, precall objectives, and postcall analysis.

Precall Analysis

During this stage, you gather all the information about the prospect and/or the prospect's company that you possibly can. Check the Internet, the local library, newspapers, and other sources. The more precall research you do, the more intelligent and informed you will sound when you finally sit down with the prospect.

If you are dealing with a business, make it a point to find out everything you can about its products, services, history, competitors, and current activities. The rule is that you should never ask a question of a prospect if the information is readily available elsewhere. Nothing undermines your credibility more rapidly than for you to ask something like "What do you do here?"

Precall Objectives

The second part of preparation is where you set your precall objectives. This is the stage where you think through and plan your coming sales call in detail, in advance.

A technique used by many of the top sales professionals is to prepare an "agenda" for the sales call before you go. Make a list of questions you would like to ask, in sequence. Space them out on the page so there is room for the prospect to make notes.

When you meet with your prospect, say, "Thank you for your time. I know how busy you are. I have prepared an agenda for our meeting with some questions that we can go over. Here is your copy."

Postcall Analysis

The third part of preparation is your postcall analysis. Immediately after the call, take a few moments to write down every bit of information that you can recall from the recent discussion.

Then, prior to seeing the customer again, take a few minutes and review all of your notes. Customers are always impressed when they are called upon by a truly professional salesperson who remembers clearly what was discussed at their last meeting and who has obviously done his or her homework.

Learn Continually

To earn more, you must learn more. You cannot get more or better results by simply working harder using your present abilities. If you want to earn more in the future, you must learn new methods and techniques.

The future belongs to the learners. The highest-paid salespeople spend much more time and money improving themselves and upgrading their skills than the average salesperson. As a result, they earn vastly more in any market.

Continuous learning is like an ongoing mental fitness program for sales champions, where you prepare and keep yourself in shape for intense competition. A continuous learning program in selling has three key parts. Consistent, persistent work in these three areas will lead inevitably to your becoming one of the highest-paid salespeople in your field, with no exceptions.

Leaders Are Readers

The first principle is simply for you to read continually in your field. Look for practical ideas you can use immediately. Imagine using them in your sales activities. Then, throughout the day, practice what you learned in the morning.

If you read about selling for one hour each day, that will amount to about one book per week. Since the average salesperson reads less than one sales book per year, if you were to read fifty books per year, that alone would give you the winning edge that will move you to the top of your sales force.

Listen and Learn

The second part of continual learning is for you to listen to audio programs in your car. As a sales professional, you spend between five hundred and one thousand hours behind the wheel each year. This amounts to between twelve and twenty-five forty-hour weeks per annum, or the equivalent of three to six months of working time in your car each year.

Turn your car into a learning machine. Enroll at "automobile university" and attend full time for the rest of your career. It can change your life. Never let your car be running without educational audio programs playing. Make every minute count. One great idea or technique can change the course of your career and dramatically increase your income.

Learn from the Experts

The third part of continuous learning is for you to take all the training you can get. Attend seminars and courses on professional selling. Ask for advice from others on the most helpful courses they have taken.

The lives of many of the highest-paid professionals have been changed dramatically as a result of attending a single sales course, boot camp, or seminar. Sometimes the ideas and strategies contained in one program have catapulted a person from rags to riches.

Practice the 3 Percent Rule

Here is a rule that will guarantee your success—and possibly make you rich: Invest 3 percent of your income back into yourself. Invest 3 percent of however much you earn back into becoming even better at what you did to earn the money in the first place.

For every dollar you invest back into yourself to improve your ability to earn even more, you will get a return of ten, twenty, fifty, one hundred, or even one thousand times your investment.

Accept Responsibility and Become Brilliant

The highest-paid sales professionals in every field accept 100 percent responsibility for their lives and for everything that happens to them. They see themselves as the presidents of their own professional sales corporations. They view themselves as self-employed.

The wonderful discovery is that the more responsibility you accept, the more you like and respect yourself. As you accept more responsibility, you become more personally powerful. You feel terrific about yourself. And the better you feel, the more you sell.

From now on, see yourself as the president of an entrepreneurial company with one employee—yourself. As the president of your own professional sales corporation, you are paid for results, not activities. If you want more money, make more sales. In the long run, you determine your own income by what you do and what you neglect to do.

Get the Prospect to Listen to You

Every sales call is an interruption of something else the customer is doing. To get a customer's attention, you must ask a question or present an idea aimed at a specific benefit that the customer wants or a specific need of the customer that your product or service can fulfill. You must answer the first question of every prospect in your opening communication, which is "Why should I listen to you?"

Get the Prospect Interested

You arouse interest by showing features of your product or service or by explaining how your product or service can improve the life or work of the prospect.

A product demonstration arouses interest. A presentation of your services, showing how they can improve the prospect's work or business, maintains interest.

The presentation or demonstration must connect with a need or desire or no purchase will take place.

Arouse Buying Desire

Features arouse interest, but desire causes the prospect to buy. If your prospect says something like "I want to think it over," what he or she is really saying is "You have not aroused my buying desire high enough for me to want to proceed at this time."

Some benefits that are most likely to stimulate buying desire are

- saving or making money;
- saving or gaining time or increasing convenience;
- being healthy, secure, popular, respected, or current;
- improving one's personal or business situation in some way.

Build Relationships and Be a Financial-Improvement Specialist

All of your selling success will be based on the quality of the relationships that you form with your customers. For most customers today, the relationship comes first. It is more important than the product or service. The building and maintaining of high-quality sales relationships proceeds in four stages:

- Stage One, roughly 40 percent of the sale, is the development of trust. This is best achieved by asking good questions and listening closely to the answers.
- Stage Two, 30 percent of the process, is focusing on identifying the true needs and wants of the prospect. Instead of talking about what you are selling, you ask questions about the prospect and his or her situation.
- Stage Three, 20 percent of the process, is presenting solutions. In this stage, you show the prospect how he or she could be better off with what you are selling than he or she is today.
- Stage Four, the final 10 percent of the process, is asking for confirmation from the prospect that what you are offering and what he or she

needs are the same. You ask the prospect to make a decision and take action on your offering. You close the sale.

Financial Improvement

When you are selling to businesses especially, you should position yourself as a "financial-improvement specialist." This requires that you focus all your attention on showing the customer how his or her business could be financially better off as a result of using your product or service. Put yourself in the position of the business owner or executive and try to see yourself as being personally involved in achieving the financial results for which he or she is responsible. Your primary aim is to demonstrate to the prospect that the financial benefit of dealing with you is greater than the cost of what you are selling.

Internal Rate of Return

Many companies use internal rate of return (IRR) to evaluate a new business expenditure. This is the return on investment that they aim to attain in purchasing new equipment of any kind. For example, a company may set 15 percent as its IRR. This means that for you to sell the company something, you must demonstrate that it will save or make the company 15 percent or more each year and eventually pay for itself.

The higher the rate of return that a business can achieve by using your product or service, the more attractive it is to buy and use because it pays for itself and yields a profit.

Time to Payback

In determining time to payback, the prospect has four key questions, spoken or unspoken, that you must answer:

1. How much does it cost?

2. How much do I get back in return on my investment?

3. How fast do I get this amount back?

4. How sure can I be that what you say is true?

The greater the clarity with which you can answer these questions, the easier it is for the prospect to buy from you. The fuzzier you are in answering these questions, the harder it is for the customer to buy from you. If neither you nor the customer can figure out the rate and speed of return, no sale will take place.

As a financial-improvement specialist, continually demonstrate and prove how the customer can achieve more of his or her business goals as a result of following your advice and recommendations. Position yourself as an unpaid member of the customer's staff, helping him or her increase sales, reduce costs, or boost profits. Show that your product or service is actually "free" in that the customer ultimately gets back far more in dollar terms than he or she pays in the first place. This is a vital key to high-level selling.

Use Educational Selling and Build Credibility

A major reason that prospects do not buy is because they do not fully understand what you are selling and how they could use and benefit from it. Many salespeople assume that after one sales presentation, the prospect is as familiar with the details of the product or service as they are. This can be a big mistake.

In educational selling, you take a low-pressure or no-pressure approach. You do not try to influence or persuade the customer in any way. You ask good questions and listen closely to the answers. You lean forward and take notes. You position yourself as a teacher rather than as a salesperson.

Show, Tell, Ask

In the "show" part of the presentation, explain or demonstrate how your product or service works to achieve a particular result or benefit. In the "tell" part of the educational selling process, explain the features and benefits of your product or service, using stories, statistics, research results, and anecdotes from other satisfied customers. In the "ask" phase, pause regularly to ask questions and invite feedback on what you have presented so far.

Risk Factors

Four factors affect a prospect's hesitancy about any sales offer. The first is the size of the purchase. The second is the length of life of the product. The third is the number of people involved. The fourth is whether or not the purchaser is a first-time buyer.

The antidote to this natural and normal skepticism and lack of trust or confidence in any sales offer is credibility. The solution is to build up the customer's concept of you as a completely believable person selling a totally trustworthy product. Today, it takes credibility for you just to get an appointment with a customer. But it takes megacredibility for you to get the sale.

Megacredibility is an idea or feeling that can be, and must be, created in the heart and mind of the prospect. It is the critical intangible factor that underlies all successful sales efforts.

Keys to Building Megacredibility

The first part of megacredibility is the credibility of the salesperson, you. Personal megacredibility has four parts: dress, grooming, accessories, and attitude.

- **Dress.** Fully 95 percent of the first impression you make on a customer will be made by your clothes. Look at the top salespeople in your field and then dress the way they do. As a general rule, you should spend twice as much on your clothes as you do now and buy half as many.
- **Grooming.** The highest-paid salespeople in almost every field tend to groom themselves in a conservative and understated way. The simplest rule about good dress and grooming is that nothing should distract the customer from your face, your person, and your conversation.
- **Accessories.** The correct accessories blend well with your clothes and your overall appearance. They enhance your overall "look" without drawing attention.
- **Attitude.** As a rule, you should always be positive, friendly, optimistic, and cheerful when you are selling.

Breaking Down Megacredibility Further The second part of megacredibility is the reputation of your company. Fully 85 percent of sales made today are based on word of mouth. This consists of what other people say about your product and your service. It is how your company is thought of and talked about by customers and noncustomers in the marketplace.

The third part of megacredibility is testimonials. One good letter from a satisfied customer may be all you need to convince a prospect that he or she is safe in buying from you. Make it a point to ask for a testimonial letter each time you get a positive comment from a customer.

The fourth part of megacredibility is the presentation. A well-thought-out, completely professional, customer-focused presentation adds value to the product or service and actually increases the price you can charge for it. A planned and prepared presentation builds your credibility to a high level.

The fifth ingredient of megacredibility is the product or service itself. Your presentation should demonstrate clearly that the product you offer is the ideal solution to the customer's needs and that the value of what you sell greatly outweighs the price you are asking.

Here is the great rule for sales success: Everything counts.

Everything counts! Everything you do in a sales situation either helps or hurts. It either moves you toward the sale or moves you away. It is either

A SIMPLE MODEL

*H*ere is a simple model you can adapt to your own product:
    "Because of [this product feature], you can [product benefit], which means [customer benefit.]"
    For example, imagine you were selling a new office computer. You could say, "Because of this Pentium microprocessor (product feature), you can run multiple programs simultaneously (product benefit), which means that you can get far more work done in a shorter period of time (customer benefit)."

increasing your credibility or decreasing your credibility. Nothing is neutral. Everything counts. All top professionals know that everything counts. They leave nothing to chance. Neither should you.

Handle Objections and Deal with Price

Your ability to answer objections effectively is a critical skill that will largely determine your level of sales and income. Your job is to master this skill. Objections are part of the normal sales process.

The first rule in handling objections effectively is that you should hear them out completely, without interrupting. Even when the prospect is objecting, you are getting an opportunity to listen, and listening builds trust. A negative prospect can be transformed into a neutral or positive prospect when you practice the "white magic" of attentive listening.

Here are three responses you can use for any objections:

- Pause, smile, and then ask: "How do you mean?" This question is almost impossible not to answer.
- You can say, "Obviously, you have a good reason for saying that. Do you mind if I ask what it is?"
- Use the "feel, felt, found" method. When a customer says something like "It costs too much," you can say, "I understand exactly how you feel. Others felt the same way when they first heard the price. But this is what they found when they began using our product or service."

Price Is Never the Main Reason

The main reason is always something else. Your job is to find it and deal with that concern effectively.

The first rule in dealing with price objections is never to argue or defend your prices. Instead, probe gently and professionally to find out the real reason that the customer is hesitating.

Another key rule with regard to price: *Price out of place kills the sale.* If you get into a price discussion before the prospect thoroughly understands what you are selling and the benefits to him or her of owning and using it, you will usually kill all possibility of a sale.

Once you postpone the price discussion, you can then go into a questioning process, positioning yourself as a consultant.

The third way to handle a price objection is this: When the prospect says, "That's more than I expected to pay," respond by asking, "How far apart are we?" Once you discover that number, as long as it is reasonably close to what you are asking, your job is to demonstrate that the difference in price is more than made up for by the increase in value that he or she will receive.

The fourth way to handle price is used when the customer opens with the question, "How much is it?" Here is a direct, "in your face" reply to the question, "How much is it?" You smile, even into the phone, and say, "That's the best part! If it's not exactly right for you, there's no charge."

Then you say, "If whatever I'm selling is not exactly right for you, you're not going to take it, are you?" Thus, you prove that if the prospect doesn't take it, then there's no charge.

The prospect will then say, "That's true. What is it, then?"

You can then proceed to arrange a face-to-face appointment.

Close the Sale and Make Every Minute Count

Your ability to ask for the order at the end of the presentation or at the end of the sales process is absolutely essential to your success. Before you move to close the sale, you can ask one of these two questions: First, you can ask, "Do you have any questions or concerns that I haven't covered so far?" If the customer says no, you can then smile and confidently ask for the buying decision. Second, you can ask, "Does this make sense to you so far?" If the prospect says yes, you can then proceed to close the sale.

Three Techniques to Ask for the Order

1. The first closing method you can use is the "Invitational Close." When the prospect says that he or she has no more questions or concerns, you could ask, "Well, then, why don't you give it a try?"

2. The second technique you can use is called the "Directive Close." With this technique you ask, "Does this make sense to you so far?" When the prospect says yes, you say, "Well, then, the next step is this." You then go on to describe the plan of action. You take out the order form of the contract and begin filling it out.

3. The third closing technique you can use is called the "Authorization Close." At the end of the sales conversation, you double-check to make sure that the prospect has no further questions. You then take out the order form, place a check mark by the signature line, push the order form across the desk, and say, "Well then, if you'll just authorize this, *we'll get started right away.*"

Time Management

Resolve today to become an expert at time management.

There are four questions that you can ask and answer continually to keep yourself focused on your highest priorities.

1. What are my highest-value activities in terms of the potential consequences of doing them or not doing them?

2. Why am I on the payroll?

3. What can I, and only I, do that, if done well, will make a significant contribution to my company and myself?

4. What is the most valuable use of my time right now?

Apply the 80/20 Rule

The 80/20 rule says that 20 percent of your activities will account for 80 percent of your results. In selling, 20 percent of your prospects will account for 80 percent of your customers, 20 percent of your customers will account for 80 percent of your sales, and 20 percent of your products and services will account for 80 percent of your sales volume.

For you to succeed greatly, you must always focus your time and energy on the few activities, the 20 percent of tasks, that can make a real difference in your life.

Three Stages of Professional Selling

Professional selling has three stages, which have been the same throughout history. They are prospect, present, and follow up.

The definition of a good prospect is "someone who can and will buy and pay within a reasonable period of time." Do not waste your precious selling time with nice people who do not have the authority, money, or ability to buy from you.

Once you are absolutely clear about what you sell, your next job is to identify exactly those customers who can most benefit the most rapidly from what you sell.

Some people are a complete waste of time. Sometimes the best use of your time is to break off discussions with a poor prospect before you waste too much time going down a blind alley. Always be polite, but don't spend time where your efforts are not appreciated.

In your market, there exist "high-probability prospects." These are the people who have an immediate need for what you are selling. Your job is to find as many of them as possible, as soon as possible, and leave the low-probability prospects for others.

You should have far more prospects in your sales funnel than you have time to see, even if you work all day long. Never allow yourself to run out of prospects. Keep the funnel full. You have to call on a lot of prospects to get a small number of sales. Be sure the ones you are calling on are the ones you can sell to easily.

Set Clear Goals and Manage Your Territory

The highest-paid salespeople have very clear sales and income goals, broken down by year, month, week, day, and even hour. Ask yourself, "Is what I'm doing right now leading to a sale?" If what you are doing is not leading to a sale, you must immediately stop doing it and get back to work.

One of the major reasons for failure in selling is poor territory management. A simple method of territory management that you can apply immediately is to divide your sales territory into four parts. Resolve to work in one of these quadrants each day or each half day. When you make appointments, cluster them so that they are close together.

Many salespeople, by recognizing their territories, have increased their income by 20 percent, 30 percent, or even 50 percent in a single month. To increase your income, you must increase the number of minutes that you spend face-to-face with customers by reducing your traveling time.

The Seven Secrets of Sales Success

Sales success is based on seven secrets, or principles. They are practiced by all the highest-paid salespeople every day. The regular application of these principles is virtually guaranteed to move you to the top of your field:

1. Get serious! Make a decision to go all the way to the top of your field.

2. Identify the skill that's limiting your sales success.

3. Be around the right people. Be around positive, successful people.

4. Take excellent care of your physical health.

5. Visualize yourself as a top person in your field.

6. Practice positive self-talk continually. Talk to yourself the way you want to be rather than the way you are today.

7. Take positive action toward your goals every single day.

STEPHAN SCHIFFMAN'S
SALES ESSENTIALS

by Stephan Schiffman

The sales profession, as anyone in it is well aware, is all about the numbers. When it comes to training sales professionals, Stephan Schiffman has numbers that are the envy of most in the industry. His D.E.I. Management Group has trained more than half a million sales professionals during its more than three decades of operation. Part of Schiffman's tremendous success stems from his belief in a simple principle: *You cannot force a prospect to do anything.* Sales professionals who struggle to make their numbers often experience the feeling that they're caught in an epic tug-of-war with their prospects. The art of selling isn't about coercion; it's dependent on the precise application of a set of skills that help the customer solve his or her problem via the salesperson's product or service.

The set of skills required to help the customer bridge his or her gap between problem and solution is the subject of *Stephan Schiffman's Sales Essentials.* He compares a salesperson's need for the book to his experience of taking a couple golf lessons with a pro. The pro instructed Schiffman on the correct grip and swing that would guarantee him a lower score. However, Schiffman felt the "correct" swing was uncomfortable and quickly reverted to his old ways. It took one year of brutal scores on the golf course for Schiffman to reconsider. He forced himself to adhere to the proven method for holding and swinging the club, and his scores dropped within months. Schiffman acknowledges that some of the techniques in *Stephan Schiffman's Sales Essentials* may cause discomfort for salespeople who are stuck in their ways. Fortunately, he offers positive reinforcement and pushes the sales professional to stick with his methods until he or she sees results.

Stephan Schiffman's Sales Essentials begins by establishing important concepts that form the foundation of Schiffman's system. It then delves into techniques specific to cold-calling before discussing basic and advanced selling skills every sales professional must master. It's important to note Schiffman's emphasis on getting the first appointment. He understands that too many salespeople look beyond getting an appointment and toward an actual presentation. The network of distractions that surrounds the average prospect continues to increase, making it all the more difficult to get the first appointment. Schiffman gives excellent advice on knocking down the door in the most professional way possible. He doesn't underestimate this single most important aspect of the sales process, and his advice in this area is not to be missed.

Stephan Schiffman's Sales Essentials doesn't limit its respect for time only to the potential customer. The sales professional operates in an environment where he or she can't afford to waste a minute. This led Schiffman to pack his book with brief, sharply delivered lessons. Many of the topics discussed in *Stephan Schiffman's Sales Essentials* will aid sales managers as well as sales professionals and are ideal to share. The book can be used as a training tool, a role that Schiffman himself had in mind when compiling the techniques he forged during decades of work.

STEPHAN SCHIFFMAN'S SALES ESSENTIALS
All You Need to Know to Become a Successful Salesperson—from Cold Calling and Prospecting with E-mail to Increasing the Buy and Closing
by Stephan Schiffman

CONTENTS
1. Foundation Concepts
2. Calling Techniques That Really Work
3. Turning Around Common Responses
4. Basic Selling Skills
5. Selling by Not Selling
6. Advanced Selling Skills
7. Establishing the Relationship
8. Epilogue

THE SUMMARY IN BRIEF

A number of years ago, Stephan Schiffman decided to take golf lessons. He had already been golfing for quite a while, without ever having taken a lesson. During the first lesson, the pro showed him the proper grip. It felt a little awkward, but the teacher assured him that the reason was simple: Schiffman had been holding the club incorrectly for many years. Once he got used to the right way of doing things, it would feel just as natural as the way he had been holding it.

When Schiffman got back on his own, he tried to hold the club and stand and swing as the instructor had told him to. But it still felt strange. He found that when he moved his grip to a more comfortable position, it just felt better. And when he stood the way he was used to standing, it just felt better. And when he swung the way he was used to swinging, it just felt better. And his average score was 150 and he couldn't understand why nobody wanted to play with him or why he wasn't getting any better.

After a year, he went back to the golf pro. This time, he followed directions, stuck it out, and practiced over and over and over again until the techniques became second nature. As the golf pro had promised, the correct way of doing things eventually became comfortable. And Schiffman's score dropped.

Schiffman opens *Sales Essentials* with this story to show that we all have our comfortable ways of doing things, swinging a golf club or connecting with people to make sales. If we take the time to do what's right over and over again until it becomes second nature, it really will deliver results.

If what you're interested in improving is your golf swing, you should talk to a golf pro. If what you're interested in improving is your sales ability, you should read this summary. *Sales Essentials* is a system written by someone who has set numerous sales appointments and closed a lot of business. Schiffman breaks his system down into simple steps. If you follow the steps, the system will work.

In this summary, you will also learn

- why it's important to always prospect for new business;
- how to master the cold call;
- how to use e-mail as a selling tool;
- why it is important to build relationships;
- how to up-sell.

THE COMPLETE SUMMARY

Foundation Concepts

The key to successful selling is getting appointments, but most salespeople don't realize that. A full 65 percent of success is finding people and telling them what you do.

There's a formula that's more important to successful salespeople than any other: A = P = S. Appointments give you prospects give you sales. If you have no new appointments today, what's your chance of getting a new prospect? It's nonexistent. If you have no new prospects, what's your chance of making a sale? That, too, is nonexistent.

The real question is, How many appointments do you need to generate one real prospect? Your appointment base is always going to be larger than your prospect base, which is always going to be larger than your sales base. It's like a pyramid, with your appointments forming the base, your prospects forming the middle and your final sales at the top. If you don't know those numbers, how can you know whether your sales approach is working?

Prospecting and the Sales Cycle

The need for perpetual sales prospecting becomes even more obvious if you consider how far your sales efforts take place in advance of your sales revenues. For example, if it takes sixty days to generate a sale, thirty days to implement the program, thirty days to use the service, thirty days to bill, and thirty days to get paid, that means six months pass between the start of the process and when you actually see the first dollar. You may think you're making sales today, but the sale you made today came from the work you did yesterday.

Even if you have a successful week, a successful month, or a successful year, that doesn't mean you should ever stop prospecting. One of the biggest mistakes you can make is to convince yourself that you don't have to prospect on a regular basis. You get happy and complacent with your existing business and think you don't have to seek new business.

The key is to keep prospecting on a regular basis. Making the sale is important, but it's not as important as managing your prospects. And the key to that is to replenish your base of prospects with new appointments. If you keep this concept in mind and act on it, you should be able to avoid the peaks and valleys.

Calling Techniques That Really Work

Have you recently seen a movie or a television show that you really enjoyed? Did the actors sound like they were reading from a script? No. It doesn't sound like a script because the actor has internalized what has to be said. That's what you must do. You have to internalize what you're going to say so it sounds natural.

The objective here is not to "handcuff" you with a script. The objective is to help you develop a script that will help you say what you need to say while freeing you to pay attention to the prospect's response—which is what's really important.

Using a script makes it easier for you to listen for crucial information, since you know exactly what you're going to say. Here are the five elements:

1. Get the person's attention. The easiest, simplest way of opening and getting the prospect's attention is by saying his or her name.

2. Identify yourself and your company. Go further. Build a brief introduction or commercial into the call.

3. Give the reason for the call, which is to set up an appointment.

4. Make a questioning statement that's going to allow the prospect an opportunity to respond in kind.

5. Set the appointment.

Six Specific Telephone Tips for Better Prospecting Numbers

Here are six specific tips that are going to help you be more effective on the telephone. It's crucial that you do all six, even though each one on its own will help you become more successful in making appointments:

1. *Use a mirror.* Take the mirror and put it where you can see it, and look at yourself while you're making calls. You're going to smile while you make calls. Why? When you smile, those smile muscles affect your larynx. The result is that you sound better.

2. *Use a timer.* Know how much time it takes you to make a good call. This is important because you don't want your calls to be any longer than they need to be. If it typically takes you two or three minutes to set the appointment, don't go beyond those two or three minutes. Here's another important rule: Block out your calling time.

3. *Practice.* Get someone to help you: your spouse, your friend, whoever. Make that person work with you until you get your cold-calling responses down perfectly. It just doesn't make sense to practice on a prospect. You're thinking about too many things; your mind is focused on connecting with that person, not on learning the fundamentals.

4. *Keep a record of your call.* Learn to manage your numbers. Successful salespeople don't merely know their numbers; they know how to use their numbers, how to analyze the ratios, and how to set appropriate goals based on them. Get in the habit of tracking three things: the number of dials, the number of completed calls, and the number of appointments you get.

5. *Tape-record your calls.* In many places, it's legal for you to tape-record your calls and then listen to them if you do so for your own use. (You should, however, check whether your state's laws require you to notify the person you're talking to.) Pay attention to both sides of the conversation.

6. *Stand up.* When you stand up and make cold calls, you're going to sound more animated. You're going to feel better about yourself. You're going to sound better, and, once again, it's going to give you the edge that you need to be more successful.

Turning Around Common Responses

You're soon going to realize that virtually every initial "no" response falls into one of these four categories:

1. "No thanks, I'm happy with what I have."

2. "I'm not interested."

3. "I'm too busy."

4. "Send me some literature."

The trick is to learn how to anticipate and handle these responses properly.

Much of the training salespeople get in cold-calling encourages empathy. The problem is, you don't have the vaguest idea how the prospect feels—and it's condescending to say you do. Let's say you're talking to a guy who's fifty-five years old, and you're just starting in sales. Can you honestly call him and tell him you understand how he feels?

Once you understand that your objective is to get in the door, not to empathize, you'll start to see how the sales process really works. So here's what to say: "Mr. Jones, a lot of people had the same reaction you did when I first called—before they had a chance to see how what we do will benefit them."

While you're at it, why not tell the person the names of the relevant companies you've worked with? If you have appropriate referrals, you should certainly use them, and this is the perfect time.

Leaving Messages That Get Results

There are a good many salespeople who swear that it's a waste of time to leave messages for prospects. Reaching someone's voice mail is common now. Excluding all those potential contacts is basically a rationalization for the bad idea of focusing your calling efforts on "warm calls" to people who are already familiar to you. The problem is, there usually aren't enough people in that category to support your revenue goals.

On the whole, good salespeople actually prefer delivering a solid, professional message to a voice-mail system and dealing with the resulting return call. Here are five reasons for that:

1. The dynamic of the call is likely to be much more favorable, and a conversational tone will often be much easier to achieve.

2. When the person calls back, you're somewhat less likely to be interrupted (because you're less likely to be perceived as an interruption).

3. When the person calls back, he or she is more likely to actually listen to what you have to say.

4. You can easily leave messages for people who are difficult or impossible to reach directly on the phone.

5. You can make prospecting calls to voice-mail systems at just about any time of the day or night, which gives you more flexibility in scheduling.

Basic Selling Skills

There are twelve simple, career-changing pieces of advice that represent the culmination of more than a quarter of a century of experience. Those who follow all twelve rules always seem to outearn those who don't.

1. Always respond to customer queries within forty-eight hours.

2. Schedule sales appointments for early (8:00 a.m.) or late (4:00 p.m.).

3. Follow through immediately on thank-you letters, letters of agreement, and internal paperwork.

4. Set two new appointments every day.

5. Strategize with your sales manager on a regular basis.

6. Don't kid yourself.

7. Create a sense of urgency in all your communications.

8. Be honest.

9. Know ten client success stories.

10. Decide on your opening question for the meeting.

11. Decide on the next step you want and ask for it directly.

12. Always try to get the other person to do something.

THE VALUE OF "NO"

Schiffman's company does a lot of work with life insurance companies and HMOs across the United States. "In fact, we train life insurance agents around the world," he writes. "When we work with a brand new life insurance agent, somebody who's just been hired, we will give that person a chart with 250 boxes on it.

"Every single time that person talks to someone about life insurance and hears, 'No, I don't want to buy,' or 'No, I'm not interested,' the salesperson puts an X in the box. When the chart is full, that is, when 250 people have said no, we give the person $1,000. Why can we do that? Well, if you stop to figure it out, you'll realize that in the process of getting 250 'no' answers, that salesperson will probably generate $10,000 in sales. In other words, we can afford to pay out $4 for every 'no,' because we know we're going to make it back.

"It's important to understand that every time someone says no, you're getting closer to a yes."

Selling Is a Conversation

Whether you realize it or not, selling is based on relationships. And the only real relationships you can count on are those that arise out of intelligent conversations between two people. Conversations are the foundation of selling.

In the end, you will sell, or fail to sell, based on the quality of your conversations with your prospects and customers. If you display genuine curiosity, and ask appropriate "do-based" questions, you will sell more of your products and services to your customers.

What are do-based questions? Do-based questions are questions that focus not on what you think the other person needs, or what you think his or her problem is, or what you think the potential pain is, but on what the other person is actually doing. If you focus only on what you consider the need, the pain, or the problem, then you won't get the whole picture of what's happening in the other person's world. You may get part of that picture, and you may close an initial sale, but to build a relationship for the future, you have to be willing to ask questions about what the other person does.

Selling by Not Selling

Each and every interaction with a customer you hope to sell to or sell more to—especially those interactions that are not directly sales oriented—is, in fact, a sales opportunity. How's that for a paradox? These nonselling discussions are chances to deepen the relationship, expand your knowledge base about what is going on in an organization and in the other person's life, and pass along relevant suggestions that parallel your own experiences and ability to add value.

For instance, let's say you have been working together for three or four years. Now, all of sudden, the person vanishes off the radar screen. E-mails go unreturned, voice-mail messages vanish, and attempts to reach out to other people in the organization go nowhere. The best answer is to give the person a reason to take the call that does not have to do with selling. In other words, send the person a book or article with a personalized note. You are giving the person an easy way to respond and giving him or her a conflict-free context for future conversation. If there's something there, you'll probably hear back from the person—or be able to reach him or her more easily the next time.

Be absolutely certain that, when you are in a meeting with your contact, interacting with him or her on the phone, or sending an e-mail, you are sending the message that this person really is more important than anything or anyone else on earth. Forget about selling. Just focus on what the other person is doing with incredible focus and attention.

If you can follow through on that type of commitment, genuine interest, and unapologetic attention, you will attract interest, build a relationship, and be able to sell more.

Offer, Timetable, Price

At any given moment during the selling initiative you may be presenting, there are three items that may be under discussion:

1. The offer itself. This means the specifics of the equipment, service, or program that you want the customer to consider as an additional purchase.

2. The timetable. This is the point in time at which you would deliver or implement your additional sale.

3. The terms. This is how your customer would end up paying for the additional purchase.

There is an interesting rule you may want to consider once you have identified these three elements of your sale. If you are having trouble dealing with one of these three elements, simply change gears and try to focus on one of the other two.

Do not let the fact that the person has grave doubts about your payment schedule keep you from discussing the specifics of the offer or the possible timetable. Get as much buy-in as you can on those other two items, and emphasize the points that are most in line with what this person is already doing. Rather than hammering on whether or not you can get a special deal on the payment terms, step back and find a way to focus on your common interests: the benefits that the person will receive from your offer and the timetable that makes the most sense for him or her to receive those benefits.

Key Communication Principles

You should identify ten initial negative responses that you hear over and over again from your prospects and customers. In particular, you should identify the types of questions, issues, and challenges that come up with your customers during your discussions about the best ways to extend your relationship with them.

You can anticipate these responses so you can know exactly the right story or anecdote from your own experience or that of someone else on your sales team to help you address whatever issue has arisen.

The one point you do have to bear in mind is that despite how similar some of the objections, responses, and issues you hear may sound, they really are coming from a unique person and a unique organization. So you will want to be very careful not to assume that the dimensions of the problem are precisely the same as those of the last person you heard this issue from. Instead, you will need to express your understanding of what the person has said, replay what you have heard, and then share an interesting anecdote from your own history.

FIVE WAYS TO DOUBLE YOUR INCOME

Double the number of calls you make.

Get through more often. One more person a day means more than two hundred more people a year.

Get more appointments.

Get more sales from your appointments.

Generate more dollars per sale.

Advanced Selling Skills

You should make a habit of identifying what you think the most difficult challenge in the relationship is going to be—and then bringing that problem up on your own, rather than waiting for the other person to do it.

By raising the most difficult issue yourself, and not waiting for the prospect to either bring it up or, even worse, fail to bring it up, you get a much better sense of exactly where you stand when it comes to the goal of getting this person to buy more from you.

When You Work for a Large Organization

The following selling rules will be of interest to people who work in companies that sometimes present bureaucratic obstacles to their customers. You really can solidify your relationships and improve your commission by adopting each of these principles. The general rule of thumb is that, if the prospect or customer calling you cannot reach you directly within one hour, you need to implement all of these ideas:

- **Make sure you are reachable.** If this means investing in your own cell phone or BlackBerry and paying for that out of your own pocket, then do so. Your customers must be able to reach you no matter what.
- **Share the Easter eggs.** Make a point of listing things that are of added value that you can deliver for your customers—all the things that nobody else within the organization is likely to tell them.
- **Introduce the family.** Do not just dash off to the Caribbean for three weeks and leave your customers high and dry. Pick someone you trust to handle their inevitable questions, crises, and suggestions.
- **Build your own company.** There are subcompanies that emerge within larger companies. These are not formal business entities, of course, but they are loosely or not-so-loosely arranged alliances and communication networks.
- **Get them a meeting with your president.** If you cannot arrange a meeting with the company president, then get the highest-ranking person you can find.
- **Give them a tour.** Salespeople are very big on touring the facilities of their prospects, but it probably is just as important that your most important customers see how your operation runs. Anyone who is critical to your sales success should have a clear sense of how your company operates, and that means firsthand experience.
- **Send a book.** Whatever book you happen to be reading, if you think it is of interest to your prospects and customers, find a reason to send a copy inscribed with your own signature.

Pull Out Your Legal Pad

One of the best strategies for moving toward "strategic partner" status is to start small and gather one fact at a time—with old-fashioned pen-and-pad technology. Most salespeople will begin a meeting with a prospect by saying,

"Let me show you a PowerPoint that we put together for the people we want to do work with."

At that point they begin paging through a generic PowerPoint that is designed specifically for nobody and generically for everybody. This is basically the twenty-first-century equivalent of the common problem of "throwing up" all over the prospect by reading verbatim from the brochure, only it feels a little less like that because the person uses the PowerPoint as a tool to hold what could be mistaken for a conversation with the other person.

This is a huge mistake and a violation of the rule that you must be sure to focus every atom of your attention on the other person during your meetings.

What's the Next Step?

One of the cardinal selling rules is that you always want to get the other person to do something. Ideally, you want the other person to take the next step. That means something someone puts in his or her calendar that shows a willingness to meet, discuss, or otherwise interact with you at some point between now and two weeks from now.

So when you say that a next step must take place at some point within the next two weeks, what you're really doing is asking the people you're interacting with to make a clear assessment to you of exactly how important this discussion meeting or conference call really is to them. That's not how you say it, of course, but it's how you can measure it.

The Art of Making People Look Good

You will know that you are not at the top of the relationship pyramid if the problem is one that you can solve, yet the customer does not call you first. In that case, you are lower down on the pyramid, and the question you should be asking is "How come you are talking to them?"

The goal is to position the up-sell properly. The key, on the most basic level, is to find something that is going to help someone do what they're trying to do and look great in the process. But what are they trying to do? That's the $64,000 question.

For most companies, what they're trying to do is

- gain market share;
- gain a competitive edge in the marketplace;
- improve/increase revenues;
- increase/improve profits.

But what companies do isn't the whole picture. What do individuals in the company try to do? Typically, they're trying to change things in their own lives. Specifically, they're trying to

- get a raise and/or a promotion;
- change the amount of work they do;
- change the amount of perceived power and status they have;
- change the actual level of control they have over specific events in their department.

So with the individual—and ultimately, it always does come down to individuals—the goal is to make the person you're working with look so good that he or she makes progress toward one or more of these goals.

Take Responsibility

One particular technique for rescuing a blown presentation is known as "taking responsibility." You probably realize that your best customers have come to rely on you and that much of your relationship with these customers is based on trust. Earning trust is really the same thing as accepting responsibility, and assuming personal responsibility for the sale as it progresses is a remarkably effective sales tool.

So how does it work? When you come to the closing stage, you simply say something like "It sounds good to me; how does it sound to you?" One of two things is likely to happen. Either the prospect will answer your question receptively—and thereby start down the road to becoming a customer—or the prospect will back off and say no flat out.

If you find yourself facing the second scenario, you take responsibility for whatever problem has arisen. What you will say will sound something like "Mr. Prospect, I'm really not sure what to say. I am so convinced that we have the best service, the best pricing, the best customization, and the best reputation of any firm in our industry that I can think of only one reason for you not to sign on with us. And that's that I must have done something terribly wrong just now in giving my presentation. So I'm going to ask you to give me a hand and tell me where I went off course. Because, to be quite frank with you, I know this service is right for you and I'd really hate to have made a mistake on something this important."

You will find that the common response you'll hear after you take responsibility for the initial "no" will sound something like this: "No, no, no, Susan, it has nothing to do with you. It's on our end." And the prospect can then be expected to go into detail about the remaining obstacles. Then you have the facts you need to continue through the cycle.

Know When to Move On

One of the great neglected truths about selling is that the very best strategy is sometimes to recognize that there is no possibility to expand a relationship with a given customer.

There comes a point when your aim is to move on and find a better opportunity. Your goal is not, and cannot be, to try to find some system that will expand every budget, improve every relationship, and allocate every organization's dollars to your company. No such incantation exists, and you should not waste your time waiting for one.

The trick is to align yourself so well with the interests of your prospects and customers that you develop a sense for whether or not the possibility really exists to expand your relationship in a way that benefits both parties.

We do not like to admit it to ourselves, but a certain percentage of the people who buy from us buy from us at the commodity level and will never buy for any other reason. We help them resolve a short-term problem or address a sudden crisis. We are not part of their long-range plans. The first decision is a "one-off." That means that the person really is not supposed to buy from us again and there is very little we can do to change that. That is not the way it is in all cases and with all customers, but it is what we face in a certain percentage of relationships. And when we do not do any meaningful exploration of the reasons that prompted the person's decision to work with us in the first place, we should not be surprised when we are not able to move the person up to the next level.

E-mail Selling Strategies

E-mail has made it easier for salespeople to communicate. That's both a good thing and a bad thing.

It's a good thing because a salesperson can now contact virtually anyone in the world. For the first time in history, you can reach out to a prospect or customer and send that person a message that reaches him or her in just a few seconds.

It's a bad thing because you can also screw up that conversation in a millisecond. The new sales culture, at least where e-mail is concerned, is one that is all too often based on instant actions, on rambling away, hitting "send," and seeing what happens.

Your sales culture may be priming you to hit "send" to as many prospects and customers as possible, but if your job is selling, you have a duty to increase the odds that the people you're trying to communicate with will actually open, read, and take action on the e-mails you send. If they do that, you will accelerate the sales process.

Ultimately, you should be using e-mail as a tool to establish momentum with people who could conceivably buy from you. If your job is to sell face-to-face, you're going to get the best results if you use e-mail to uncover reasons to get face-to-face with your prospects and customers.

Screwing Up the Sales Process

Now you have this technology that makes it much, much easier to "touch" the person to whom you are trying to sell. But notice that a meaningful "touch" only takes place after you have already established some kind of relationship with the person.

It is tempting to believe that e-mail has rendered prospecting obsolete. After all, nobody really enjoys making cold calls, and we're always on the lookout for evidence that some technological advance has rendered obsolete something we really don't like to do. But the sad truth of the matter is that even superior, seasoned, experienced salespeople find themselves in an income crisis when they neglect prospecting for extensive periods of time.

Learn how to use e-mail to support your sales process—but do not expect e-mail to replace the prospecting that is a natural part of your sales process.

Top of the Mind

Your job is to increase the odds that your e-mail does not get lost in the shuffle. To do that, you have to make certain that you are putting only relevant information in front of the other person.

Because most unfamiliar e-mail messages are ignored, e-mail is simply no replacement for prospecting by phone. Therefore, it shouldn't distract you from prospecting by phone. Even so, e-mail may occasionally be useful for reaching out to specific contacts with whom you otherwise couldn't connect. Some people really will react more quickly to an e-mail message than they will to a telephone call. And they will react positively—if the message reaches them in the first place, if they open the message, if the message has meaning to their day, and if the message is perceived as helpful.

Here are nine ways to increase the odds that the e-mail prospecting message you send will accelerate your selling cycle:

1. *Choose a heading that gets you noticed.* In the subject line, try using a reference name, someone you can list as a referring party, or someone the recipient might know.

2. *Get to the point.* The message should be no more than two or three sentences long. The shorter it is, the more likely it is to be understood and acted upon.

3. *Use the person's name in the body of the message.* Otherwise, he or she may assume that this is an e-mail that a thousand other people are receiving.

4. *Emphasize commonality.* If you can, point out that your company has been doing business with other firms in this person's industry.

5. *Don't try to sell.* Don't include long monologues about how great your company is. Say clearly that the reason for the message is to set up an appointment. Offer a specific time and date that you want to get together.

6. *Don't hound the person.* Send one message a week, maximum.

7. *Don't make getting this particular individual to answer your message your life's work.* After three e-mail attempts, move on.

8. *Don't try to turn an appointment into a prolonged premeeting correspondence.* Send a polite, short message of thanks and confirmation and then show up at the appointed day and time.

9. *Give your address.* Include the name and physical address of your company, as well as a way for the recipient not to receive unsolicited messages in the future.

Establishing the Relationship

Once you make the effort and invest the time to sit down face-to-face with a person and open up the relationship, you can hasten the progress by means of e-mail. You can stay on the person's radar screen, remind him or her of certain key points from previous conversations, even get the prospect involved in circulating your message to the important people in the organization, thus involving other players to help you expand your influence and access within the sale.

The people you are talking to can help you move the sale forward more quickly because you can stay in contact with them not only through face-to-face and voice communications, but in a very direct way by means of tactful, nonharassing e-mail messages.

Epilogue

Two lumberjacks were given axes and told to go into the forest and cut down trees. The first lumberjack went up to his first tree and started to chop away. He chopped all day long without stopping.

The second lumberjack also did his share of chopping and cutting, but at various points during the day, he would stop, walk away, and come back a few minutes later. At the end of the day, the lumberjack who had worked nonstop had cut *less* wood. Why?

The lumberjack who took breaks went to sharpen his ax. Both men were given the same tool, but only one of them learned how to use the tool properly.

We're all given the same tools. We all play on the same field. We all play by the same rules, yet certain people really learn how to use those tools properly. In the end, it's not the playbook that's important; it's the execution. What will make you better than the next person? What will give you the success you need? Your execution. Your ability to carry out the plan.

THE WINNING ATTITUDE

by John C. Maxwell

S uccess in the sales profession requires talent, determination, self-confidence, and a good deal of faith. Selling is a difficult profession because
of its long hours, frequent travel, and never-ending pressure to deliver the
numbers. A talented sales professional must harden him- or herself to frequent
rejection. This requires an attitude that can cast aside even the darkest clouds
to reveal the blue sky behind them. Leadership expert John Maxwell provides one
path to developing and maintaining the outlook needed to weather the storms of
the selling life in his book *The Winning Attitude*.

Belief in oneself and faith in a higher power go hand in hand with Maxwell.
Growing up as the son of a minister in Michigan, Maxwell followed his father's path
to the pulpit. The ability to lead a congregation to pursue better and more faith-
filled lives sparked Maxwell to begin a career writing and speaking about leadership and success. Originally published in the early 1990s, *The Winning Attitude*
rapidly became a must-read for executives as well as anyone seeking personal
motivation. In the sales realm, the book continues to be an important force to help
professionals develop a positive attitude as a means of defense. When one considers that salespeople face more rejection than people in any other profession,
the need for the attitude equivalent of a suit of armor becomes obvious.

The Winning Attitude is rooted in faith. While Maxwell's religious examples stem
solely from the Bible, and the New Testament in particular, this should not discour-
age readers from delving into the heart of his message. The power of belief, be it
in oneself or in something larger, is a necessity if one hopes to achieve any level
of success. As Maxwell writes, "Almost daily we witness jobs that are held but
hated . . . all because people are waiting for others, or the world, to change." It
is not a stretch to imagine that there are some sales professionals reading this
collection of titles who may be considering leaving the profession and its various
stresses behind. This book is intended for those individuals, as well as the ones
who need to refresh their outlook both personally and professionally.

The Winning Attitude takes readers on a journey of personal discovery and
development. What gives it an extra edge for sales professionals is Maxwell's
discussion of the problems that can "crash" an attitude. The demands on

salespeople are merciless and tied entirely to the company's bottom line. The impression, whether accurate or embellished, is that the sales department is a playing field on which anyone is capable of being replaced. It's a cold environment in which to earn a living, and the ability to maintain a positive demeanor is a more difficult skill to acquire than people realize. *The Winning Attitude* examines the impact of problems that occur around an individual and, more important, the effect of internal issues on an attitude. It's not coincidental that the sales profession is cited specifically during Maxwell's discussion of dealing with a lack of immediate success. However, as he points out, getting up and trying again and again pays off for those brave enough to take this course of action.

THE WINNING ATTITUDE
Your Key to Personal Success
by John C. Maxwell

CONTENTS

THE SUMMARY IN BRIEF

In *The Winning Attitude*, leadership expert John C. Maxwell describes why it is important to maintain a positive attitude. Then he explains how to adopt a positive attitude and how to develop one. Along the way, Maxwell explains how to make the choice to keep this attitude and how to recognize and learn to overcome obstacles that threaten it.

Written while Maxwell was a senior pastor at Skyline Wesleyan Church, *The Winning Attitude* includes biblical references throughout, adding resonance and support to his observations.

Maxwell makes the case that having a positive attitude makes life better and more rewarding. Success or failure in any undertaking, he says, is caused more by mental attitude than by mental capacity.

The Winning Attitude provides not only inspiration for those who would like to establish a positive attitude but also a practical guide for how to accomplish that goal.

Maxwell explains how fear of failure, dread of discouragement, and struggles with sin hold people back; how criticism, conflicts, and problems get in the way, and then he delineates the choices people can make to help them achieve a positive attitude.

In addition, you will learn the following:

- What an attitude actually is
- Why a positive attitude is important
- What ingredients make up an attitude
- How to create an attitude
- Mistakes involved in constructing an attitude
- How an attitude can crash
- What opportunities exist for developing the right attitude

THE COMPLETE SUMMARY

The Consideration of Your Attitude

Doesn't an individual's attitude dictate his or her performance? Does he or she have an "attitude indicator" that continually evaluates his or her perspective and achievements in life?

What happens when the attitude is dictating undesirable results? How can the attitude be changed? And if the attitude changes, what are the ramifications to other people?

Christ gives us a perfect example to follow. His high standard was not given to frustrate us but to reveal areas in our lives that need improvement. Philippians 2:3–8 reminds us: He was selfless. He was secure. He was submissive.

The attitude dictates performance.

The Attitude—What Is It?

The attitude is an inward feeling expressed by behavior. That is why an attitude can be seen without a word being said. Since our attitude is often expressed by our body language and by the looks on our faces, it can be contagious. Have you noticed what happens to a group of people when one person, by his or her expression, reveals a negative attitude? Or have you noticed the lift you receive when a friend's facial expression shows love and acceptance?

When the attitude is positive and conducive to growth, the mind expands and the progress begins. What is an attitude?

- It is the "advance man" of our true selves.
- Its roots are inward but its fruit is outward.
- It is our best friend or our worst enemy.
- It is more honest and more consistent than our words.
- It is an outward look based on past experiences.
- It is a thing that draws people to us or repels them.
- It is never content until it is expressed.
- It is the librarian of our past.
- It is the speaker of our present.
- It is the prophet of our future.

The Attitude—Why Is It Important?

For some, attitude presents a difficulty in every opportunity; for others it presents an opportunity in every difficulty. Some climb with a positive attitude, while others fall with a negative perspective. The very fact that the attitude "makes" some while "breaking" others is significant enough for us to explore its importance.

1. *Attitude Axiom #1: Our attitude determines our approach to life.* One of the valid ways to test your attitude is to answer this question: Do you feel your world is treating you well? If your attitude toward the world is excellent, you will receive excellent results. If you feel so-so about the world, your response from the world will be average. Feel bad about your world, and you will seem to have only negative feedback from life. It would be impossible to estimate the number of jobs that have been lost, the number of promotions missed, the number of sales not made, and the number of marriages ruined by poor attitudes. But almost daily we witness jobs that are held but hated and marriages that are tolerated but unhappy, all because people are waiting for others, or the world, to change instead of realizing that they are responsible for their behavior.

2. *Attitude Axiom #2: Our attitude determines our relationships with people.* When the attitude you possess places others first and you see people as important, your perspective will reflect their viewpoint, not yours. Until you walk in the other person's shoes and see life through another's eyes, you will be like the man who angrily jumped out of his car after a collision. "Why don't you people watch where you're driving?" he shouted. "You're the fourth car I've hit today."

Usually the person who rises within an organization has a good attitude. The promotions did not give that individual an outstanding attitude, but an outstanding attitude resulted in promotions.

3. *Attitude Axiom #3: Often our attitude is the only difference between success and fail-ure.* History's greatest achievements have been made by men and women who excelled only slightly over the masses of others in their fields. This could be called the principle of the slight edge. Many times that slight difference was attitude. Certainly aptitude is important to our success in life. Yet success or failure in any undertaking is caused more by mental attitude than by mere mental capabilities. There is very little difference among people, but that little difference makes a big difference.

4. *Attitude Axiom #4: Our attitude at the beginning of a task will affect its outcome more than anything else.* The right attitude in the beginning ensures success at the end. You are acquainted with the saying "All's well that ends well." An equal truth is "All's well that begins well." Many times we are guilty of viewing our future challenges as the sunset of life rather than the sunrise of a bright new opportu-nity. For instance, there's the story of two shoe salesmen who were sent to an island to sell shoes. The first salesman, upon arrival, was shocked to realize that no one wore shoes. Immediately he sent a telegram to his home office saying, "Will return home tomorrow. No one wears shoes." The second salesman was thrilled by the same realization. Immediately he wired the home office saying, "Please send me 10,000 shoes. Everyone here needs them."

5. *Attitude Axiom #5: Our attitude can turn our problems into blessings.* When con-fronted with a difficult situation, a person with an outstanding attitude makes the best of it while getting the worst of it. Life can be likened to a grindstone. Whether it grinds you down or polishes you depends upon what you are made of. Great leaders emerge when crises occur. In the lives of people who achieve, we read repeatedly of terrible troubles that force them to rise above the com-monplace. Not only do they find the answers, but they also discover a tremen-dous power within themselves.

6. *Attitude Axiom #6: Our attitude can give us an uncommonly positive perspective.* The individual whose attitude causes him or her to approach life from an entirely positive perspective is not always understood. This is an individual some would call a "no-limit person" who doesn't accept the normal limitations of life like most people; who is unwilling to accept "the accepted" just because it is accepted. This individual is determined to walk to the very edge of his or her potential, or the potential of a project, before accepting defeat. Not only does the future look bright when the attitude is right, but also the present is much more enjoyable. The posi-tive person understands that the journey is as enjoyable as the destination.

7. *Attitude Axiom #7: Our attitude is not automatically good just because we are Christians.* The apostle Paul tells us about the proper Christian attitude: Do things for the right reasons; regard others as more important than yourself; look out for the interests of others; possess the attitude of Christ, who was not power hungry, but rather emptied Himself, demonstrated obedience, and fulfilled God's purpose.

Murphy's Law:
"Nothing is as easy as it looks; everything takes longer than you expect; and if anything can go wrong, it will, and at the worst possible moment."

Maxwell's Law:
"Nothing is as hard as it looks; everything is more rewarding than you expect; and if anything can go right, it will, and at the best possible moment."

The Construction of Your Attitude

We quickly blend into the color of our surroundings. Similarities in thinking, mannerisms, priorities, talk, and opinions are very common within individual cultures. Unquestionably, our surroundings help construct our attitudes, too.

In our early years, our attitudes are determined mainly by our conditions. A baby does not choose his or her family or environment. But as the child's age increases, so do his or her options.

Foundational Truths About the Construction of the Attitude

Before we look at specific things that help construct attitudes, we must understand some basic principles about attitude formation:

1. A child's formative years are the most important for instilling the right attitudes. Attitudes we accept as children are usually the attitudes we embrace as adults.

2. An attitude's growth never stops. As long as we live, we are forming, changing, or reinforcing attitudes. There is no such thing as an unalterable attitude.

3. The more our attitude grows on the same foundation, the more solid it becomes. Reinforcement of our foundational attitudes, whether positive or negative, makes them stronger.

4. Many builders (specialists) help construct our attitudes at a certain time and place. Certain people come into our lives at various times who help make or break our perspective.

5. There is no such thing as a perfect, flawless attitude. Our attitudes need adjustment with every change that comes into our lives.

Materials That Are Used in Constructing an Attitude

- **Personality.** We are born as distinct individuals. A set of attitudes accompanies each personality. Generally, people with a certain temperament develop specific attitudes common to that temperament.
- **Environment.** Our environment is a greater controlling factor in our attitude development than our personality or other inherited traits. Environment is the first influencer of our belief system. Therefore, the foundation of an attitude is laid in the environment to which we were born.
- **Word Expression.** Words can encourage either the stretching or shrinking of our lives. If most of our conversations contain a negative bent, it is better to say nothing.
- **Adult Acceptance.** Leaders should know about the importance of acceptance/affirmation of the ones they are leading. The truth is, people don't care how much you know until they know how much you care.
- **Self-image.** It is impossible to perform consistently in a manner inconsistent with the way we see ourselves. We usually act in direct response to our self-image. Nothing is more difficult to accomplish than changing outward actions without changing inward feelings. How we see ourselves affects how others see us. If we like ourselves, it increases the odds that others will like us. *Self-image is the parameter for the construction of our attitude.* We will never go beyond the boundaries that stake out our true feelings about ourselves.
- **Exposure to New Experiences.** We always have a number of opportunities in our hand. We must decide whether to take a risk and act on them. Nothing in life causes more stress yet, at the same time, provides more opportunity for growth than new experiences.
- **Association with Peers.** What others indicate about their perceptions of us affects how we perceive ourselves. Usually we respond to others' expectations.
- **Physical Appearance.** Our looks play an important part in the construction of our attitude.

The Costliest Mistake People Make in Constructing an Attitude

What are a person's capabilities? No one knows. Therefore, no one should be consciously instilling life-limiting thoughts into others.

Let's talk about the "sap strata."

The sap strata line represents our self-imposed, limiting barrier. The effort it would take to break through that sap strata level takes the "sap" out of us. Every time we make an attempt to break through the line, there is accompanying pain. We pay a physical and emotional price when we actually break through our perceived limitation and enter a new area of further potential.

Sadly, many people accept their sap strata and never reach their potential. Here are a few comments we unconsciously make that can limit our potential and keep us from breaking through the sap strata:

"It's never been done before."

"I'll never try that again."

"Take it easy."

The Crashing of Your Attitude

Here are some rules to remember when you have one of those very bad days and your attitude starts to plummet:

Rule 1: Maintain the right attitude when the "going gets tough." Our natural reaction is to bail out of the right attitude to compensate for our problems. During our flight of life our attitude is most critical during the "tough times." That is when we are tempted to panic and make bad attitude decisions. When the external circumstances lead to wrong internal reactions, we really have problems.

Rule 2: Realize that the "rough weather" will not last forever. When you're caught in the middle of touchy situations, it is often difficult to remember this truth. We become consumed with the problems. Many times it is not the size of the problem but the duration of it that weighs heavily on us.

Rule 3: Try to make major decisions before the storm. Many storms can be avoided by thinking and planning ahead. Not all storms can be avoided. Yet I wonder how many we encounter because we fail to check all the resources available to us. Too many times our troubles are a result of our own poor planning and not the conditions that surround our lives. To avoid some potential storms in life we need to know and rely on tough weather indicators. Here are some indicators and important questions to ask oneself when dealing with them:

Lack of experience: Do I know someone with successful experience in this area?

Lack of knowledge: Have I studied sufficiently to direct my course effectively?

Lack of time: Did I allow the process of time to work on me as well as the storm?

Lack of facts: Are all the facts gathered to allow a proper decision?

Rule 4: Keep in contact with the control tower. Every pilot knows the value of communicating with knowledgeable people during times of trouble. The natural reaction when having difficulty in the sky is to radio for help. We do not always do this in our daily living. Our tendency is often to try to make it on our own.

The Crash from Within

There are certain storms within a person's life that contribute to an attitude crash. The three storms are predominantly inward, not outward. They are part of us and must be constructively dealt with to bring inner peace and a wholesome attitude.

The First Inward Storm: The Fear of Failure

We do everything but accept it. Acceptance doesn't mean resignation and apathy. It means understanding that failure is a necessary step to success.

The person who lived a life free of mistakes likely never attempted anything. Failures are footprints on the road to achievement. Accepting failure in the positive sense becomes effective when you believe that the right to fail is as important as the right to succeed.

Take a risk. Climb out on a limb where the fruit is. The greatest hazard in life is to risk nothing. The person who risks nothing does nothing, has nothing, and is nothing. That person may avoid suffering and sorrow, but he or she simply cannot learn, grow, feel, change, love, or live. Chained by personal certitudes, this person is a slave; he or she has forfeited freedom.

Fear of failure grips those who take themselves too seriously. While we were growing up, many of us spent a great deal of time worrying about what the world thought of us. By the time we reach middle age we realize that the world wasn't paying much attention all the time we were worrying. Until we accept the fact that the future of the world does not hinge on our decisions, we will be unable to forget past mistakes.

Attitude is the determining factor in whether our failures make or break us. The persistence of a person who encounters failure is one sign of a healthy attitude.

The Second Inward Storm: The Dread of Discouragement

Discouragement hurts our self-image. Discouragement causes us to see ourselves as less than we really are. Discouragement causes us to evade our responsibilities. Discouragement causes us to blame others for our predicament. Discouragement comes when we:

- *Feel that the opportunity for success is gone.* We need the spirit of the boy in the Little League. A man stopped to watch a Little League baseball game. He asked one of the youngsters the score. "We're behind eighteen to nothing," came the answer. "Well," said the man, "I must say you don't look discouraged." "Discouraged?" the boy asked. "Why should we be discouraged? We haven't come to bat yet."
- *Become selfish.* Usually people who are discouraged are thinking mainly about one thing—themselves.
- *Are not immediately successful in our attempts to do something.* A study conducted by the National Retail Dry Goods Association points out that unsuccessful first attempts lead almost half of all salespeople to certain failure. Note: 48 percent of all salespeople make one call and stop; 25 percent of all salespeople make two calls and stop; 15 percent of all salespeople make three calls and stop; 12 percent of all salespeople go back and back and back and back. They make 80 percent of all sales.
- *Lack purpose and a plan.* Another characteristic of discouragement is inactivity. You seldom see a discouraged activist running to and fro trying to help others. When you are discouraged, you tend to withdraw. Many times discouragement comes right after a successful venture. You may be totally discouraged, thinking there is little you can do to overcome those feelings of discouragement and inadequacy.

The Third Inward Storm: The Struggle of Sin

Your attitude begins to falter when sin enters your life. A withdrawal, a hardness, and a fleshly nature begin to invade us, all caused by sin. It is first appealing, then appalling; first alluring, then alienating; first deceiving, then damning; it promises life and produces death; it is the most disappointing thing in the world.

If your attitude is threatening to crash, check the internal indications. See if you are afraid of failure, dealing with discouragement, or struggling with sin.

The Crash from Without

Our attitude sometimes crashes when the storms around us begin to take their toll. Here are four of these outward storm causes.

The First External Storm: The Closeness of Criticism

The word "closeness" is used because the criticism that hurts always comes close to where we live or what we love. We always hurt ourselves when our reaction to those who criticize us becomes negative.

In spite of experiencing misunderstanding, ingratitude, and rejection, our Lord never became bitter, discouraged, or overcome. Every obstacle was an opportunity. Broken-heartedness? An opportunity to comfort. Disease? An opportunity to heal. Hatred? An opportunity to love. Temptation? An opportunity to overcome. Sin? An opportunity to forgive.

The Second External Storm: The Presence of Problems

When our attitude crashes, we have two alternatives. We can either alter the difficulty or alter ourselves. What can be changed for the best we must change. When that is impossible, we must adjust to the circumstances in a positive way.

The Third External Storm: The Conflict of Change

We resist nothing more than change. With the proper attitude, all change, positive or negative, will be a learning experience that results in a growing experience.

I have spent much time observing why and when people start resisting change. Some strive until they are comfortable, then they settle in and don't want to grow. For most, a negative experience has made them pull back and say, "Never again."

Change is essential for growth. Each generation is a bank in which the previous generation deposits its valuables. The new generation examines those valuables, rejects what is no longer needed, and uses what is left to create new treasures. This whole process of conserving, criticizing, and creating adds up to the one thing we fear: change.

WHY CUSTOMERS QUIT

A few years ago, I was traveling in the South and stopped at a service station. It was a rainy day, yet the station workers were diligently trying to take care of the customers. I was impressed by the first-class treatment and fully understood the reason when I read this sign:

1% die

3% move away

5% other friendships

9% competitive reasons (price)

14% product dissatisfaction

BUT . . . 68% quit because of an attitude of indifference toward them by some employee!

In other words, 68% quit because the workers did not have a customer mind-set working for them.

Just suppose each new generation had to discover numerals or language or medicine or the gospel. The world would see no progress. But because each generation conserves what previous generations have discovered, we can continue to make progress in the important areas of life.

The Fourth External Storm (Which Causes More Attitude Fatalities Than Anything Else): The Night of Negativism

Our challenge is to think right in a negative world.

Negative thinking and living does many detrimental things to our lives.

Negative thinking creates clouds at critical decision times. We become tense instead of relaxing.

Negative talking is contagious. Negative thinking blows everything out of proportion. Negative thinking limits our potential. Negative thinking keeps us from enjoying life. Negative thinking hinders others from making a positive response.

The Changing of Your Attitude

One of the great discoveries we make, one of our great surprises, is to find that we can do what we were afraid we couldn't do. Most of the prison bars we beat against are within us; we put them there and we can take them down.

That statement includes some good news and some bad news. The bad news is that we bring many of our problems on ourselves. The good news is that, beginning today, we can break out of our prison of bad attitudes and become free for effective living.

Most people who have negative attitudes do not realize that attitudes know no barriers. The only barriers that bring our attitudes into bondage are those we place upon them. Attitudes, like faith, hope, and love, can cross over any obstacle.

The Choice Within You

We are either the masters or the victims of our attitudes. It is a matter of personal choice. To change means to choose to change.

Choice #1: Evaluate your present attitudes. This will take some time. The following evaluation process was developed to help you search for the right answers in the most efficient way:

1. Identify problem feelings. What attitudes make you feel the most negative about yourself? Feelings can usually be sensed before the problem is clarified. Write them down.

2. Identify problem behavior. What attitudes cause you the most problems when dealing with others? Write them down.

3. Identify problem thinking. We are the sum of our thoughts. What thoughts consistently control your mind? Although this is the first step in correcting attitude problems, these are not as easy to identify as the first two.

4. Clarify biblical thinking. What do the Scriptures teach about you as a person and about your attitudes?

5. Secure commitment. "What must I do to change?" now becomes "I must change." Remember, the choice to change is the one decision that must be made, and only you can make it.

6. Plan and carry out your choice. This evaluation will take time. If you have an encouraging friend who knows you well, perhaps you should enlist his or her help.

Choice #2: *Realize that faith is stronger than fear.* The only thing that will guarantee the success of a doubtful undertaking is the faith from the beginning that you can do it.

There is a biblical way to handle fear so that an endeavor can be successful and not be limited by it: Understand that God sees your problems. Ask for a filling of confidence and love that is greater than fear; possess positive emotions and seek positive reinforcements that are stronger than the negatives. Believe God is working a miracle in your life; place the changes you seek in attitude, thinking, and behavior at the top of your prayer list. Be filled with the Holy Spirit.

Don't be fearful or hesitant. You can't cross a chasm in two small jumps. The future is worth the risk.

Choice #3: *Write a statement of purpose.* In order to have fun and direction in changing your attitude, you must establish a clearly stated goal. This goal should be as specific as possible, written out and signed, with a time frame attached to it. The purpose statement should be placed in a visible spot where you see it several times a day to give you reinforcement.

You will attain this goal if each day you do three things: Write specifically what you desire to accomplish each day. Verbalize to your encouraging friend what you want to accomplish each day. Take action on what you write and verbalize what you wrote each day.

Choice #4: *Have the desire to change.* No choice will determine the success of your attitude change more than desiring to change. When all else fails, desire alone can keep you heading in the right direction. It is a sad day when a person becomes so satisfied with his or her life, thoughts, and deeds that he or she ceases to be challenged to do greater things in life.

Choice #5: *Live one day at a time.* Anyone can fight the battle for just one day. It is only when adding the burdens of those two awful eternities, yesterday and tomorrow, that we tremble. It is not the experiences of today that drive people to distraction; it is remorse or bitterness over something that happened yesterday and dread of what tomorrow may bring. Let us, therefore, live but one day at a time—today!

Choice #6: Change your thought patterns. That which holds our attention determines our actions. We are where we are and what we are because of the dominating thoughts that occupy our minds. We can control our feelings by learning to change one thing: the way we think.

Choice #7: Develop good habits. Attitudes are nothing more than habits of thought. Habits aren't instincts; they're acquired actions or reactions. They don't just happen; they are caused. Once the original cause of a habit is determined, it is within your power to accept or reject it. Most people allow their habits to control them. When those habits are hurtful, they damage our attitudes.

Choice #8: Continually choose to have a right attitude. Once you make the choice to possess a good attitude, the work really begins. Now comes a life of continually deciding to grow and maintaining the right outlook. Attitudes have a tendency to revert back to their original patterns if not carefully guarded and cultivated.

Our decision to continually choose the right attitude will bring many benefits. To improve continually, we must change continually.

You are the key to changing your attitude. No one but you can determine what you will think and how you will act.

The Opportunities Around You

Once you have made the choice to change your attitude, you are ready to allow the opportunities around you to make this decision a success.

Opportunity #1: Enlist the cooperation of a friend. Few people are successful unless a lot of people want them to be. Change has a tendency to intimidate us. Add to that intimidation the realization that we have a long way to go before proper attitudes are established, and we begin to feel sort of inadequate. To overcome this feeling you need the help of a friend. Find someone who has the spirit of Tenzing Norgay, the native guide of Edmund Hillary, who made the historic first climb of Mt. Everest.

Coming down from the peak, Hillary suddenly lost his footing. Tenzing held the line taut and kept them both from falling by digging his ax into the ice. Later Tenzing refused any kind of special credit for saving Hillary's life; he considered it a routine part of the job. As he put it, "Mountain climbers always help each other."

Conditions needed for successful cooperative effort: A friend you can see or talk to daily. Someone who loves you and is an encourager. Someone with whom you have mutual honesty and transparency. A person who is successful in overcoming problems. Someone who has strong faith in God and believes in miracles.

Opportunity #2: *Associate with the right people.* Many times people blame circumstances for their problems. But usually it is the crowd we run with, not the circumstances we encounter, that makes the difference in our lives. Good circumstances with bad friends result in defeat. Bad circumstances with good friends result in victory. Although it is unrealistic to surround yourself with only positive people, it is possible to choose friends who have a proper outlook on life.

Opportunity #3: *Select a model to follow.* Visual messages last longer than those we just hear. You could select someone to follow who would give you a constant visualization of what you want to become. Making a single decision to alter an attitude is not enough. The vision of what you desire must be constantly before you. To achieve the kind of life you want, you must act, walk, talk, and conduct yourself as the ideal person that you visualize yourself to be.

Begin looking for someone to stretch your life. Ask that individual to disciple you for a few months. Enjoy the experience of growth by example.

Opportunity #4: *Learn from your mistakes.* You cannot control all circumstances. You cannot always make right decisions that bring right results. But you can always learn from your mistakes. When you strike out, forget it. If you made some mistakes, learn from them and do better the next time.

One reason some people never grow through change is that they can't stand failure. Even the best people have a lot more failure than success. The secret is that they don't let the failures upset them. They do their very best. Let the chips fall where they may, then go on to the next attempt.

Opportunity #5: *Expose yourself to successful experiences.* It takes five positive experiences to overcome one negative situation. When faced with the possibility of failure, our tendency is to sit back and be anxious. Fear is nature's warning signal to get busy. We overcome it by successful action.

Experiences that are continually unsuccessful can increase our desire to sit out the game in the arena of life. Action that produces confidence and a degree of success will encourage us to attempt new challenges. Nothing intimidates us more than constant exposure to failure. Nothing motivates us more than constant exposure to success. Therefore, people change more quickly if they are continually given situations in which they can be successful.

Start exposing yourself today to successful people and experiences. Read books that will make you a better person. Find something that you can do well, and do it often. Help make someone who needs your spiritual gifts a better person. Feed your right attitudes and, before you know it, your bad ones will starve to death.

Share your growth with those who are interested in you and already have excellent attitudes. Take time daily to congratulate yourself and thank others for making this change of attitude possible.

INDEX